THE EMPEROR JUSTINIAN AND THE BYZANTINE EMPIRE

Greenwood Guides to Historic Events of the Ancient World

The Peloponnesian War
Lawrence Tritle

The Reign of Cleopatra
Stanley Burstein

The Decline and Fall of the Roman Empire
James W. Ermatinger

The Trojan War
Carol G. Thomas and Craig Conant

The Establishment of the Han Empire and Imperial China
Grant Hardy and Anne Kinney

THE EMPEROR JUSTINIAN AND THE BYZANTINE EMPIRE

James Allan Evans

Greenwood Guides to Historic Events of the Ancient World
Bella Vivante, Series Editor

GREENWOOD PRESS
Westport, Connecticut • London

Library of Congress Cataloging-in-Publication Data

Evans, J. A. S. (James Allan Stewart), 1931–
  The Emperor Justinian and the Byzantine Empire / James Allan
Evans.
      p.   cm.—(Greenwood guides to historic events of the ancient
world)
    Includes bibliographical references and index.
    ISBN 0–313–32582–0 (alk. paper)
    1. Justinian I, Emperor of the East, 483?–565. 2. Emperors—
Byzantine Empire—Biography.   3. Byzantine Empire—History
Justinian I, 527–565   I. Title.   II. Series.
    DF572.E83   2005
    949.5'013'092—dc22   2004017997
    [B]

British Library Cataloguing in Publication Data is available.

Library of Congress Catalog Card Number: 2004017997
ISBN: 0–313–32582–0

First published in 2005

Greenwood Press, 88 Post Road West, Westport, CT 06881
An imprint of Greenwood Publishing Group, Inc.
www.greenwood.com

Printed in the United States of America

The paper used in this book complies with the
Permanent Paper Standard issued by the National
Information Standards Organization (Z39.48–1984).

10 9 8 7 6 5 4 3 2 1

CONTENTS

Photo essay follows Chapter 6.

SERIES FOREWORD

As a professor and scholar of the ancient Greek world, I am often asked by students and scholars of other disciplines, why study antiquity? What possible relevance could human events from two, three, or more thousand years ago have to our lives today? This questioning of the continued validity of our historical past may be the offshoot of the forces shaping the history of the American people. Proud of forging a new nation out of immigrants wrenched willingly or not from their home soils, Americans have experienced a liberating headiness of separation from traditional historical demands on their social and cultural identity. The result has been a skepticism about the very validity of that historical past. Some of that skepticism is healthy and serves constructive purposes of scholarly inquiry. Questions of how, by whom, and in whose interest "history" is written are valid questions pursued by contemporary historians striving to uncover the multiple forces shaping any historical event and the multilayered social consequences that result. But the current academic focus on "presentism"—the concern with only recent events and a deliberate ignoring of premodern eras—betrays an extreme distortion of legitimate intellectual inquiry. This stress on the present seems to have deepened in the early years of the twenty-first century. The cybertechnological explosions of the preceding decades seem to have propelled us into a new cultural age requiring new rules that make the past appear all the more obsolete.

So again I ask, why study ancient cultures? In the past year, after it ousted that nation's heinous regime, the United States' occupation of Iraq has kept that nation in the forefront of the news. The land base of Iraq is ancient Mesopotamia, "the land between the rivers" of the Tigris and Euphrates, two of the four rivers in the biblical Garden of Eden (Gen. 2). Called the cradle of civilization, this area witnessed the early development of a centrally organized, hierarchical social system that utilized the new technology of writing to administer an increasingly complex state.

Is there a connection between the ancient events, literature, and art coming out of this land and contemporary events? Michael Wood, in his educational video *Iraq: The Cradle of Civilization*, produced shortly after the 1991 Gulf War, thinks so and makes this connection explicit—between the people, their way of interacting with their environment, and even the cosmological stories they create to explain and define their world.

Study of the ancient world, like study of contemporary cultures other than one's own, has more than academic or exotic value. First, study of the past seeks meaning beyond solely acquiring factual knowledge. It strives to understand the human and social dynamics that underlie any historical event and what these underlying dynamics teach us about ourselves as human beings in interaction with one another. Study of the past also encourages deeper inquiry than what appears to some as the "quaint" observation that this region of current and recent conflict could have served as a biblical ideal or as a critical marker in the development of world civilizations. In fact, these apparently quaint dimensions can serve as the hook that piques our interest into examining the past and discovering what it may have to say to us today. Not an end in itself, the knowledge forms the bedrock for exploring deeper meanings.

Consider, for example, the following questions. What does it mean that three major world religions—Judaism, Christianity, and Islam—developed out of the ancient Mesopotamian worldview? In this view, the world, and hence its gods, were seen as being in perpetual conflict with one another and with the environment, and death was perceived as a matter of despair and desolation. What does it mean that Western forms of thinking derive from the particular intellectual revolution of archaic Greece that developed into what is called rational discourse, ultimately systematized by Aristotle in the fourth century B.C.E.? How does this thinking, now fundamental to Western discourse, shape how we see the world and ourselves, and how we interact with one another? And how does it affect our ability, or lack thereof, to communicate intelligibly with people with differently framed cultural perceptions? What, ultimately, do we gain from being aware of the origin and development of these fundamental features of our thinking and beliefs?

In short, knowing the past is essential for knowing ourselves in the present. Without an understanding of where we came from, and the journey we took to get where we are today, we cannot understand why we think or act the way we do. Nor, without an understanding of historical development, are we in a position to make the kinds of constructive changes necessary to advance as a society. Awareness of the past gives us the resources necessary to make comparisons between our contemporary world and past times. It is from those comparisons that we can assess both the advances we have made as human societies and those aspects that can still benefit from change. Hence, knowledge of the past is crucial for shaping our individual and social identities, providing us with the resources to make intelligent, aware, and informed decisions for the future.

All ancient societies, whether significant for the evolution of Western ideas and values, or whether they developed largely separate from the cultures that more directly influenced Western civilization, such as China, have important lessons to teach us. For fundamentally they all address questions that have faced every human individual and every human society that has existed. Because ancient civilizations erected great monuments of themselves in stone, writings, and the visual arts— all enduring material evidence—we can view how these ancient cultures dealt with many of the same questions we face today. And we learn the consequences of the actions taken by people in other societies and times that, ideally, should help us as we seek solutions to contemporary issues. Thus it was that President John F. Kennedy wrote of his reliance upon Thucydides' treatment of the devastating war between the ancient Greek city-states of Athens and Sparta (see the volume on the Peloponnesian War) in his study of exemplary figures, *Profiles in Courage*.

This series seeks to fulfill this goal both collectively and in the individual volumes. The individual volumes examine key events, trends, and developments in world history in ancient times that are central to the secondary school and lower-level undergraduate history curriculum and that form standard topics for student research. From a vast field of potential subjects, these selected topics emerged after consultations with scholars, educators, and librarians. Each book in the series can be described as a "library in a book." Each one presents a chronological timeline and an initial factual overview of its subject, three to five topical essays that examine the subject from diverse perspectives and for its various consequences, a concluding essay providing current perspectives on the event, biographies of key players, a selection of primary documents, illustrations, a glossary, and an index. The concept of the series is to provide ready-reference materials that include a quick, in-depth examination of the topic and insightful guidelines for interpretive analysis, suitable for student research and designed to stimulate critical thinking. The authors are all scholars of the topic in their fields, selected both on the basis of their expertise and for their ability to bring their scholarly knowledge to a wider audience in an engaging and clear way. In these regards, this series follows the concept and format of the Greenwood Guides to Historic Events of the Twentieth Century, the Fifteenth to Nineteenth Centuries, and the Medieval World.

All the works in this series deal with historical developments in early ancient civilizations, almost invariably postdating the emergence of writing and of hierarchical dynastic social structures. Perhaps only incidentally do they deal with what historians call the Paleolithic ("Old Stone Age") periods, from about 25,000 B.C.E. onward, eras characterized by nomadic, hunting-gathering societies, or the Neolithic ("New Stone Age"), the period of the earliest development of agriculture and hence settled societies, one of the earliest dating to about 7000 B.C.E. at Çatal Höyük in south-central Turkey.

The earliest dates covered by the books in this series are the fourth to second millennia B.C.E. for the building of the Pyramids in Egypt, and the examination of the Trojan War and the Bronze Age civilizations of the eastern Mediterranean. Most volumes deal with events in the first millennium B.C.E. to the early centuries of the first millennium C.E. Some treat the development of civilizations, such as the rise of the Han Empire in China, or the separate volumes on the rise and on the decline and fall of the Roman Empire. Some highlight major personalities and their empires, such as the volumes on Cleopatra VII of Ptolemaic Egypt or Justinian and the beginnings of the Byzantine Empire in eastern Greece and Constantinople (Istanbul). Three volumes examine the emergence in antiquity of religious movements that form major contemporary world systems of belief—Judaism, Buddhism, and Christianity. (Islam is being treated in the parallel Medieval World series.) And two volumes examine technological developments, one on the building of the Pyramids and one on other ancient technologies.

Each book examines the complexities of the forces shaping the development of its subject and the historical consequences. Thus, for example, the volume on the fifth-century B.C.E. Greek Peloponnesian War explores the historical causes of the war, the nature of the combatants' actions, and how these reflect the thinking of the period. A particular issue, which may seem strange to some or timely to others, is how a city like Athens, with its proto-democratic political organization and its outstanding achievements in architecture, sculpture, painting, drama, and philosophy, could engage in openly imperialist policies of land conquest and of vicious revenge against any who countered them. Rather than trying to gloss over the contradictions that emerge, these books conscientiously explore whatever tensions arise in the ancient material, both to portray more completely the ancient event and to highlight the fact that no historical occurrence is simply determined. Sometimes societies that we admire in some ways—such as the artistic achievements and democratic political experiments of ancient Athens—may prove deeply troublesome in other ways—such as what we see as their reprehensible conduct in war and in brutal subjection of other Greek communities. Consequently, the reader is empowered to make informed, well-rounded judgments on the events and actions of the major players.

We offer this series as an invitation to explore the past in various ways. We anticipate that from its volumes the reader will gain a better appreciation of the historical events and forces that shaped the lives of our ancient forebears and that continue to shape our thinking, values, and actions today. However remote in time and culture these ancient civilizations may at times appear, ultimately they show us that the questions confronting human beings of any age are timeless and that the examples of the past can provide valuable insights into our understanding of the present and the future.

Bella Vivante
University of Arizona

PREFACE

Emperor Justinian dominates the history of the Mediterranean world in the sixth century. Not only was his own reign, from 527 to 565, remarkably long, but it was preceded by the nine-year reign of his uncle Justin, which was treated by contemporaries as at best a prelude to Justinian's. Justin was an old man when he was unexpectedly elevated to the throne, and though he was a shrewd old soldier, he was uneducated by the standards of the ruling elite and as his health deteriorated, he depended increasingly on his ambitious nephew. Justinian was succeeded by his sister's son, Justin II, whose wife, Sophia, was the niece of Empress Theodora, Justinian's wife. Justin's reign was unlucky; he ruled briefly and disastrously before he went insane. Sophia ably filled the power vacuum, chose the next emperor, Tiberius, and had a hand in choosing Tiberius' successor, Maurice, whose reign was a prelude to calamity. It is estimated that the empire's population at the end of the sixth century was only 60 percent of what it was at the beginning. Justinian's reign was a turning point for the empire, and his legacy was a mixed blessing.

The sources for Justinian's reign are abundant. There are the chroniclers, the most important of whom is John Malalas, who lived through the period, but other than that, we know nothing about Justinian. There are the historians: the greatest of them, Prokopios of Caesarea, wrote a history of Justinian's wars in seven books up to 550, and later added a final book that brought the history down to 552, when the Goths in Italy were finally defeated. Prokopios was on the staff of the greatest general of the day, Belisarios, and consequently we are well informed about Belisarios, both as a military officer and as a husband. His wife, Antonina, was a formidable lady, a crony of Empress Theodora and, like Theodora, a former actress. Agathias of Myrina continued Prokopios' history, covering the years 552 to 559, and Menander Protector continued Agathias for the years 558 to 582, which brought his history down to the accession of Emperor Maurice. Menander's complete history does not survive, but the fragments of it that we still have, are extensive. As well as his history, Prokopios wrote a remarkable commentary on Justinian's reign, the *Anekdota* (Unpublished Work), which is better known by its popular title, *Secret History*. In it, Prokopios claims to report what he could not publish in his history for fear of the vengeance of Justinian and his formidable wife. Justinian was a reformer, tirelessly issuing new laws to improve the administration of the empire and the church, and to establish a Christian faith that was acceptable to all churchmen. The sixth-century society had no liking for innovators, and Justinian made many enemies, as the *Secret History* attests.

Justinian's most lasting achievement was his legal reform. The law code (Justinian issued two editions, of which only the second survives); the *Digest*, which summarized previous legal decisions; and the *Institutes*, which was a textbook for lawyers, formed the basis of European law. But Justinian continued to issue a multitude of new laws after the second edition of his code was published. These *Novels* (New Laws) give us a vivid insight into Justinian's character, for each law was prefaced by a little essay in which Justinian explained why the law was necessary and how it fitted into the Roman legal tradition. The actual words may not have been written by Justinian, but they express his ideas. They reveal a man who was an inveterate reformer. He was intolerant and despotic, but at the same time he believed that he was working for the general good of his subjects. He claimed to respect the traditions of Rome, but his knowledge of Roman history was sketchy. In that he was no different from most Byzantines of his day.

The archaeological remains are impressive. In Istanbul, as Constantinople is known today, Justinian's churches of Hagia Sophia, Hagia Eirene, and Saints Sergius and Bacchus are still standing. The first two are now museums, and the last is the mosque of Little Ayasofya, separated from the shore of the Sea of Marmara by an elevated railway. On the eastern frontier, the great fortress of Dara exists as impressive ruins. In 530, outside Dara's walls, Belisarios won the first victory that the Byzantines had won for over a hundred years. The monastery of Saint Catherine is still standing at the foot of Gebel Musa (according to tradition, Mount Sinai, where Moses received the Ten Commandments). On three beams of the monastery church there are inscriptions: one honoring Theodora; one, Justinian; and the third, the builder of the church. But it is at Ravenna in northern Italy that we feel closest to the age of Justinian. The tomb of the great Ostrogothic king, Theodoric, is there. So is the church of San Vitale, dedicated one year before Theodora died of cancer in 548. In its chancel, on the sidewalls, there are mosaics, one showing Justinian and his entourage and the other, Theodora and her attendants. Justinian and Theodora never visited Ravenna, and the mosaics were perhaps made by Italian craftsmen, but it is very likely that the imperial pair saw and approved their designs.

This book is part of the series Greenwood Guides to Historic Events of the Ancient World. Two other volumes in the series complement it: *The Decline and Fall of the Roman Empire*, by James W. Ermatinger, and the *Emergence of Christianity*, by Cynthia White. For the purposes of comparison, *The Establishment of the Han Empire and Imperial China*, by Grant Hardy and Anne Kinney, is also useful. China was the source of silk, the luxury fabric of the period, used not only for the garments worn at the Byzantine court but also for the vestments of the clergy. One achievement of Justinian was to acquire silkworm eggs smuggled out of China, which allowed the Byzantine Empire to establish a silk industry of its own. These two empires at either end of the Asian landmass each lived in its own world, but they present interesting parallels.

CHRONOLOGY OF EVENTS

All dates are C.E.

330	The dedication of Constantinople, founded by the first Christian emperor, Constantine I, six years earlier.
395	Emperor Theodosius I (the Great) dies, leaving the empire to his two sons, Honorius (395–423), who ruled the western half, and Arcadius (395–408), who ruled the eastern half.
402	Emperor Honorius moves his capital from Milan to Ravenna, which is less exposed to barbarian attacks.
406	The Rhine frontier breaks as the Vandals, Alans, and Sueves surge across it, taking advantage of an unusually cold winter that froze the river.
410	The Visigoths under Alaric sack Rome.
429	The Vandals cross from Spain and commence the conquest of Africa. In 439 they capture Carthage.
451	The Chalcedonian Creed is formulated at an ecumenical church council held at Chalcedon, across the Bosporus from Constantinople.
455	Rome is sacked by the Vandals under King Gaiseric.

468	A naval expedition that Emperor Leo I launches against the Vandal kingdom is annihilated.
476	Deposition of the last western emperor, Romulus Augustulus. The conventional date for the fall of the western Roman Empire.
482	Emperor Zeno issues the *Henotikon*, an edict of "unity" that is intended to reconcile the Chalcedonians and the Monophysites. The *Henotikon* ignores the decisions of the Council of Chalcedon and condemns both the doctrine of Nestorios, who taught that Christ has two distinct natures, and the doctrine of Eutyches, that Christ's divine nature subsumes his human nature.
484	Pope Felix III condemns the *Henotikon*, thus giving rise to the Akakian Schism between Rome and Constantinople, so called for the patriarch Akakios, who was responsible for the wording of the *Henotikon*.
491–518	Reign of Emperor Anastasius, who favors the Monophysites.
518–527	Reign of Emperor Justin I, the uncle of Justinian.
519	The Akakian Schism ends. Constantinople and Rome are reconciled on Rome's terms. Justin authorizes the persecution of the Monophysite clergy in the empire, though he does not extend the persecution to Egypt.
527–565	Reign of Justinian.
530	The battle of Dara is fought outside the walls of the fortress of Dara on the eastern frontier. Belisarios defeats a superior Persian force. It is the first Roman victory over the Persians in over a century.
531	Belisarios is defeated by the Persians at Callinicum on the Euphrates River, and is recalled after an in-

vestigation indicates that his leadership had been less than competent.

532	January 13–18: The *Nika* riot in Constantinople nearly overthrows Justinian and destroys large areas of the city.
532	February 23: Work begins on the churches of Hagia Sophia and Hagia Eirene.
533	Belisarios leads an expeditionary force of some 16,000 troops against the Vandal kingdom in Africa. He defeats the Vandals in two pitched battles, and in 534 Gelimer, the Vandal king, surrenders.
534	Belisarios returns to Constantinople for a triumph. The Berbers in Africa rise in revolt.
535	Belisarios leads an expeditionary force totaling some 7,500 troops against Sicily. By the end of the year, he has conquered Sicily.
536	Belisarios crosses the Strait of Messina and begins his campaign against the Ostrogoths. In December he enters Rome unopposed.
537–538	The Goths besiege Rome for a year and nine days. They abandon the siege when a Byzantine force under John, the nephew of Vitalian, threatens Ravenna.
537	December 27: The great church of Hagia Sophia is dedicated in Constantinople.
540	The Goths surrender Ravenna to Belisarios. In the same year, the shah of Persia, Khusru, destroys Antioch, and Slavs and Kutrigur Huns raid the Greek peninsula and plunder it. One spearhead reaches the defenses of Constantinople.
541	Bubonic plague breaks out in Alexandria.
542	Bubonic plague reaches Constantinople and causes enormous loss of life.

544–549	Belisarios campaigns against the Ostrogoths in Italy, without success. In 548, he sends his wife, Antonina, to Constantinople to beg Empress Theodora to intervene and persuade Justinian to send reinforcements.
548	Theodora dies of cancer before Antonina reaches Constantinople.
550	Justinian appoints his cousin Germanos as commander of the war against the Ostrogoths in Italy. Germanos collects an army, but dies before he can leave for Italy.
551–552	Justinian sends an expedition under Liberius to Spain.
552	Narses, leading an army of some 30,000 troops, defeats Totila at Busta Gallorum, effectively ending Gothic resistance.
554	Justinian issues the "Pragmatic Sanction," a decree intended to restore the social order in Italy to what it had been before the Ostrogothic War.
557	December 14: Great earthquake in Constantinople, which cracks the dome of Hagia Sophia.
558	An embassy of Avars arrives in Constantinople to ask for an alliance, land within the empire, and a subsidy. They are granted a subsidy but no land.
558	May 7: Partial collapse of dome of Hagia Sophia while repairs are being made. In the same year, the plague returns to Constantinople.
559	Invasion of the Balkans by the Kutrigur Huns, led by their *khagan*, Zabergan. One spearhead threatens Constantinople, but it is routed by Belisarios, whom the emperor has summoned from retirement to deal with the crisis.

562	A peace treaty is negotiated with Persia that is to last for fifty years. Persia is to receive a subsidy of 30,000 gold *nomismata* annually, with the subsidy for the first seven years to be paid immediately, to be followed by payment for the next three years, and thereafter payments made annually.
562	November: There is a conspiracy against Justinian, and Belisarios is accused of being implicated. He is restored to favor in July 563.
562	December: Dedication of the restored church of Hagia Sophia with a redesigned dome.
564 (end of the year)	Justinian issues a decree proclaiming that the Aphthartodocetist heresy must be accepted as orthodox and insists that the patriarchs countersign it. The patriarch of Constantinople refuses, and is replaced.
565	November 15: Justinian dies. He is succeeded by his nephew Justin II, whose wife, Sophia, is a niece of Empress Theodora.
567	The Avar khan Baian and Alboin, king of the Lombards, who had settled in Pannonia (modern Hungary), make an agreement to destroy the Gepids who live in Dacia, on the left bank of the Danube.
568	The Lombards take half the spoils from the destruction of the Gepids and invade Italy. The invasion is gradual but relentless, and the Byzantine realm in Italy is reduced to Ravenna, Venice, and, in the south, Calabria and Sicily.
c. 570	The prophet Muhammad is born.
572	Justin II refuses to pay the annual subsidy due to the Persians by the peace treaty signed ten years earlier. He launches a war against Persia, though his army is unready.

573	The fortress of Dara falls to the Persians. News of the fall affects Justin II so severely that he becomes insane. Empress Sophia buys a one-year truce with Khusru at the cost of 45,000 gold *nomismata*.
574	The Persians and the Byzantines agree to a five-year truce, for which the Byzantines are to pay an annual subsidy of 30,000 gold *nomismata*.
574	Justin II is persuaded, in a moment of lucidity, to appoint Tiberius as caesar with the name Tiberius Constantine. When Justin II dies in 578, Tiberius becomes emperor.
578–582	Reign of Tiberius II.
582–602	Reign of Emperor Maurice, son-in-law of Tiberius II.
c. 587	A raid by a horde of Avars and Slavs destroys Athens and Corinth. In the aftermath, Slavic immigrants overrun mainland Greece.

THE WORLD OF
LATE ANTIQUITY:
A HISTORICAL
OVERVIEW

THE EMPIRE OF JUSTINIAN: THE BACKGROUND

The era known as late antiquity or the proto-Byzantine period reached its climax with the reign of Emperor Justinian (527–565).[1] The Roman Empire in the west had been taken over by barbarian kingdoms by the time Justinian became emperor. Italy was ruled by the Ostrogoths; North Africa, by the Vandals; most of Gaul, by the Franks; and Spain, by the Visigoths. What remained of the Roman Empire was the region east of a line drawn through the Balkans. When Justinian died, he had reconquered North Africa and Italy, and the empire had a foothold in Spain. Yet the grandeur of it all masked the seeds of decline. Wars and an extravagant building program had emptied the treasury, and recurrent epidemics of bubonic plague from 541 onward had decimated the population. Yet this reign was the final flowering of the Roman Empire, which had ended in western Europe when the last emperor in Italy, Romulus Augustulus, was dethroned and forced to retire in 476. The first emperor had been Julius Caesar's grandnephew, *Imperator* Caesar Augustus, who made himself master of the Roman Empire in 31 B.C.E. Five centuries later, the last of the line abdicated.

Enormous changes had taken place over those five centuries. The greatest of them happened in the early fourth century when Emperor

---

1. All dates are C.E. unless otherwise indicated.

Constantine adopted Christianity as his religion. Henceforth, all the emperors save one were Christian. The Christian Church enjoyed imperial favor, and paganism would move from being tolerated to being persecuted before the end of the century. Constantine's other change that was to color the future of the empire was to move its capital to a new foundation, Constantinople (modern Istanbul). It was a refoundation: the Greeks had established a colony called Byzantium on the site in the seventh century B.C.E., and this colony gave the name "Byzantine" to the empire that Constantinople ruled. Protected by its huge walls, built by Emperor Theodosius II, Constantinople lasted until 1453, when the Ottoman Turks captured it and made it the capital of the Ottoman Empire.

The other great change was the failure of the western Roman empire. Following the death of Emperor Theodosius I in 395, the empire was divided, with the west going to his ten-year-old son Honorius and the east to Honorius's older brother Arcadius. Neither was especially intelligent or energetic, but the eastern empire was less exposed to invasion. In the west, the Rhine frontier broke on the last day of 406; a wave of barbarians crossed the frozen river and pushed into Gaul, Spain, and eventually Roman Africa. Emperor Honorius, lacking the resources for effective resistance, had already moved his capital from Milan to Ravenna in northeast Italy, which was easy to defend, and tried feebly to cope. The eastern empire was luckier: the Balkans were vulnerable to invasion across the Danube frontier, but the Asian provinces and Egypt were relatively safe. Commerce continued, and taxes were collected. The east was relatively prosperous and its population was increasing. When Emperor Anastasius (r. 491–518) died, he left the treasury full for his successors, Justin I and Justin's nephew Justinian.

THE RECONQUEST

Anastasius died suddenly and was succeeded by the commander of the palace guard known as the Excubitors, Justin I. He was an unexpected choice: a peasant from the region of modern Skopje, where the native language was Latin, who had migrated to Constantinople; there he joined the Excubitors and rose through the ranks. He was barely literate, and his wife, Lupicina, was an ex-slave whom he had bought, freed, and then married. He had at his side his nephew Justinian, for as Justin's fortune improved, he brought family members to Constantinople and saw to it that they got the education he had been denied. One of them was his sister's son, Flavius Petrus Sabbatius, who took the name "Justinian" when his uncle adopted him.

It is not clear that Justinian had any grand plan for reconquest when he succeeded his uncle. War with Persia had broken out two years before Justin's death, and it did not end until 532, when a peace was negotiated that was to last forever. In January of the same year, Justinian was almost overthrown by the *Nika* riot in Constantinople, which began as a commotion in the Hippodrome and rapidly grew into an insurrection backed by powerful senators in Constantinople. But Justinian emerged more secure than ever. In 533, he dispatched an expeditionary force of some 16,000 troops against the Vandal kingdom in Africa. Its commander was Belisarios, the best-known of Justinian's generals, for on his staff was the historian Prokopios. Thanks to Prokopios' great work on the wars of Justinian down to 552, we have a detailed account of the fall of the Vandal kingdom and its aftermath.

The Vandals were defeated in two pitched battles, and in 534 the Vandal king Gelimer surrendered. Belisarios returned with his captives and plunder to Constantinople and was honored with a triumph. The conquest of the Vandal kingdom did not bring peace to Africa, however, for the Berbers (or, as the Byzantines called them, the Moors) rose in revolt, and the war dragged on until the Byzantines at last won a decisive victory in 548.

Justinian now saw a chance to take Italy from the Ostrogoths, who had established themselves in Italy under their king, Theodoric the Amal (r. 493–526). The Ostrogothic kingdom was showing its age. Theodoric's young grandson, Athalaric, who succeeded his grandfather with his mother, Amalasuntha, as regent, died after a brief life of dissipation, and Amalasuntha secured the throne for her cousin Theodahad, whom she thought she could manipulate. But Theodahad threw her into prison and put her to death, thereby giving Justinian a just cause for war. In 535, Belisarios was dispatched to Sicily with a force only half as large as the one he had led against the Vandals, for the Ostrogothic kingdom looked like easy prey. Theodahad was no warrior, and the prospect of war frightened him. Sicily fell easily, and next year Belisarios invaded Italy.

The conquest proved far more difficult and expensive than Justinian had anticipated. The Ostrogoths rid themselves of Theodahad after he allowed Naples to fall to the Byzantines without any effort to relieve it, and they chose a new king, Witigis, who forced Belisarios to stand siege in Rome for a year and nine days. Belisarios had 5,000 troops and Witigis reputedly had 150,000, though probably the number is exaggerated. Yet in the end, about the middle of March 538, Witigis and his Ostrogoths had to abandon the siege. However, the imperial army suffered from a familiar problem: dissension among the officers of the general staff, particularly between Belisarios and Narses. Narses had been sent with reinforcements, and one result was that the two men operated independently until their failure to cooperate led to the fall of Milan to the Ostrogoths, who massacred all the men in the city—some 300,000, according to Prokopios—and sold the women into slavery. On hearing the news, Justinian recalled Narses and made it clear that Belisarios held supreme command. The Ostrogoths surrendered Ravenna only because Belisarios duped them into believing he would rebel against Justinian once he had Ravenna under his control, and would rule as western Roman emperor in partnership with the Ostrogoths. Instead, Belisarios returned to Constantinople with King Witigis captive, plus the royal treasure.

Justinian gave Belisarios a correct but distinctly cool reception. After Belisarios' victory over the Vandal kingdom, he had been granted a triumph in Constantinople that was an updated, Christianized version of the triumphs of ancient Rome, but the honor was not repeated after Belisarios' capture of Ravenna. Justinian would probably have preferred to leave the Ostrogoths in control of Italy north of the Po River, where they could serve as a buffer kingdom shielding Italy from invasions from the north. The Ostrogoths soon realized that Belisarios had cheated them, and regrouped under a new king, Totila, who soon reconquered much of Italy. Belisarios was sent back to Italy in 544, but he was starved for troops. Bubonic plague was raging throughout the empire, decimating the population and making recruits scarce. Belisarios was recalled in 549, and the campaign of reconquest dragged on until 552, when Justinian finally dispatched a large army, commanded by Narses, that defeated the Ostrogoths decisively. It was a brief triumph. In 568, after Justinian died, the Lombards invaded from the north, and Byzantine Italy was soon reduced to a few footholds.

The reconquest should be seen in the context of the defense of the empire as a whole. In 540, the year that Ravenna surrendered to Belisarios, a horde of Slavs and Huns invaded the Balkans and one spearhead reached the walls of Constantinople. In that year, too, the shah of Persia, Khusru, broke the "Endless Peace" that was to last forever and invaded the eastern provinces, destroying Antioch and looting and burning other cities. Justinian stitched together a truce with Persia in 545, but he had to pay handsomely for it. At the eastern end of the Black Sea, in Lazica (modern Georgia), Persia and Byzantium dueled year after year, for both powers considered this a strategic area. Justinian thought that if Persia controlled this region, it could launch an attack along the north coast of the Black Sea and cut the trade routes over which goods were brought from the Ukraine and Russia south to Constantinople. Yet, these distractions notwithstanding, Justinian pushed the reconquest of the west with whatever resources he could spare. Even before the defeat of the Ostrogoths was complete, he saw a chance to intervene in Spain and dispatched a force that carved out a Spanish province called Baetica, which Byzantium held for seventy years.

THE END OF PAGANISM

When the fourth century began, the great majority of citizens in the empire were still pagan, but once Constantine I extended imperial favor to the Christian Church, the number of Christians increased rapidly. Within twenty years, probably half the population or more was Christian, and after Constantine, there was only one emperor who was a pagan: Julian, the last of the Constantinian dynasty. His attempt to revitalize paganism during his brief reign (361–363) succeeded only in throwing into sharp relief the weakness of paganism as a vital creed that could compete with Christianity. Yet Constantine I made no clean break with the past: like the emperors before him, he held the office of high priest of "Jupiter, Best and Greatest," the chief god of the Roman state, as did all the emperors who succeeded him until Gratian (r. 367–383). But Constantine banned pagan sacrifice and his son Constantius II reiterated the interdict; since festivals involving sacrifice lay at the heart of pagan cults, the ban was a heavy blow.

On the popular level, paganism's bitterest enemies were the monks. The monastic movement began in Egypt early in the fourth century, spread rapidly to Palestine and Syria, and then to the rest of the empire. Two main types of monastic communities emerged, eremetic and cenobitic. The hermit Saint Antony (d. 355–356) is credited with the first variety, in which ascetics lived in caves or cells, often connected by pathways called *laurai*—hence the term "laura" for this type of monastic community. The second variety, the cenobitic (from the Greek *koinos bios,* meaning "life in common"), went back to Saint Antony's contemporary, Saint Pachomius (d. 346), who established the first cenobitic monastery at Tabennisi in Upper Egypt, where the monks lived together within a group of buildings surrounded by a wall, their lives governed by a rule that divided the day into hours for worship and hours for work. Monks took an active part in controversies about correct Christian doctrines. For instance, the "Sleepless Monks" in Constantinople, so called because they took shifts praising God twenty-four hours a day, hunted down any threats to orthodoxy like bloodhounds; in 512 they even incited a riot that nearly dethroned Emperor Anastasius when they detected a new, heretical addition to the liturgy of Hagia Sophia, the cathedral of Constantinople. Monks had no mercy for pagans. When mobs destroyed pagan temples, monks were generally in the thick of it.

Paganism did not die easily, but the reign of the virulently anti-pagan Emperor Theodosius I (r. 379–395) marks the end of toleration. In 392, the great temple of Serapis in Alexandria, Egypt, was destroyed. The pagans expected that the god Serapis would show his wrath by withholding the annual flood of the Nile River on which the fertility of Egypt depended, but the next year, to their dismay, the flood occurred as usual. Theodosius I, who was a fervent Christian, repeated the ban on pagan sacrifices in 391 and 392, and prescribed a heavy fine for disobedience. There was a reaction in Rome, where the Roman senators were still largely pagan: the western emperor Valentinian II was assassinated in 392 on the orders of his master of the soldiers, Arbogast, who made an obscure rhetorician named Eugenius emperor in Valentinian's place. Eugenius was a Christian but held pagan sympathies, and the pagan senators supported him. Theodosius I defeated Arbogast in 394 at a battle on the River Frigidus (modern Wippach), and the Christians saw the victory as the turning point when God showed his wrath against the pagans. Subsidies to pagan priests and cults were finally withdrawn, and mob violence against pagan temples and images increased.

The reign of Justinian marked the death throes of paganism, even though it still lingered in some corners of the empire. Justinian launched an attack against paganism as soon as he took the reins of power into his hands. His first law against the pagans dates to the period between April

1 and August 1, 527, while he was still co-emperor with Justin I. It applied to all who rejected the Catholic Church and the orthodox creed:
his empire was to have one faith, and it was his purpose to achieve that
end. He followed this law with a group of anti-pagan statutes which repeated all the previous anti-pagan laws that had not been strictly enforced. Pagans were barred from posts in the civil service. Baptized
Christians who lapsed into paganism were to be put to death. Citizens
who had never received baptism should seek it forthwith or lose their
property rights. Anyone caught making secret sacrifices to the gods was
to be put to death. In 529, a law appeared that threatened pagan teachers with confiscation of their property and exile if they did not accept
Christian baptism forthwith.

This law is of particular interest because, as a result of it, the Neoplatonic Academy in Athens was closed down. Plato had founded the Academy about 385 B.C.E., and though it had suffered various vicissitudes and
the original Academy itself had long since disappeared, Athens had remained a center for the teaching of philosophy for more than nine centuries. The future emperor Julian had studied there in the fourth century,
and so had the church fathers Basil of Caesarea and Gregory of Nazianzus.
The Neoplatonic Academy, which claimed to be the heir of Plato's Academy, had been founded in the last quarter of the fourth century by the
last native philosopher that Athens produced, Plutarch, whose house on
the south slope of the Acropolis became the center of his school. In the
next century, one of Plutarch's successors as the *diadochos* (head of the
school), Proklos, transmuted the philosophy that was taught there by in-
fusing it with the transcendentalism of late Neoplatonism. The Academy
became a kind of pagan monastery with its sacred books, the dialogues
of Plato and, even more, a series of divine revelations called the *Chaldean
Oracles*. Contemplation, prayer, and hymns of praise to the gods became
as important in the Academy as they were in any Christian monastery.

In 529, Justinian closed the school. If we are to assign a date to the
end of paganism, 529 is as good as any. Seven of the philosophers from
the Academy, led by the *diadochos* Simplikios, emigrated to Persia, where
Shah Khusru I welcomed them, but the philosophers found the atmos-
phere in Persia no more tolerant than that within the Byzantine Empire
and they soon returned. However, Khusru saw to it that a clause was in-
serted into the "Endless Peace" of 532 which allowed these philosophers
to practice their ancient religion unmolested. Some pagan philosophers

continued to teach in Alexandria, for Roman laws were never strictly enforced, and in the towns and villages the half-life of paganism lingered on. In 542, while bubonic plague was raging in Constantinople, Justinian sent a mission headed by John of Ephesus to Asia Minor to wipe out paganism, and John reported that he had made 80,000 converts. Yet even though pockets of paganism survived, Justinian's reign can rightly be regarded as the period when the last embers of pagan vitality were finally extinguished.

JEWS AND SAMARITANS

In mid-535 Justinian issued a constitution on ecclesiastical matters in North Africa, which had just been conquered, and the Catholic Church had been freed from the oppression of the Vandals, who were Arian heretics. The chief targets of this constitution were pagans and Christian heretics, but Jews were included. They were forbidden to possess Christian slaves, and their synagogues were to be made into churches. The decree against the Jews was not enforced, but it was indicative of Justinian's attitude. Judaism had been a *religio licita* (a permitted religion) under Roman law when the Roman Empire was pagan, which meant that Jews could practice their religion—a right not conceded to Christianity until the conversion of Constantine I. In the fourth and early fifth centuries, the Roman law codes contained a number of laws directed against Jews; for instance, marriage between a Christian and a Jew was treated as adultery, and no Jew should assail another Jew who converted to Christianity, whereas Christians who converted to Judaism were to have their property confiscated. Ownership of Christian slaves by Jews was a sore point. The law banned it, but the ban seems to have met determined resistance from the Jews, and in 438 Emperor Theodosius II softened the measure: he ruled that Jewish masters should not convert their Christian slaves to Judaism on pain of death, but he was prepared to accept Jewish ownership of Christian slaves so long as the slaves could practice their religion freely. After 438, we know of no more laws promulgated concerning Jews until we reach the reign of Justinian.

Judaism remained a *religio licita* under Justinian, and his anti-Jewish measures were pinpricks. In fact, archaeology shows that there was a boom in synagogue construction in Palestine during Justinian's reign. Yet this period was a watershed in Jewish–Gentile relations. In the cities of the empire, bishops of the Christian Church were exercising more and more secular power. In some places they were the only effective authority. The Roman Empire was becoming a Christian empire with little room for dissent, and Jewish communities found themselves increasingly isolated. At one time, educated Christians and Jews alike shared the Greek *paideia*, the education in the Greek classics that was the mark of an educated man, but in Justinian's reign this shared heritage was becoming frayed. Jews withdrew increasingly into their own culture, and it is a symptom of the change that this was the time when Hebrew was replacing Greek as the language for services in the synagogues.

For the Samaritans, Justinian had no mercy. They were the remains of the old northern kingdom of Israel, the "Lost Ten Tribes," though they claimed descent from the tribes of Ephraim and Manasseh. Their center was the old holy city of Shechem (Roman Neapolis, modern Nablus), and nearby, on Mount Gerizim, they had built their temple with the permission of Alexander the Great. At the start of the sixth century they probably made up the majority of the rural population in Palestine. They rebelled in 484, and Emperor Zeno retaliated by turning their temple on Mount Gerizim into a church dedicated to the Virgin. Under Zeno's successor, Anastasius, there was another rebellion that was suppressed. In 529, they rebelled again. The empire was at war with Persia, and the Samaritans hoped for Persian help. Justinian suppressed the uprising ruthlessly; the historian Prokopios, who sympathized with the Samaritans, put the number of their dead at 100,000, and we hear of 20,000 who were sold into slavery. The result was a shortage of farmers in Palestine, and Justinian, responding to an appeal from the bishop of Caesarea, the chief city of the province of First Palestine, rescinded his harshest measures against the Samaritans. But in 556 they rose again, and the master of the soldiers in the East repressed them without pity. After Justinian's death, there was a last uprising in 572, after which the Samaritan "problem" was effectively extinguished. Only a handful of Samaritans survive today.

THE PROBLEM OF CHRISTIAN HERESY

However, what aroused Justinian's greatest rancor was heresy. Arianism, which had roiled the empire in the fourth century and had claimed some emperors as adherents, was finally ruled heretical at the Council of Constantinople in 381, but Arian churches were still tolerated. Justinian's uncle, Justin I, tried to curb their rights, but his measures brought a protest from Theodoric, the king of the Ostrogoths in Italy, who ordered the pope to journey to Constantinople to plead on behalf of the Arians. By 538, however, there was no longer any need to worry about Ostrogothic protests, and Justinian closed the Arian churches in the eastern empire and confiscated their property. The Montanists, followers of a certain Montanus in Phrygia, who in the second century preached a doctrine that rejected marriage, stressed asceticism, and looked forward to the world to come, were ruthlessly persecuted. Some shut themselves up in their churches and set the buildings afire rather than accept baptism, but in spite of it all, Montanism lingered into the ninth century. Nestorianism, which taught that there were two separate, distinct natures in Christ, one completely human and the other completely divine, still flourished in Persia, but within the Byzantine Empire it was universally vilified. But the greatest danger to the empire was the opposition to the Chalcedonian Creed, for on the one hand it split the Latin western empire from the Greek eastern empire, and on the other, it split Greek-speaking believers in the east from the non-Greek: the Christians who spoke ancient native tongues, such as Syriac, descended from Aramaic, or Coptic, derived from the language of the pharaohs of Egypt.

The question that divided the theologians was the nature of the Trinity. What was the relation of God the Father to His son, Jesus? What did the Gospel of Saint John mean when it stated in its opening verse that the "Word" (that is, the *Logos*) existed in the beginning, and it became flesh? In 451, a church council met across the Bosporus from Constantinople at Chalcedon, and drew up the "Symbol" of Chalcedon to supplement the Nicene Creed, which had been formulated at Nicaea in 324 to counter the earlier heresy of Arianism. The "Symbol" stated: "We, then, following the Holy Fathers . . . confess the one and same Son our Lord Jesus Christ, the same perfect in Godhead and also perfect in manhood . . . consubstantial with the Father according to His Godhead and consubstantial with us according to His Manhood. . . ." That is, Christ was contained within a human and a divine nature, neither subordinate to the other.

The Creed of Chalcedon was the credo of Rome, expressing the theology enunciated by Pope Leo the Great. The western Roman Empire accepted it wholeheartedly. In the east, it had some adherents as well, but the majority opinion favored a less bald statement of the "two natures" doctrine. It is usual nowadays for historians to refer to these anti-Chalcedonians as Monophysites, that is, believers in a single, divine nature of Christ, but the term was not used in Justinian's day, and it disguises the fact that among the anti-Chalcedonians there was considerable difference of opinion. Emperor Zeno (r. 474–491) tried to paper over the rift between the Chalcedonians and the anti-Chalcedonians by promulgating a statement of faith, called the *Henotikon*, that satisfied the moderate anti-Chalcedonians, but Rome would have nothing to do with it. When Justinian's uncle, Justin I, came to the throne in 518, the patriarchate of Constantinople and the papacy were not in communion, and one of Justin's first acts was to abandon the *Henotikon*, accept the Chalcedonian Creed, and begin a persecution of the anti-Chalcedonians. Following Justin, one emperor after another would waste his energy trying to find a new *Henotikon* which would replace the one that Justin had abandoned, but none succeeded. Justinian was to devote an inordinate amount of effort to the task.

Justinian was a Chalcedonian, reared in a region of the empire that belonged to the see of Rome, and spoke Latin as its native tongue. However, his wife, Theodora, favored the anti-Chalcedonians. Cleavages within families over theology were by no means unknown, but in the case of Justinian and Theodora, it meant that they had separate agendas in matters of religious policy, though both aimed at finding a creed that was acceptable to all. Even before Justinian and Theodora became emperor and empress, Theodora was known as a friend at court for the anti-Chalcedonians, and once she became empress, she established a place of refuge for persecuted anti-Chalcedonian clergy in Constantinople in the Palace of Hormisdas, which was an adjunct of the Great Palace of the emperors. The Monophysite Christian churches in the east look on her today as a saint, for she was, at least indirectly, responsible for their foundation.

Theodora died in 548, while Justinian was in the midst of a major effort to find some common ground between the Chalcedonians and the anti-Chalcedonians. This was the "Three Chapters" dispute. The Three Chapters were the writings of three theologians who had lived in the previous century, and had argued that Christ had two entirely separate natures: one perfectly human and the other perfectly divine. This was the heresy of Nestorios, which was anathema to both the Chalcedonians and the anti-Chalcedonians, and yet the Council of Chalcedon in 451 had received the authors of the Three Chapters into communion with the Catholic Church. The anti-Chalcedonians pointed this out as evidence that Chalcedonian theology was really Nestorianism, and consequently heretical. Justinian decided to destroy this impediment to church unity by placing the Three Chapters under anathema.

Pope Vigilius in Rome had owed his elevation to the papacy to Empress Theodora, but that did not make him any more malleable. He put up a determined defense of the Three Chapters. He could not read them, for like most of the Latin clergy, he could not read Greek; and when the patriarch of Constantinople, Menas, had excerpts translated into Latin for him, he recognized immediately that they were heretical. Yet Justinian was claiming the right as emperor to define Christian doctrine, and that claim was caesaropapism: Caesar (that is, the emperor) was usurping the right of the pope to rule on church doctrine. On that point, the Roman Church was not prepared to concede, and Vigilius, with the fervent backing of the Latin clergy, particularly those in North Africa, defended the rights of the papacy with all his might.

In the end, Vigilius lost. Justinian forced him to give way, and the Three Chapters were declared heretical by the Fifth Ecumenical Council that opened in May 553 in Justinian's new cathedral, Hagia Sophia, in Constantinople. Vigilius, a broken man suffering from a kidney stone, set out from Constantinople for Rome, but died in Sicily, and the Roman see, bitter at his surrender, refused him burial in St. Peter's basilica. Yet the condemnation of the Three Chapters did nothing to heal the split between the Chalcedonians and the anti-Chalcedonians. In the eastern provinces of the Roman Empire, a separate Monophysite Church was already coming into being, with its own priests and bishops. When Justinian died, the divisions in Christian theology were as great as ever, perhaps even greater.

The effort to find a creed acceptable to both Chalcedonians and anti-Chalcedonians became an obsession of Justinian. He continued to ponder the question and to consult: in 557 he convoked a meeting of Monophysite clergy in Constantinople, but it achieved nothing. Then, in late 564, he proclaimed an edict that affirmed the heresy of Aphthartodocetism, an extreme form of Monophysitism, and he required the patriarchs of the church to give their assent. The patriarch of Constantinople refused and was packed off to a monastery, and a replacement was found whom Justinian thought would be more malleable—in fact, he was only more cunning. All the patriarchs opposed Justinian's edict, and a showdown was in the offing when Justinian died in his sleep in mid-November 565. His successor, Justin II, immediately revoked the Aphthartodocetist decree.

THE FINAL YEARS

When Justinian's reign began, he surrounded himself with bright young men, often from obscure backgrounds. Many of them grew wealthy, for high office in the civil service or the army was a road to self-enrichment. Some fell from favor, but Justinian was always reluctant to discard an efficient minister, even when that individual used questionable methods. As Justinian grew old, his officials grew old with him. Liberius, the general in charge of the Byzantine expedition into Spain in 552, was over eighty years old. So was the eunuch Narses when he succeeded where Belisarios had failed in Italy, and finally crushed the Ostrogoths in 552. Justinian's knack of finding bright young men to serve him seems to have deserted him.

Yet the old problems kept recurring. The imperial treasury was empty, for Justinian's lavish building program had helped to empty it, and the demands of the army were expensive. Justinian resorted to forced loans to get money. Bubonic plague, which smote Constantinople in 542, traveled across the empire and returned to Constantinople for a new crop of victims in 558. In the same year, the dome of Justinian's great church of Hagia Sophia collapsed, and it had to be rebuilt with a less daring design. In 559, a horde of Kutrigur Huns, led by their *khagan* Zabergan, crossed the Danube on a cold March day when the river was frozen. They swept into the Balkans. One spearhead reached Constantinople, and there were no troops to resist them. Justinian had to call his old general Belisarios out of retirement, and he put together a scratch force that caught the Huns in an ambush and routed them. It was a close call.

The menace of the Kutrigurs on the Danube frontier faded after 562, but a new ethnic group appeared: the Avars, mounted warriors who introduced the stirrup into Europe. An Avar embassy first appeared in Constantinople in 558, asking for land within the empire and calling for an annual subsidy. Justinian granted them a subsidy, but for land he directed them elsewhere. The Avars would be a problem in the future. At least on the eastern frontier, Justinian succeeded in buying peace. In 561, a new peace treaty, calling for an annual subsidy of 420 gold pounds, was negotiated with Persia. But in 563, the Berbers in North Africa revolted again. The cause was Byzantine misgovernment, and the revolt had not yet been suppressed when Justinian died.

Justinian left an empty treasury and many unpaid debts for his successor, Justin II, who was the son of Justinian's sister and whose wife, Sophia, was the niece of Empress Theodora. They were the last of the dynasty that began when Justin I was unexpectedly chosen emperor in 518. In their reign, the Lombards would invade Italy and the Byzantine Empire would lose control of most of Justinian's reconquest there. In the east, Justin II would provoke a new war with Persia which was so disastrous that he lost his sanity and Sophia, who was not Theodora's niece for nothing, stepped into the power vacuum and saved the situation. At the start of his reign, Justin II continued the fruitless search for reconciliation between the Chalcedonians and anti-Chalcedonians, but it was not long before he resorted to persecution. Yet the empire that Justinian built outlived Justin and Sophia, and it did not begin its long decline until after the death of the Prophet Muhammad in 632.

CHAPTER 1

THE SHAPE OF THE EMPIRE IN LATE ANTIQUITY

AN OVERVIEW OF THE EMPIRE

The Roman Empire that Justinian inherited no longer stretched over the whole Mediterranean region. It had been reduced to its eastern Greek-speaking half. In the Balkans, it controlled the area now occupied by Greece, Macedonia, Bulgaria, Albania, and Serbia, which together made up the prefecture of Illyricum. Its northern frontier was the Danube River, north of which were various Germanic, Hun, and Slavic peoples who made constant incursions into imperial territory but thus far had made no permanent settlements. In Asia, the prefecture of the Orient comprised an area west of a frontier that ran roughly from the eastern tip of the Black Sea south to the Euphrates River, and from there across the desert of Jordan to the Gulf of Aqaba. In Africa, it controlled Egypt and the southern part of present-day Libya. The western empire was occupied by barbarian kingdoms: the Vandal kingdom in North Africa, the Visigoths in Spain, the Franks in France, and the Ostrogoths in Italy.

The premier city of the eastern empire was the capital and seat of the emperor, Constantinople. Founded on the Bosporus by the first Christian emperor, Constantine, it had grown into a city of some half-million. Smaller, but still large by the standards of the time, were Antioch, the capital of the diocese of the Orient, and Alexandria, the capital of Egypt, each with a population of over 100,000. The fourth city of the empire was Thessaloniki, the seat of the praetorian prefect of Illyricum. Besides the foregoing there were, all told, more than 900 cities of various sizes, urban centers with churches, public baths, schools, and the homes of the important landowners, each surrounded with its own territory where the majority of the empire's population lived in country villages. The cultural divide was often sharp: in the cities the language spoken was Greek, whereas in the villages one might find native tongues. In Egypt, the natives spoke Coptic, and in Syria, Syriac, derived from Aramaic. Most of the old kingdom of Armenia was under Persian control and was known as Persarmenia, but the empire still possessed part of it and its language was Armenian.

Every city had a bishop, and the bishop of the metropolis or capital of a province was the metropolitan, with jurisdiction over the other bishops of the province. The bishops were often the most powerful officials in a city, and increasingly exercised civil as well as ecclesiastical power. The bishoprics were subject to the great patriarchates of Alexandria, Antioch, Constantinople, and Jerusalem. Rome, which claimed primacy over them all, was under the physical control of the Ostrogothic kingdom, and the Ostrogoths were Arians. The relationship between the popes and their Ostrogothic rulers was marked by mutual respect but there was little warmth to it, and the Ostrogothic kings Theodoric and Theodahad did not hesitate to issue orders to the popes and expected to be obeyed. Yet Rome claimed the allegiance of the Latin west, and its authority extended into the Balkans.

THE GOVERNING POWER

Sprawling over the southeastern tip of Constantinople, taking up an area of some 250 acres, was the Great Palace, the seat of the emperor and his ministers. It was not one building, but an enclosed area like the Kremlin in Moscow, and within its walls were churches, palaces, audience halls, porticoes, even a riding stable. Flanking its west side was the great Hippodrome, connected to the palace by a private passageway that allowed the emperor to reach the imperial loge, where he showed himself to his subjects. The vestibule of this palace complex was a mini-palace itself, called the Brazen House, because of either its bronze roof or its great bronze doors, and it looked out on the Augustaeum, the central square of Constantinople, across which stood the church of Hagia Sophia, the seat of the patriarch.

The imperial office was a legacy of the Roman Empire, and the presumption still lingered that the emperor was elected by the Roman Senate and the people. When a new emperor was chosen, the populace gathered in the Hippodrome ratified his election with the acclamation *Tu vincas*, that is, "May you be victorious!" But in the case of Emperor Anastasius, it was actually the widow of Zeno, the previous emperor, who made the choice, and Emperor Marcian was chosen by Pulcheria, the elder sister of the dead emperor Theodosius II, who might have preferred to rule herself if Constantinople had been ready to accept a female emperor. Once crowned, the emperor became the vicar or representative of God, holding a special relationship with Heaven that was spelled out in numerous pamphlets on kingship and its responsibilities. Unlike his predecessors in pagan Rome, he was not himself a god, but he held his appointment from God; he was the friend of the *Logos*, the Divine Word, and everything about him was sacred. The principle enunciated by the third-century jurist Ulpian had long been accepted—that what the emperor decided had legal force—but it is not until Justinian that we first encounter the claim in a law (*Novel* 105.4) that the emperor is "Law incarnate," and hence the source of all laws.

The emperor was surrounded by ceremony. His public appearances were choreographed as carefully as any dramatic production. The ceremony increased markedly under Justinian and Theodora, who were the first to insist that senators prostrate themselves before both of them and kiss their feet. Crimson garments and slippers, colored with the costly dye that had once been the stock in trade of the ancient Phoenicians, were now reserved for the imperial family, and silk imported from China was a major drain on the treasury: one of developments of Justinian's reign was the acquisition of silkworm eggs, smuggled from China by two monks, and the establishment of a domestic silk industry. A coronation ceremony in the imperial loge in the Hippodrome was introduced for Emperor Marcian in 450, and seven years later, Leo I, on his accession, had a second coronation in the cathedral of Hagia Sophia. With Emperor Anastasius, a coronation oath was added to the ceremony. Justinian was crowned co-emperor with his uncle Justin I three months before Justin's death, and he received the diadem from the patriarch in a ceremony held within the imperial palace.

The emperor's privy council, called the *consistorium*, replaced the *concilium principis* (advisory council of the emperor) of the earlier Roman Empire. It apparently took its name from the hall where it met. It consisted of the five important ministers of state, plus important members of the central administration and sometimes a sprinkling of senators. Despite their importance, neither the praetorian prefect nor the urban prefect was a member, but they could be invited to attend. The senate of Constantinople, which had been founded by Emperor Constantius II, had little power, but it could serve as a supreme court and take part in the preparation of laws. Its members belonged to one of the three upper classes, the *illustres* (illustrious persons), the *spectabiles* (notable persons), and the *clarissimi* (celebrated persons); of these, only the *illustres* had the right to speak in the Senate.

Of the five important ministers of state, first and foremost was the master of offices, in charge of the civil service. There were various corps (*scholae*) of personnel under him, such as the *scholae palatinae*, which by now was a largely ornamental palace guard, and the Excubitors (*excubitores*), commanded by the Count of the Excubitors, who were more effective guardsmen. Justin I was Count of the Excubitors before he became emperor. The master of offices also oversaw the corps of *agentes in rebus*, the agents, spies, and couriers who kept their fingers on the pulse of public opinion, as well as the various corps of stenographers, bookkeepers, filing clerks, and so on. He also looked after the imperial arsenals and factories that manufactured arms and armor, and the imperial post, which took messages and sometimes important functionaries across the empire, using relays of horses. The tentacles of the master of offices stretched into other offices as well; by Justinian's day, he also served as minister of foreign affairs.

After the master of offices in order of importance came the *quaestor* of the Sacred Palace, the emperor's spokesman and legal consultant, who was responsible for the wording of the laws that the emperor promulgated. Then came the three ministers in charge of finance: the Count of the Sacred Largesses, the Count of the emperor's private fortune (*res privata*), and the Count of the Patrimony. They supervised the revenues and expenditures of the state. Finally there was the immensely powerful grand chamberlain (*praepositus sacri cubiculi*), who was in charge of the domestic services of the Sacred Palace and in a position to control access to the emperor. By tradition he was always a eunuch, and since castration was outlawed within the boundaries of the empire, the grand chamberlain was usually of foreign origin, a boy who was castrated and then imported as a slave into the empire.

PROVINCIAL ADMINISTRATION

Justinian inherited the system of provincial administration that resulted from the reforms of Emperor Diocletian over two centuries earlier. There was a large number of small provinces, each ruled by a governor (*praeses*) who probably purchased his office, a practice that Justinian tried unsuccessfully to abolish. The governors had two main functions: seeing to it that the taxes were collected and administering justice. The command of the military detachments belonged not to the governor but to a duke (*dux*), who might be in charge of the military in more than one province, and hence could exercise more authority than the governor, in practice if not in law.

The provinces were grouped into dioceses and the dioceses into prefectures. The prefecture of Illyricum had two dioceses, and the prefecture of the Orient had five, taking in all the Asian possessions as well as Thrace in Europe and Egypt in Africa. Heading the dioceses were vicars, but their importance had been declining over the years, and Justinian was to abolish the dioceses altogether. At the top of the pyramid were the praetorian prefects. The praetorian prefect of the Orient, with his headquarters in Constantinople, was arguably the most important public official in the empire, rivaling the master of offices. His office supervised the collection of taxes in kind, which meant that his oversight extended to agriculture generally. He determined the quotas that were assigned to rural districts. It was his task to supply the army with rations and to see to it that sufficient grain reached Constantinople each year to feed its population, and it was through his office that imperial instructions were sent to provincial governors. He had, however, no military function. He carried the title of prefect of the praetorian guard, who had been the only troops in Italy in the first century, and the two prefects consequently had clout in the early Roman Empire. But the old praetorian guard had been disbanded by Emperor Constantine, and now the praetorian prefect was a purely civil official.

The praetorian prefect's jurisdiction did not extend to the city of Constantinople and its suburbs. Its administration was vested in an urban prefect. He oversaw commerce and industry in the city, and kept law and order. He headed the municipal police, called the *taxiotai*, who were adequate for day-to-day policing but too few in number to suppress a major riot. The urban prefect's dwelling, the *praetorium*, housed the city jail in its basement. Among the prefect's duties was presiding over the senate, and when he did, he wore a toga, the distinctive costume of the citizens of ancient Rome who were known as *togati* (men of the toga).

THE BYZANTINE ARMY

Since war somewhere in the empire occupied almost every year of Justinian's reign, we should take a close look at the army at his disposal. The old units of the Roman army, the legions and cohorts, no longer existed. The standard military unit now was the *numerus* of between 200 and 400 fighting men, commanded by a tribune. The troops fell into five main categories. First there were the regulars: the *stratiotai*, a word that in classical Greek meant simply "soldiers." They made up *comitatenses*, the field army, and they were the elite. There were five armies of *comitatenses* in the empire that Justinian inherited, each under a master of the soldiers (*magister militum*). There were two with headquarters in Constantinople under Masters of the Soldiers in the presence. Two were in Thrace and Illyricum, and one was in the east, under a master of the soldiers stationed in Antioch.

On the frontiers there were the *limitanei*, militia who garrisoned the forts on the *limes* (the frontier). They were commanded by the dukes in the provinces. In Justinian's day it is hard to differentiate the *limitanei* from the *stratiotai*, for sometimes the *limitanei* appear to be regular soldiers operating on the frontier, and not peasant militia at all. Many of the forts in areas vulnerable to invasion that the *limitanei* were supposed to man were simply places of refuge where the rural folk in the neighborhood took shelter when the barbarians made raids, staying there until the raiders were driven out by the regular army or moved on because they had had their fill of plunder.

Then there were the federate troops (*foederati*), originally recruited from among the barbarians. In Justinian's army they differed very little from the *stratiotai*. Like them, they received their pay and provisions from the imperial treasury, and they were recruited from among Roman citizens as well as barbarians. The term "allies" (*symmachoi*) was used now for the barbarian contingents bound by treaty to the empire, fighting under their native leaders who were paid subsidies and granted land for their services. Finally there were the private retainers (*bucellarii*) of the military commanders, who recruited and supported them, though they owed their primary loyalty to the emperor. They were a commander's trusted guardsmen whom he might use as his subordinate officers when he was on campaign. The great field marshal Belisarios began his career as a *bucellarius* of Justinian, and once he became renowned and wealthy, he was famous for the number of *bucellarii* he maintained: up to 7,000.

The most effective part of the army was its mounted archers. They rode into battle protected by body armor and greaves; on their right side they had a quiver of arrows, and on their left, a sword. Even the heavy cavalry, the *catafractarii*, who wore mail armor and carried a lance, also used the bow. The mounted archers could shoot their arrows while riding at full gallop, and their bows were fearsome instruments of war, able to shoot missiles that pierced shields and corselets. The Byzantine army came to depend on them more and more.

On the eastern frontier, where the Byzantines faced Persia, Arab allies were important, and both Persia and Byzantium had their friendly sheikhs. The Persians had the Lakhmid tribe, which was pagan, and to counter them, Justinian made a treaty with the Ghassanids, recognizing their sheikh al-Harith as "phylarch" (tribal leader). The Ghassanids secured the southern sector of the frontier facing Persia, so that Justinian could concentrate his forces in the more vulnerable central and northern sectors. The Ghassanids were Christian, which was an added bond between them and the Byzantine Empire, though they were Monophysite. When al-Harith asked Empress Theodora for a Monophysite bishop for his tribe, and Theodora saw to it that he was granted his request, it marked a turning point in the relations between the Chalcedonians and the anti-Chalcedonians. It was the first step toward establishing a breakaway Monophysite Church.

THE CLERGY

The wealth of the church had increased greatly since the early fourth century, and the clergy made up a substantial portion of the population. The great church of Hagia Sophia in Constantinople had a small army of clergy; a law of Justinian from the year 535 attempted to reduce its number to 525, which is some indication of the size to which it had grown. Bishops might receive salaries higher than provincial governors, and several times higher than professional men such as professors and public doctors. The lower clergy also drew stipends according to their rank. Priests and deacons, who served at the altar, were classed in the highest order. Then came the subdeacons, readers, acolytes, singers, exorcists, and doorkeepers. Farther down the scale were the grave diggers and the hospital attendants (*parabalani*). There were deaconesses as well, who superintended the baptism of women. Add to these the monasteries and convents that owned a substantial amount of property, and it is clear that the Christian Church absorbed a large portion of the gross domestic product.

Yet the church had become part of the fabric of society. It dominated private life. The year was marked by a succession of church festivals celebrating the lives of Christ, the Virgin Mary, and the saints. The church had Christianized many pagan customs and incorporated them into its rituals: thus, on August 15, when the pagans had once celebrated the grape harvest, the emperor and the patriarch would lead a procession from Constantinople to celebrate a harvest festival in a vineyard in a suburban area. The church maintained hospitals for the ill and provided what relief there was for the poor. Moreover, in the cities of the empire, it was often the bishops who provided leadership. The municipal councils consisted of decurions, whose membership was hereditary. These councils, which had once governed the cities and collected the taxes, had died a slow death over much of the empire, though Justinian continued to pass laws directing the council members to fulfill their duties. The bishops stepped into the vacuum of power, though they were assisted by ad hoc advisory councils of local notables. Their relationship with the monasteries in the territories of their cities was not always harmonious, particularly in the eastern provinces, where the monasteries were in closer contact with the country folk than the bishops, and were often anti-Chalcedonian.

THE PEOPLE

The Byzantine Empire was a multicultural society in which ethnicity mattered less than cultural background and social status. The great division was between the *potentes* (influential men) and the *humiliores* (lowly folk). The first of these was the group with clout, who possessed wealth and power. Their privileges were recognized in law, which granted them preferred treatment in the law courts and various fiscal immunities.

Among the *potentes*, the senators were particularly privileged. The Constantinople Senate had been established by Emperor Constantius II (r. 337–361), and the number of senators increased rapidly, for among the privileges a senator enjoyed was immunity from the duties of the curial class (men of property) that provided the decurions for the municipal councils in the cities. There was a hierarchy within the senatorial class, with the *illustres* at the top, then the *spectabiles*, and, at the bottom, the *clarissimi*; by Justinian's reign, only the *illustres* had the right to be called senators and to speak in the senate. The historian Prokopios of Caesarea, who was an *illustris*, accused Justinian of anti-senatorial bias with some justice, for though the senators did not start the *Nika* riots of 532, they joined the drive to unseat the regime once they sensed it had a chance of success.

The *humiliores* were the great majority. They were the tradesmen, small-scale merchants, soldiers, small landholders, tenant farmers, and laborers, both slave and free. In the western Roman Empire, agriculture was dominated by great estates worked by tenant farmers who were tied to the land and were little better than serfs. There were great estates in the eastern empire as well, but the free peasant working his own small farm had survived in far greater numbers than in the west. But the laws tied the *humiliores* to their trades, and prescribed harsh punishments if they transgressed. The picture that we get from the laws is of an unfree economy in which tradesmen were required to follow the trades of their fathers, and social mobility was blocked by legal obstacles.

Yet the picture is untrue. This was a society in which we find a great deal of social mobility. We have numerous examples, among them Justin I, a peasant who rose through the army ranks until he became emperor, using his position to help his family ascend into the upper class, and Empress Theodora, who advanced not only her own family but also actresses whom she had known during her career on the stage. The laws that made trades hereditary clearly could not be enforced. The fact that they are repeated in the law codes is evidence for increased social mobility, for in the heyday of the Roman Empire, it was customary for a son to follow his father's trade without any law to force him to do so. This system was breaking down, and the laws that attempted to freeze men in hereditary trades and professions were an attempt to halt the process.

THE NEIGHBORS OF THE EMPIRE

When Justinian came to the throne, the old Roman Empire of the west was occupied by barbarian kingdoms. In Africa it was the Vandal kingdom, established a hundred years earlier. Luxury and settled life as proprietors of large estates confiscated from their former Roman owners had made the Vandals soft, but that was not their only problem. The native Berber tribes on the edges of the Vandal-occupied region were pressing them hard, and the Vandals, who fought as horsemen armed with spears and swords, found it hard to cope with an enemy that threw javelins and rode camels. The Byzantines were to inherit the Berber problem from the Vandals.

In Italy, the great Ostrogothic king Theodoric died in 526 after reigning for thirty-seven years. The Ostrogoths occupied one-third of the landholdings in Italy, though there is some argument as to whether they took over the land itself, or merely the revenues from the land. The Roman landed proprietors continued to enjoy much of their wealth even after they had lost a share of it to the Ostrogoths. The Roman senate continued as before, with one consul chosen each year in Rome and the other in Constantinople. Theodoric discouraged any fraternization between his Goths and the Romans, and his policy of apartheid was made easier by religious division: the Goths were Arians, while the Romans were Catholics who supported the Chalcedonian Creed. The Romans still considered themselves to be subjects of the emperor, but as long as Emperor Anastasius ruled, his Monophysite sympathies prevented the Romans from giving him their wholehearted allegiance. Once Justin I became emperor and healed the schism between the pope and the church of Constantinople, the Romans were more inclined to collaborate, and Theodoric's last years were filled with paranoia and suspicion. When he died, his little grandson succeeded him with Theodoric's daughter Amalasuntha as regent.

Justinian's conquests brought both Africa and Italy back into the empire, but at great cost. After the African campaign of 533–534, led by Belisarios, destroyed the Vandal kingdom, Justinian organized it into a new prefecture and took the unusual step of putting both the civil and the military authority in the hands of the prefect. The Berbers, however, had risen in revolt even before Belisarios left Africa for his triumph in Constantinople in 534. His successor, Solomon, campaigned against them with some success until 544, when he fell in battle as a result of disaffection among his troops. What followed was a sorry tale of incompetence, army rebellion, and blundering until Justinian transferred to Africa the duke of Mesopotamia, John Troglita, who defeated the Berbers and restored the situation. No doubt the revolts caused much devastation and loss of life, but the archaeological evidence indicates that Byzantine Africa recovered its prosperity. The chief source of its wealth seems to have been its export trade in olive oil with markets in the eastern empire.

Italy also became a prefecture with its capital at Ravenna after the Ostrogothic kingdom was wiped out. The military and civil commands were nominally separate, but in fact Narses was de facto supreme ruler until he was dismissed by Justinian's successor, Justin II. One of Totila's acts during the struggle with the Byzantines had been to break up the large estates in Italy and free the tenant farmers who had been virtual serfs of the great proprietors. Justinian tried to turn the clock back with a law known as the Pragmatic Sanction, but the agony of Italy was to continue. Three years after Justinian's death, it was invaded by the Lombards. Byzantine resistance was ineffective, and Justinian's conquest of Italy was reduced to a few footholds.

We can say less about Justinian's conquests in Spain at the expense of the Visigothic kingdom there. In 552, Justinian, taking advantage of a dynastic quarrel within the Visigothic royal family, sent a small force to Spain to help Athanagild, who was in revolt against King Agila and was secretly Roman Catholic. Once Athanagild won the throne, he found his Byzantine allies unwilling to leave, and the Byzantine Empire retained a province in Spain until 624.

North of the Danube were the Bulgars and Slavs, known by various names, such as the Huns, who were Bulgars, and the Antai and Sclaveni, who were Slavs. The Bulgars were a Ural–Altaic group who had migrated westward from central Asia and reached the Volga River in the fourth century. There they split into two groups, the Kutrigurs north of the Black Sea and the Utigurs farther east. At the end of Justinian's reign, a new threat appeared: the Avars, who had been driven westward from their homes on the borders of China by the Turks and first made contact with the Byzantines in 558. They were mounted warriors who introduced the stirrup into Europe, and with their long lances and efficient reflex bow, they were a fearsome enemy. However, Justinian kept peace with them by diplomatic means, giving them a subsidy and finding new enemies for them outside the frontiers, but he refused their demand for land inside the empire.

The Balkans were terribly vulnerable. Prokopios of Caesarea reports that the Huns, Antai, and Sclaveni overran Illyricum and Thrace in almost every year of Justinian's reign. In 530, the master of the soldiers in Illyricum, Moundos, defeated a horde of Bulgars and won a breathing space during which peace prevailed for a decade. In 540, a horde of Bulgars invaded Illyricum and Thrace, menacing Constantinople itself, and returned home with some 100,000 captives. In the same year, another raid got as far south as the Isthmus of Corinth, where a wall across the isthmus, the ruins of which may still be seen, barred their advance. Four years later there was another Bulgar raid into Illyricum, and the next year Narses, while on his way to Italy, encountered a horde of Sclaveni in Thrace and destroyed it. There were more raids in 550, and in 559 a horde of Kutrigurs descended on the Balkan Peninsula. One spearhead got as far south as Thermopylae, another reached the Gallipoli Peninsula, and a third thrust threatened Constantinople, which was without an adequate defending force. Desperate, Justinian called Belisarios out of retirement, and the old warrior laid an ambush for the Kutrigurs and put them to flight. Yet in spite of all the raids, there were no permanent settlements of Slavs south of the Danube until nearly the end of the century, and at Justinian's death the Danube frontier was still intact.

On the eastern frontier, there was the Persian Empire. Persia bitterly resented the great fortress of Dara on the frontier, which Anastasius had built during a period of peace, in contravention of a treaty dating to 442. Persia was under attack by raiders from the Russian steppes known as the Ephthalites (White Huns), which allowed Anastasius to take advantage of Persian weakness. When Justinian came to the throne, he inherited a war that was not going well, but in 530 the Byzantines, led by Belisarios, won a victory outside the walls of Dara, and in the same year they won another success farther north at Satala, on the main east–west road to Anatolia. The general in charge there was Sittas, who had just married Empress Theodora's elder sister, Komito. Neither victory was decisive, however, and the following year, Belisarios suffered an ignominious defeat at Callinicum on the Euphrates River.

Both sides were now ready for peace. Negotiations took place in 532, and the "Endless Peace" came into effect the next year. It did not last long. In 540 the shah of Persia, Khusru, invaded the eastern provinces, destroying Antioch; and though these hostilities ended in a six-year truce in 545, it was not until the end of 561 that a permanent peace was signed again. It called for substantial subsidies to Persia, which Justinian's successor, Justin II, would refuse to pay, and a war would break out again in which the Byzantines would lose Dara.

The rivalry between Byzantium and Persia extended to the eastern end of the Black Sea, where the prize was Lazica (modern Georgia). The struggle was religious as well as political, for Lazica had been a client kingdom of Persia, and Zoroastrianism, the Persian state religion, had quasi-official standing there until 522, when the Laz king Tzath, who had just come to the throne, journeyed to Constantinople to request baptism. Persia reacted angrily. But by 540, Lazica had had enough of the Byzantines, and a new Laz king, Gubazes, took advantage of the Byzantine defeats in that year to renew the ties with Persia. The truce of 545 between Persia and Byzantium did not extend to Lazica, and in 548, Gubazes switched sides again because Persia had alienated the Laz by attempting to impose Zrorastrianism. The war dragged on in Lazica until the peace of 561. Persia renounced Lazica, and the long, expensive war there came to an end.

Justinian is often charged with neglecting the defense of the east in order to concentrate on recovering the western empire. The grounds for this accusation are weak. Justinian did not launch his offensive against Vandal Africa until the "Endless Peace" was signed, and after war broke out again with Persia, he starved the campaign against the Ostrogoths in Italy in order to defend the east and maintain control of Lazica. What upset his calculations was the plague that broke out in Egypt in 541 and reached Constantinople the next year. During Justinian's last years, the army was hard-pressed for recruits. The contemporary historian Agathias of Myrina (5.13.7) states that the army shrank to only 150,000 men, spread over the whole of the empire. When Justinian died, he left an empire that included North Africa, Italy, and part of Spain, but it was dangerously overextended.

CHAPTER 2

THE *NIKA* REVOLT OF 532

In January 532, after hostilities with Persia had ceased but before the "Eternal Peace" was sealed and came into force, the regime of Justinian and Theodora survived its most serious challenge. The Constantinople mob rioted and nearly dethroned the emperor and empress. There had been many riots in Constantinople before; in 512, one of them had almost driven Emperor Anastasius from office. He survived only by appearing in the imperial loge in the Hippodrome, bareheaded and clutching the Scriptures in his hands, and the sight of the old man without his crown aroused the pity of the mob. Its change of mood saved Anastasius. What had sparked the revolt of 512 was a small change in the liturgy of Hagia Sophia that smacked of anti-Chalcedonian doctrine. In 532, what ignited the insurrection was a protest in the Hippodrome by the Blue and Green demes, but it was fueled by resistance to Justinian's reforms that challenged the old social order of Constantinople, and also by the aversion that the old ruling classes felt for Justinian, and even more for his empress, the former actress Theodora.

Perhaps to compensate for their lowly origins, Theodora and Justinian set new standards for protocol. Senators who came into their presence were expected to prostrate themselves before both of them and kiss their shoes. The ceremony must have wounded the pride of the old ruling classes of the empire, for in earlier reigns, senators were not required to prostrate themselves before the emperor and no formal greetings were given to the empress. Theodora had been born into the lowest stratum of society, for before she became Justinian's partner, she had been a burlesque star and a courtesan. Senators who prostrated themselves before her must have done so with silent disgust and bitterness. There were other reasons for discontent, too, including the fact that among the unemployed in Constantinople there was a growing number of persons from the provinces who had been driven from their homes by the harsh methods of the imperial tax collectors on the staff of John the Cappadocian, the praetorian prefect. But personal dislike for Justinian and Theodora led many senators to support the insurrection once it got under way.

The riot began with a demonstration in the Hippodrome. Chariot racing had always been popular, and it enjoyed imperial patronage. In Rome, the great Circus Maximus, where the chariot races were held, flanked the imperial palace on the Palatine Hill, and the emperor could make his way from his palace to the imperial loge in the Circus Maximus by a private passageway. In Constantinople, which was the "New Rome," the Hippodrome, which could seat about 100,000 spectators, was situated immediately to the west of the imperial palace, and there was a private passage from the palace to the emperor's box, the *kathisma*, where the emperor showed himself to his subjects. One of Justinian's first acts on becoming emperor was to rebuild the *kathisma*, making it loftier and more impressive. Like all emperors, he patronized the chariot races, and like other emperors, he had his favorite teams. They belonged to the Blue faction.

The factions were the companies that entered the four-horse chariots in the races. They were known by the colors that their horses wore: the Blues, Greens, Reds, and Whites. In Constantinople, the Reds and the Whites had fallen into a secondary position, and although charioteers still wore their colors, their horses were provided by the Blues and the Greens, and possibly even the Blue and Green factions may have used horses from the imperial stables. But the Reds and Whites still had fans who sat together in the Hippodrome and cheered the Red and White charioteers. Emperor Anastasius had been a Red.

Yet it was the Blue and Green factions that attracted the most devoted fans. Chariot racing was the equivalent of football, baseball, or hockey games in modern North American cities. In Constantinople it had no rivals as a spectator sport. Combat in which pairs of gladiators fought in the arena, often until one combatant was killed, had fallen under the disapproval of the church. Wild beast fights had lasted longer, but their popular appeal was diminishing as well. The Hippodrome was what drew the youth in Constantinople. Blue and Green gangs of young men sat together in their own sections and cheered on their favorite charioteers.

On the streets, their rivalry often erupted into gang warfare. Contemporary sources refer to these young men as demes, as if they had some official standing. But the Greek word *demos* (singular; plural, *demoi*) means only "people." The demes were the general populace: the upper classes might have called them the "rabble" or the "mob."

Street violence had been on the rise in the reign of Justin I, and some contemporaries blamed Justinian. He was not yet emperor, and he seems to have thought there was some political gain in identifying himself with the Blues, for he was a Blue and Theodora had been a Blue since her days in the theater. If Blue gang members got in trouble with the law, they knew they had a friend in Justinian, and that made them all the bolder. The Greens, who probably outnumbered the Blues, fought back. The streets became unsafe at night.

Gang members cultivated the "Hunnic" look, with long ponytails and shaved hairlines, and they wore shirts with puffed sleeves (as if to make room for their bulging biceps). This made some property owners nervous, so much so that they freed their slaves and treated their debtors with special consideration. Eventually, however, the gangs went too far and murdered a citizen in the church of Hagia Sophia. Emperor Justin realized what was going on, and took measures to restore order, and when Justinian himself became emperor, he issued an edict demanding respect for the law in the cities of the empire. But both Justinian and Theodora remained Blues.

Nowadays few historians accept the hypothesis that once was popular: that the Blues were orthodox Catholics and the Greens were anti-Chalcedonians. Nor do they accept another hypothesis that has been put forward: that the demes were a sort of city militia, though this theory has better support, for the demes were made up of physically fit young men who could contribute to a city's defense, and sometimes did. When the Persians captured Antioch in 540, for instance, the young men in the demes waged a bitter street battle to drive back the attackers. The truth seems to be that a person became a Blue or a Green for much the same reason as one might choose to support one football team or another nowadays, and if the Blue and Green fans resorted at times to fisticuffs, the reason was irrational exuberance. Yet the Blues and the Greens could become politicized, and in 532 that happened.

In the opening days of the year, there had been a crackdown on street violence, and the city prefect, Eudaimon, whose duty it was to keep the peace, had made arrests. He found seven of his prisoners guilty of murder, some of them Greens and others Blues, and he sentenced four to be beheaded and three to be hanged. But in the case of two of those sentenced to be hanged, the hangman was incompetent. Twice the rope broke and the prisoners fell to the ground, still alive. Then monks from the nearby monastery of Saint Conon intervened and, seizing the two felons, rowed them across the Golden Horn to the church of Saint Lawrence, where they took refuge. One was a Blue; the other, a Green. The city prefect sent troops to guard the church and prevent their escape.

Three days later, on the Ides of January (January 13), it was customary to hold races in the Hippodrome. When Justinian appeared in the imperial loge, the Blue and Green fans sitting in their sections opposite him beseeched him to show mercy to the poor felons in the church of Saint Lawrence. The emperor made no reply. The shouts continued during twenty-one of the twenty-five races scheduled for the day, and then, while the twenty-second race was being run, there suddenly arose a cry in unison from both the Blues and Greens: "Long live the merciful Greens and Blues!" The two rival factions had united against Justinian. The riot had begun.

That evening, the mob attacked the Praetorium, which was the headquarters of the city prefect, and attempted to set it ablaze. Then there was a rush to the square known as the Augustaeum, between the imperial palace and the cathedral of Hagia Sophia, and the conflagration spread. Hagia Sophia burned, as well as the vestibule of the palace, known as the Brazen House, and one of Constantinople's two senate houses. Next day, Justinian, hoping to calm the uproar, ordered races to be held again in the Hippodrome, but the mob had already forgotten the two felons, and turned its anger against three of Justinian's ministers: the city prefect Eudaimon, the *quaestor* Tribonian, and the praetorian prefect John the Cappadocian. John was a merciless tax collector; Tribonian was the brilliant but corrupt jurist who oversaw the new codification of the law; and Eudaimon policed Constantinople. They were servants of an unpopular government. Justinian gave way, and replaced them.

But by now it was clear that a number of disgruntled senators had taken over the direction of the riot, and their aim was to replace Justinian. Justinian had nowhere to turn, for Constantinople had nothing like a modern police force. His palace guard was unreliable, because they were waiting to see who would win before they made a move. Fortunately, Belisarios was in the imperial palace, and he had his own guard, battle-hardened troops from the eastern front. So, by chance, was Moundos, who had been appointed master of the soldiers in Illyricum but was still in Constantinople with a force of Herulians. Taken together, there were perhaps 1,500 reliable troops. Belisarios attempted a sortie, and there was a sharp fight in the streets outside the palace, but his force was too small to achieve anything.

The mob was still out of control as the weekend approached. It again set fire to the Praetorium, and the wind spread the flames. Justinian was now besieged in the imperial palace, wondering whom he could trust. He doubted the loyalty of the handful of senators shut up in the palace with him, and ordered them to return to their homes. Among them were two nephews of Emperor Anastasius, Hypatios and Pompeios. They begged to remain, for they feared that if the mob was looking for a new emperor, it might choose one of them. But Justinian's paranoia was aroused. He insisted that they leave.

Sunday arrived. Justinian made a last effort to appease the mob, appearing in the imperial loge in the Hippodrome with the Gospels in his hands and promising to accede to the demands of the people and grant the rioters amnesty. But the mob replied with insults. Learning that Anastasius' nephews were no longer in the palace, the mob rushed to Hypatios' house, dragged him out, and took him to the Forum of Constantine (where visitors to Istanbul can still see the stump of a column that once supported a statue of Emperor Constantine). There, at the foot of the column, Hypatios was crowned with a gold chain. He was terrified at first, but then a false rumor reached him that Justinian and Theodora had fled, and he took heart. The imperial throne was attractive.

Within the palace, Justinian and his handful of supporters were panicky. Most of the emperor's advisers counseled flight. But Empress Theodora would have none of it. She said that she, at least, would not flee; she would live by the old maxim that the imperial purple made a good burial shroud. She carried the day. The mob, packed in the Hippodrome, was acclaiming Hypatios emperor, but as he looked down on the people below, he heard the cheers turn to cries of fear and pain. Belisarios, with his guardsmen at his back, entered the Hippodrome by one entrance, while Moundos with his Herulians entered by another. They began to cut down the rioters, who were crammed too closely together to defend themselves. It was estimated that 30,000 were killed. It was a brutal solution, but it left the regime of Justinian and Theodora secure.

Hypatios and Pompeios were put to death and their property was confiscated. Justinian was inclined to spare them, but Theodora insisted that they be killed. Their bodies, cast into the sea, were later washed up on the beach and recovered. Eighteen other senators were banished and lost their property. But once Justinian felt secure, he allowed them to return and gave them back the remainder of their property (he had already bestowed some of it on others). Likewise, he restored the property of Hypatios and Pompeios to their children. The bloodletting had been immense, but Justinian wanted the healing process to begin as soon as possible.

The result was, however, that the levers of power were now firmly in Justinian's hands. John the Cappadocian was soon back in office, cutting costs where he could and squeezing taxes out of reluctant taxpayers. Tribonian continued his work on the laws. The Senate in Constantinople, lacking the long tradition of the Senate in Rome, had never been a very effective instrument, but now it was powerless. Like it or not, the old ruling class of Constantinople had to accept this new dynasty descended from Balkan peasants on Justinian's side, and from the riffraff of the theater on Theodora's.

CHAPTER 3

THE LEGAL ACHIEVEMENT OF JUSTINIAN

THE STATE OF THE LAW

"The vain titles of the victories of Justinian are crumbled into dust; but the name of the legislator is inscribed on a fair and lasting monument." That was the verdict of Edward Gibbon in his *The Decline and Fall of the Roman Empire*, written more than two centuries ago and still the most widely read treatment of late antiquity. The "fair and lasting monument" is Justinian's codification of Roman law, the *Corpus Iuris Civilis*. In its modern edition it fills three large volumes with a total of over 2,200 closely printed pages, and its influence is still felt in the law courts of Europe and Latin America.

The Justinianic period inherited a vast quantity of jurisprudence from the past. The first Roman law code, the Twelve Tables, which has survived only in fragments, dates to 451 B.C.E. Since then a great accumulation of laws and legal literature had mushroomed. Some were case-made laws, legal interpretations in the law courts that were regarded as binding on later judges. Roman emperors issued edicts and "constitutions" (Latin, *constitutiones*, "decisions" or "regulations"), which had the force of law. If a provincial governor queried an emperor on a point of law, the emperor's response had legal force. In addition, there were the opinions of the legal experts, the *jurisconsulti*, men who made a special study of law and were consulted by the practicing lawyers. In the Roman Empire a lawyer would have a gentleman's education—training in rhetoric and classical literature—but his training in law might be rather sketchy. For the finer points in law, he went to a *jurisconsultus*.

By Justinian's day, legal education had been regularized, and Justinian fine-tuned the curriculum. Lawyers were still expected to have adequate training in rhetoric and to be familiar with classical literature. In the east, that meant the classics of ancient Greece, such as Homer, Herodotos, and Thucydides and the lyric poets, for the Latin classics never attracted many readers among the Greeks. But Latin was the language of law, and an aspiring lawyer had to learn it. A papyrus found at Nessana, a village on the edge of the desert in Palestine, is a vocabulary list for Virgil's *Aeneid*, a Latin epic read in school, and the list must have been used by a schoolboy there in the early sixth century. After elementary school, the would-be lawyer had to seek higher education, and if his family was wealthy enough, he might go to one of the great schools in Alexandria, Gaza, Constantinople (where Emperor Theodosius II had founded a university), or Athens, where the Neoplatonic Academy was still a stronghold of pagan philosophy until Justinian closed it down in 529 by banning all pagan teachers from the classrooms. But, pagan or not, the teachers instructed their pupils in a curriculum that emphasized the classics from a pagan past.

Then came a four-year course in law, and training for lawyers was no longer sketchy. Before Justinian's reforms, there had been law schools in Alexandria and in Caesarea in Palestine, but Justinian closed them down and concentrated legal education in Berytos (modern Beirut) and Constantinople. The Berytos school was famous for the high caliber of its faculty and for its excellent Latin, though Greek had taken over as the language of instruction in the fifth century. By contrast, the metropolitan school at Constantinople was a recent foundation, only a century old when Justinian ascended the throne. But in 551, a great earthquake destroyed the Berytus school and it was never rebuilt. Constantinople remained the only school that offered a four-year course in law, and gaining acceptance into it must have been very competitive.

Once the would-be lawyer graduated, he would look for a niche in the civil service; with a little luck, he could expect a remunerative career. He was known as a *rhetor* in Latin, or *scholastikos* in Greek, and he joined the educated elite of the empire that was proud of its familiarity with the heritage of the classical past. He was also proud of the traditions of Roman law. He liked the fact that it was written in Latin, a language most people in the East did not understand, and the chaotic condition of the law did not greatly bother him. A clever lawyer might win a case by producing a half-forgotten edict several centuries old, for an opinion written 400 years earlier still had legal weight. Men like him were not overjoyed at Justinian's zeal to organize the law and make it more efficient. Efficiency sinned against the legal traditions of Rome; it cast light on the obscure corners of the law that delighted lawyers; and, even more important, it threatened the perquisites that a lawyer expected.

THE CODIFICATION OF THE LAW

We know of three efforts to codify the law before Justinian's code; one of these, the Theodosian Code, has survived and may be read in English translation. But it was more than a century old when Justinian came to the throne. It contained no edicts or constitutions later than the reign of Emperor Theodosius II (408–450), who had commissioned it. Justinian wanted a code that was up-to-date and based on more thorough research, and barely seven months after Justin I's death, he got the project under way.

He convened a ten-man commission headed by John the Cappadocian to make a new code. The task was done with the dispatch and efficiency for which John was famous. The new code came into effect in April of the next year. No copy of this first code of Justinian has survived.

Twenty months later, Justinian assigned another project to a new commission. Since the first code had been produced, there had been a purge of pagans from the civil service. The chair of the new commission, Tribonian, had probably profited from it, for like most bureaucrats, he regarded the office as a source of wealth. Tribonian came from Pamphylia in Asia Minor and his origins were lowly, but he had proved his worth as a member of the commission that drew up the first law code and now held the office of *quaestor sacri cubiculi*, whose duty it was to draft new laws and countersign them. The task that Justinian assigned his *quaestor* and the commission he chaired was to read through the great mass of jurisprudence from the past, and reduce it to a useful form.

The commission scanned 1,528 books written by Roman lawyers from the first to the fourth centuries, making excerpts from them. Then it organized them into fifty books divided into 432 chapters or "titles." The task took three years to complete. In the *Nika* riot of January 532, the mob demanded that Tribonian be dismissed as *quaestor* and Justinian yielded, but Tribonian's work on the commission continued. By December 533 the work was done. Its name was the *Digest* (Greek, *Pandects*).It contains fifty books, each divided into various "titles" or topics dealing with separate points of law, and presenting the pronouncements of leading Roman jurists' specific points. Most of the authorities cited belong to the second and third centuries, before the Roman Empire became Christian, but a few are earlier. Some go back to the time of Cicero, a contemporary of Julius Caesar (first century B.C.E.). The *Digest* is a great monument to the traditions of Roman law.

It became clear, while the *Digest* was being written, that law students needed a new, up-to-date textbook, and one was produced under the general supervision of Tribonian. The *Institutes* was more than an ordinary textbook, for like the *Digest*, Justinian gave it the force of law. Lawyers could cite it in court. The introduction to the *Institutes* begins with a splendid manifesto that defines the spirit of Justinian's regime: the imperial office, it says, should be supported not only by the armed forces of the empire but also by the law: with the one it can be victorious over its enemies, and with the other it can extirpate injustice and lawlessness.

Justinian continued to promulgate new laws, for he was a zealous reformer. His new code of laws that John the Cappadocian's commission had published was soon obsolete, and in late 530 or 531, it was supplemented by the *Fifty Decisions*, a collection of laws dating after the publication of the code. No copy of it has survived, for once Tribonian's commission finished the *Digest*, Justinian gave it a new task. He wanted a new edition of the code. This is the *Codex Justinianus*, which we still have. It sets forth the laws in twelve books, and in each book the laws are grouped under titles, each dealing with the laws on a specific topic. The date of the law is given, and the name of the emperor who enacted it. No longer could a lawyer unearth some ancient and obscure law and use it in court to support his case. The laws cited in the *Codex* go back as far as Emperor Hadrian (r. 117–138), and laws that the *Codex* omitted no longer had legal force.

Yet Justinian did not cease issuing laws. His output diminished after 542, the year of the bubonic plague, of which Tribonian was a victim. But his zeal to reform never died. He never commissioned a collection of the laws dating after the publication of the *Codex Justinianus*, but unofficial collections were made, and three of these have survived. The largest of them, containing 168 laws, was drawn up probably within fifteen years of Justinian's death. These were the "Novels" (*Novellae Con-*

stitutiones, New Decrees), and most of them were written in Greek. Justinian's native tongue was Latin, for he came from a Latin-speaking region of the empire, but he preferred efficiency to tradition; so when he was addressing laws to Greek-speaking subjects, he used Greek. In Constantinople, knowledge of Latin was declining. Likewise, in the west—in Italy, Africa, and Gaul—fewer persons knew both Latin and Greek, and the language divide was to contribute to misunderstandings between the east and the west.

Partly because Latin was becoming a foreign language in the east, Justinian's new law code, written in Latin, never became the sole source of law in the Byzantine Empire. In the Greek-speaking cities there were already competing legal traditions that went back to ancient Greek customs. There were several efforts to make Justinian's law more user-friendly, which culminated in a great new codification called the *Basilica* (Imperial Law), produced under Emperor Leo VI the Wise (r. 886–911). In the centuries that followed, private scholars also made their contributions: handbooks that condensed Roman law and made it more serviceable. One of these, the *Hexabiblos*, published in 1345, remained an official source of law in modern Greece until 1940, when a new civil code replaced it.

It was in western Europe and its colonies in the Americas that Justinian's code had its greatest impact. Late in the eleventh century, the *Digest* was rediscovered. A manuscript found at Pisa was taken in 1406 as the spoils of war to Florence, where it still is, and another manuscript was found about the same time. The time was ripe to receive it, for Italy was at the beginning of a period in history known to medievalists as the "Renaissance of the twelfth century," when universities were reviving or being founded. A teacher of the liberal arts at Bologna, Irnerius, started a painstaking study of the *Digest* and the rest of Justinian's jurisprudence as far as he was able, and began to offer lectures on Roman jurisprudence in 1088, the year that the University of Bologna regards as its foundation date.

Bologna became a center for legal studies, and Irnerius' successors there continued his work, writing "glosses" or explanatory notes on the corpus of Roman law. The Roman legal concepts that resulted from the studies of these "Glossators," as they were called, filtered into the universities and the law courts of Europe. The major exception was England. There King Henry II (r. 1154–1189) had set up a system of royal courts before the influence of Roman law began to be felt, and along with the royal courts there arose a legal profession trained in English common law. These English jurists preferred their own judicial procedures to Rome's, though even in England, Roman law had an impact. From England, English judicial procedure passed to her colonies. But in the Spanish and French colonies in the Americas, jurisprudence still looks back to Justinian and the achievements of his jurists.

JUSTINIAN'S REFORMS

The *Codex* and the *Digest* look back to the past, but Justinian was a reformer at heart. He felt that he had a vocation vouchsafed him by God to set the laws on an even keel. He was a tireless worker, and his laws give us some measure of the man. They reveal both his concerns and his prejudices.

There is a group of laws directed against the heterodox: pagans, heretics, Samaritans, and Jews. In 527, while Emperor Justin was still alive, though gravely ill, and Justinian was co-emperor, he issued a sweeping measure directed against all who rejected the Catholic Church and the orthodox faith. Then in the next two years there appeared a group of specific laws. Pagans were barred from the civil service, where the most profitable jobs in the empire were to be found. The rights of pagans to inherit and to leave legacies to designated heirs were curtailed. Anyone who was caught sacrificing secretly to the pagan gods was to be put to death. Pagan teachers were denied salaries from the imperial treasury, and another law threatened pagan teachers with confiscation of their property and exile if they did not accept baptism.

The Samaritans, the remnants of the northern kingdom of Israel, claimed to be the descendants of the Israelite tribes of Ephraim and Manassah. Until Justinian, the Samaritan religion, like Judaism, had the status of a "permitted religion" (*religio licita*). The law guaranteed its freedom and granted certain privileges. But in 529, the Samaritans rose in a revolt that was ruthlessly crushed and their religion lost its favored status. In 551, Justinian relaxed his measures, but in 556 the Samaritans rose again in revolt and were suppressed without pity.

As for Judaism, it retained its status as a *religio licita*. The Jewish Sabbath was respected by law. Jewish male children might be circumcised, whereas Gentile children might not, though there were exceptions for the Egyptians. Rabbis and synagogue elders had the same exemptions as the Christian clergy from the burdens of serving on town councils. Synagogues were protected by law against attacks, and if a mob of fanatical monks burned a synagogue and then consecrated the site for a church to prevent the Jews from rebuilding, the Jews were to receive another site of equal value. The rabbinical school at Tiberias in Palestine, which was the intellectual center of Judaism, continued unhindered by the imperial authorities. At the same time, the Jewish community did not consider Justinian a friend. For one thing, Justinian's zeal for legal reform extended even to the synagogues: one of his laws stipulates that the Scriptures might be read in the synagogues either in Greek or in the local language of the congregation—probably an effort to discourage Hebrew, which was being used increasingly in synagogues. For another, it is clear Justinian classed Judaism as a heresy, even though he allowed it freedom. In one of his laws, Justinian wrote "I hate heresy" and among the heresies that he listed by name was Judaism.

The status of women was also a concern of Justinian. Women in Roman society never enjoyed equality with men in all aspects of life, but since the fourth century, the law had been evolving in a direction favorable to women. Justinian quickened the pace. Rape was punished severely, whether the victim was a virgin, a married woman, or a widow. A woman caught in adultery was no longer to be put to death, though her lover might still suffer the death penalty. Instead, she was to be sent to a convent. A wronged husband was not required to divorce his wife before her adultery was proved, and Justinian gave the husband the right to pardon her if he wished (which the law had previously not permitted). He recognized infidelity as a legitimate reason for divorce, but he applied it equally to a husband who strayed as well as to a wife. Yet the husband's adultery was judged less strictly than the wife's. The same tilt toward the male applied to the sins of the clergy: a deaconess who married or took a man as her partner was punished more severely than a priest or deacon who took a wife or a concubine.

Justinian protected a wife's right to her dowry, and promulgated an interesting measure to safeguard her antenuptial donation, which was a counterdowry that a husband gave to his wife upon marriage. Justinian ruled that the same rules should apply to both the dowry and the antenuptial donation. Moreover, before a husband could encumber his wife's antenuptial donation with debt, his wife had to give her consent *twice*. This safeguarded her right to change her mind in case she was persuaded by her husband's blandishments and then thought better of her decision later.

Concubines had hitherto had no protection. Constantine had tried to outlaw concubinage entirely, but his prohibition could not be enforced. Emperor Anastasius had ruled that if a man married his concubine, their offspring would become legitimate, provided that the father did not already have legitimate children. Justinian removed the proviso: even if a father already had children by a wife who was dead or divorced, he could legitimate his children by his concubine by marrying her.

Morality mattered to Justinian, and he tried to bolster it with legislation. One law reveals his mind-set; it forbade swearing and blasphemy because it was due to such offenses that famines, earthquakes, and plagues occurred. Like his contemporaries, Justinian feared the wrath of God, which could manifest itself in natural disasters. A number of serious earthquakes happened in Justinian's reign, one of which cracked the dome of his new church of Hagia Sophia and caused a partial collapse; and as for pestilence, the empire had never encountered one like the bubonic plague that ravaged Constantinople in 542 and returned in 558. Two laws directed against homosexuals repeated a law found in the Theodosian Code that prescribed death by the sword for men caught in the "sin of sodomy." Foundlings abandoned by their parents, and brought up by the church, should be free for all time, Justinian ruled, for it seems that some parents were trying to reclaim as slaves the children they had abandoned. If a slave who fell ill was abandoned by his master and then recovered, the master could not reclaim him. Justinian never attacked the institution of slavery itself—it was never seriously questioned in the ancient world—but he repealed an ancient law dating back to Emperor Augustus that restricted the number of slaves one master might manumit, and banned the manumission of slaves under the age of thirty. Henceforth the age of the slave did not matter. Moreover, the ancient distinction between freeborn citizens and freedmen disappeared, though the proviso remained that freedmen should show respect for their former masters. Justinian summed up his personal convictions when he wrote in a law of 535, "In the service of God, there is no male or female, nor freeman nor slave."

Empress Theodora's footprint is visible in a group of laws that improved the rights of actresses. Justin I, at Justinian's urging, had already allowed a penitent actress who had reached the rank of patrician to marry whomsoever she pleased. Justinian went further. A free woman who had left the stage was given permission to marry even men who held the highest offices, and daughters of actresses were given the same right. Then Justinian proclaimed a law that removed all barriers to marriage between persons of unequal rank, and in 541 this law was made retroactive. Theater managers continued to try to bind actresses to the stage by making them take an oath to continue in what Justinian calls "their immoral profession," thus preventing them from retiring from the stage. Justinian ruled that women caught in this trap would be doing a duty to God by breaking their oaths. He prescribed a heavy fine for any theater manager who made an actress take an oath to continue acting; the fine was to go to the actress to help her begin a new life.

No woman was to be sent to jail. If she could not post bail, then she should go to a nunnery if detention was necessary. The reason was that the male prison guards sometimes violated women. The sanctity of marriage was also a concern. Justinian listed a number of just reasons for divorce. For instance, if a husband was impotent or had been a captive for five years, or if either marriage partner turned out to be a slave, the marriage could be dissolved. A husband could divorce his wife if she went to the Hippodrome or the theater, and a wife could divorce a husband found guilty of conspiring against the emperor. The list was extensive, but Justinian omitted divorce by mutual consent, in spite of its standing in past Roman law. This omission did not please everyone, and Justinian's successor, Justin II, restored it. The basis for marriage, ruled Justinian, with his own marriage to the former actress Theodora no doubt in his mind, was not dowry or other property considerations, but mutual love. This marked a break with the concept of the classical past, that regarded love and sexual passion as a disruptive force, a poison infused into the veins of young men and women by the toxic arrows of the god Cupid, which led them to lose their reason and forget that what mattered in the Roman marriage was property settlements and prestigious family alliances.

Efficiency was another cause dear to Justinian's heart. He proclaimed a number of measures intended to increase efficiency and honesty in the administration. He frowned on the sale of offices, which was the bane of Byzantine administration. But the practice did not end; in fact, Prokopios in his bitter *Secret History* claimed that the sale of offices increased enormously in Justinian's reign. It was a method of raising money, and the imperial treasury needed money. The emperor's concern extended to the church. No member of the clergy was to be charged a fee for installation in a benefice. There was one exception: the Great Church, called Hagia Sophia, in Constantinople. Delinquent clergymen were another concern of the emperor. Many clergymen, it seems, were absenting themselves from their churches, though they did not forget to collect their salaries. Justinian decreed that bishops should appoint other clergy to take over the posts of these delinquents. Clergy were forbidden to gamble or go to the theater, and no man who was illiterate, heterodox, or immoral was to be ordained. These measures give a glimpse of the governance of the clergy, for laws are rarely passed to forbid imaginary offenses. If a bishop was forbidden to leave his diocese except with the permission of his metropolitan, the patriarch of Constantinople, or the emperor himself, we can be sure that some bishops did spend time away from their dioceses.

'In the cities of the empire, the collection of taxes had been the responsibility of the local town councils, or "senates" (*curiae* in Latin or *boulai* in Greek). The members of these city senates belonged to the curial class (men of property), and at one time it was an honor to belong to the *curia* of a city. That had long ago ceased to be the case. The *curiae* had to make good any shortfall in the taxation quota; hence membership in a *curia* was a road to poverty, or at least a much reduced fortune. Thus escape from the curial class became a fine art. One way was to become a member of the clergy, which made ordination popular. Another way was to become a member of the Constantinople senate, which had been founded by Emperor Constantine I's son, Constantius II, in imitation of the senate of Rome on the Tiber. But the more members who managed to escape their curial duties in their home cities, the more onerous the duties became for the curials who were left.

Emperor Anastasius had tried to remedy the situation by appointing tax collectors called *vindices*, who would take the burdens off the shoulders of the *curiales*. The *vindices* seem to have made matters worse. Justinian's solution was old-fashioned: he passed laws to prevent the *curiales* from evading their financial responsibilities. He seemed oblivious to the fact that in many cities, there were no longer any *curiae*. Instead, the bishops were becoming the most important men in the cities of the empire. The bishop would meet with the leading men in his city, the *protoi* (first men), local persons of influence whom it was prudent to consult.

But these "first men" held no offices. Rather, they were the heads of powerful families with networks of friends and supporters. The power to maintain law and order and to represent the city shifted to the bishops.

The general picture that emerges from Justinian's laws is of an emperor who was a self-confident reformer, authoritarian and intolerant particularly in matters of theology, which was dear to his heart, but at the same time concerned for the welfare of his subjects and the well-being of the empire. Prokopios in his *Secret History* alleges that he stole the property of the well-to-do, and certainly Justinian's laws show that he was determined that the rich should pay their share of taxes. He was also extraordinarily hardworking. The laws themselves were drafted by the *quaestor sacri cubiculi* (*quaestor* of the imperial chamber), but the work was done under Justinian's watchful eye. In particular we can recognize his personality in the prefaces to the laws, which are often little essays designed to show why the laws were needed and to put them in the context of Roman legal tradition. If Justinian did not write them himself, he at least saw to it that they echoed his sentiments.

THE RESULTS

What difference did all this legislative activity make? Laws can take effect only when there is machinery in place to enforce them, and in Justinian's empire, there was no public prosecutor—no official corresponding to a district attorney or, in Canada, a crown attorney. Thus all cases brought before the law courts were like our civil suits, when an aggrieved party sues another party for wrongdoing. A person might safely ignore a law if no one made it his business to summon him into court. Nor was finding a court always easy. Provincial governors held assizes or court sessions, as they had in the past; in fact, the usual title for a governor now was *iudex* (judge). But governors generally purchased their offices and expected to make a profit from their investments. A poor man who could not afford a generous *sportula*, the fee that every official expected for his services, could not expect justice from a *iudex*. However, Justinian allowed anyone who suffered injustice at the hands of a provincial governor to have recourse to his bishop. The clergy were becoming a second tier of government, and the bishop of a city was often the most powerful civil authority there. But in the villages where the peasants lived, it was often the monasteries that offered protection. If a village was fortunate enough to have a holy man who was respected for his asceticism, he might act as a kind of ombudsman, speaking out on behalf of the oppressed. He served as the resource for the poor and the powerless, for whom the law code meant little.

One of the charges that Prokopios levied against Justinian in his *Secret History* is that he promulgated laws and then promptly broke them. Justinian banned the sale of public offices, but then, barely a year later, he began selling them to the highest bidder. He needed money, and the demands of the treasury overruled the emperor's good intentions. Moreover, compliance with many of the laws had to be voluntary, for it was beyond Justinian's power to enforce them. He ruled, for example, that when soldiers were billeted in private houses, they were to take whatever quarters were vacant and leave the principal rooms in the house for the owners. Prokopios complains that the soldiers always took the best rooms in the house, and he also claims that Justinian and Theodora encouraged corruption even though Justinian's laws try to put an end to it. Prokopios is a baleful critic, but he demonstrates that the trickle-down effect of Justinian's laws was meager.

CHAPTER 4

EMPRESS THEODORA

THEODORA, PARTNER OF JUSTINIAN

In 521, the year when Justinian first held the consulship during the reign of his uncle Justin I, or perhaps in 522, he met the woman he would marry. Theodora was a former actress whose father had worked for one of the factions of the Hippodrome. She had a lurid past, though all the details about it come from one source, the historian Prokopios of Caesarea, who nourished a burning hatred for both Justinian and his empress. Theodora left behind her two very different reputations. In the Roman Catholic west, she was a wicked woman, another Delilah who had betrayed Samson, the strongman of the Bible and the thirteenth Judge of Israel. In the eastern churches, however, she is still regarded as a saint.[1] In the year 2000, the supreme head of the Syrian Orthodox Church proclaimed the 1500th anniversary of the "Righteous Queen Theodora," who, according to the belief of his church, was the daughter of a Syrian priest from Mabbug (modern Manbej). During her life as empress, she looked after Justinian's outreach policy. While Justinian remained loyal to the Chalcedonian Creed, Theodora kept the lines of communication open with the heretics, both the anti-Chalcedonians and, to a lesser extent, the Nestorians. She and her husband seemed at times to be following religious programs that were diametrically opposed, which bewildered contemporaries and puzzles modern historians. Yet they were

---

1. See Susan A. Harvey, "Theodora the 'Believing Queen': A Study in Syriac Historiographical Tradition," *Hugoye: Journal of Syriac Studies* 4, no. 2 (July 2001): 1–32.

partners, and Justinian never made any move to curb his wife's freedom of action, even when she seemed to thwart his policies.

Most historians agree that the story of Theodora's youth and upbringing that Prokopios relates in his *Secret History* is largely true. Prokopios was a contemporary and thus in a good position to know. Moreover, there is a scrap of corroborating evidence from the Syriac historian and churchman John of Ephesus, who, in contrast to Prokopios, liked Theodora and shared her religious beliefs. He calls her at one point "Theodora from the brothel." It is a clear reference to her early life when she was an actress; actresses in Constantinople practiced prostitution.

The future empress Theodora, her elder sister, Komito, and her younger sister, Anastasia, were the daughters of Akakios, who kept the bears for the Green faction. Wild beast hunts were still staged as public entertainments in the early sixth century, but it is perhaps more likely that the bears which Akakios tended were trained for use in the acrobatic acts that kept the crowd in the Hippodrome amused between chariot races. Bearkeepers ranked low in the social hierarchy, but it was a steady job, and in Constantinople, steady jobs for unskilled men were hard to find.

While Theodora was still very young, her father died, leaving his little family with no means of support. Her mother, however, was a resourceful woman, and she remarried quickly, expecting that her new husband would take over Akakios' job. So he might have, except that it was the prerogative of the head ballet dancer of the Green faction to make the choice, and he took a bribe from another candidate and chose him instead. Theodora's family was left destitute. Desperate, her mother dressed her three little daughters as suppliants, putting garlands on their heads, and set them before the block of seats reserved for the Green fans in the Hippodrome. The Greens rejected their appeal. But by chance, the Blue faction had just lost its bearkeeper, and the Blues took pity on the destitute little family. They hired Theodora's stepfather, and Theodora never forgot the kindness of the Blues. She remained their devoted supporter as long as she lived.

As soon as the three sisters were old enough, their mother put them on stage. The eldest, Komito, soon became a star, and Theodora made her debut on stage as a little slave girl waiting on her sister. Proper women did not attend the theater; in fact, Justinian in his reform of the laws governing marriage would make a wife's theater attendance a legitimate cause for divorce. Yet women could play female roles in mimes and pantomimes, which were the box office hits of the day. The plots of the pantomimes were taken from the store of Greek myths that was a legacy of the pagan past, and it was the raunchy tales that pleased the crowds most. Theodora became well known for her "Leda and the Swan" act, which told how Leda, while taking a bath in a pool, was raped by the god Zeus in the shape of a swan. Leda's offspring included Helen of Troy and the twin gods Castor and Pollux. As Theodora interpreted the act, she appeared on stage, and while she performed a simple dance—she was not a talented dancer—she disrobed until she wore only the minimum amount of clothing the law prescribed, for complete nakedness was illegal. She then reclined on stage while attendants sprinkled wheat around her groin. Then a gaggle of geese appeared and gobbled up the grain. It was a crude representation of the myth, but the all-male audience liked it. It was no wonder that respectable women ostentatiously turned their backs on Theodora if they met her in the marketplace.

Actresses practiced prostitution, though they were a step above the harlots who plied their trade outside the imperial palace on the main street of Constantinople. Theodora was no exception. She became a courtesan. At this stage of her career, she gave birth to an illegitimate daughter, and once she became empress, she found a husband for her from the family of Emperor Anastasius. The hope of every courtesan was a generous patron, and Theodora thought she had found one when the governor of Cyrene, Hekebolos, took her with him to his province. Provincial governorships were lowly posts in the imperial bureaucracy, and Hekebolos had no doubt purchased his office, for buying such offices was the rule even though there was a law against it. But the relationship did not last. Hekebolos and Theodora quarreled, and Theodora was cast adrift.

She made her way to Alexandria, which was full of anti-Chalcedonian refugee clergy driven there by Justin's persecution. Up to this point in her life, Theodora had probably had had little contact with the church. Stage players were beyond the pale. Priests would not administer the sacraments to them unless they were on their deathbeds, and even then, they were careful to see that the dying person was really beyond recovery, for if a performer took the sacraments and then regained health, it was unthinkable that he or she should return to the stage. That would profane the last rites of the church. But at the same time, the shows had to go on. The crowd had to be entertained, and emperors passed a series of laws prohibiting public entertainers from abandoning the stage unless they sought a life of holiness as monks or nuns. As an actress, Theodora was not yet baptized and quite possibly had never attended a church service.

Yet it seems that in Alexandria, Theodora underwent a change of heart. Exactly what happened, we do not know. One source reports that she met the patriarch of Alexandria, Timothy III, who gave refuge to the anti-Chalcedonian clergy. At least, even after Theodora became empress, she always regarded Timothy as her spiritual father. Another anti-Chalcedonian churchman whom she may have met was Severos, the patriarch of Antioch. Severos in exile was still the foremost Monophysite churchman, and the anti-Chalcedonians regarded him as their leader, though his position was not unchallenged. A bishop who had fled to Egypt with him, Julian of Halikarnassos, had begun to develop a Monophysite doctrine that was far more extreme than what Severos taught: Julian claimed that Christ not only had a single divine nature, but that His divine nature so completely absorbed His human element that His body was incorruptible from the moment He was conceived. However, Julian saved the Passion by teaching that although Christ was totally divine, He consented to suffer on the cross as if He were a human being. Thus Julian answered the objection that a divinity would not suffer pain. Christ was divine, he claimed, but He felt the pain of crucifixion because He wished to suffer it. This Julianist doctrine, sometimes called Aphthartodocetism, the "doctrine of incorruption," soon gained a great number of fanatic believers in Egypt and, in fact, was embraced by Justinian in the last months of his life.

Theodora became a Monophysite, yet she did not abandon her contacts with the theater. She made her way to Antioch, and there she encountered a dancer named Makedonia, who was employed by the Blue faction. But Makedonia had a second profession as well: she belonged to Justinian's secret service. Justinian was Emperor Justin's nephew and adopted son, but his position as heir apparent was not yet entirely secure. He had his own cadre of informants—many of them, it seems, recruited from among the Blues—and in return for Blue support, he gave them his patronage and protection. Street violence was epidemic in the early years of Justin's reign, and people believed that Justinian encouraged it as a tactic for securing power. His support of the Blue rioters was blatant.

Makedonia denounced any persons in Antioch whom she recognized as Justinian's enemies.

Theodora confided in Makedonia, and Makedonia told her that her luck would change. We cannot prove that Makedonia was the person who introduced Theodora to Justinian, for Makedonia's encounter with Theodora in Antioch is related by only one source, the *Secret History*, which implies that the Devil himself engineered the meeting of Justinian and Theodora. But the hypothesis solves one mystery: How did Theodora and Justinian meet? Among the anti-Chalcedonians who revered Theodora's memory, more flattering legends arose: one related that Theodora was living a virtuous life in Constantinople, supporting herself by spinning wool, when Justinian met her. Another related that she was the daughter of a Monophysite priest who lived at Callinicum on the Persian frontier, and Justinian met her when he was leading an expedition against Persia. This story stated that her father made Justinian swear never to make his daughter accept the "accursed" Chalcedonian Creed before he would consent to the marriage. But Justinian never led an expedition against Persia. These stories are efforts to give Theodora a respectable and pious background, and they come from relatively late sources. The story that Prokopios relates of Theodora's past includes gossip from the streets of Constantinople, but it is contemporary gossip purveyed by people who may have seen Theodora on stage.

Very soon, as early as 522, Theodora was living as Justinian's mistress in the Palace of Hormisdas, a mansion on the shore of the Sea of Marmara near the imperial palace. She was made a patrician, an honor that gave her social standing. But a law passed by Emperor Constantine I forbade marriage between a man of senatorial rank and an actress. It would have to be changed if Justinian were to wed Theodora. Empress Euphemia, however, was adamantly opposed. It was not merely that Theodora was a former actress and prostitute, for Euphemia was a former slave whom Justin had bought from her owner, who had tired of her, then freed and married her. Theodora, however, was already known as a Monophysite sympathizer, and Euphemia was a stout supporter of Chalcedon. But Euphemia was dead by 523 or 524, and without her, Justin was easily won over. He issued an edict that allowed marriage between a penitent actress and a man of rank. This edict[2] has survived, and though it

---

2. *Cod. Just.* 5.4.23.

makes no mention of Justinian and Theodora by name, it is tailored to their situation. Their marriage soon followed.

Justin was by now old and ill, troubled by an old wound. On April 1, 527, he made Justinian co-emperor, and four months later, when he died, Justinian succeeded smoothly to the throne. His reign would last thirty-eight years. Theodora would die before him, in 548, but while she was alive, it was clear to contemporaries that she was more than a wife; she was Justinian's partner in power. Governors setting out for their provinces took an oath of allegiance to Justinian *and* Theodora. In one matter, however, Justinian and Theodora were opposed. Justinian supported Chalcedon and the doctrine of the two natures of Christ, whereas Theodora was a convinced Miaphysite who considered the faith of Severos, the anti-Chalcedonian patriarch of Antioch now in exile in Egypt, the correct view of the nature of the Trinity.

THEODORA AS EMPRESS

Theodora must have enjoyed her position as empress with all its perquisites. Constantinople's ruling elite had despised her as an actress and a courtesan in her youth, and now she took pleasure in lording it over them. Court protocol had always been important, but with Justinian and Theodora it reached new heights. Theodora insisted upon every mark of respect. Justinian was approachable, but Theodora made men who wanted an audience with her wait in an antechamber until she was ready to see them, and then they had to prostrate themselves before her and kiss her feet. She enjoyed luxurious living. Unlike Justinian, who was abstemious and needed little sleep, Theodora slept late and loved gourmet food. Moreover, she did not turn her back on her old friends from the theater. On the contrary, she invited actresses into the palace and clearly liked their company. She even found upper-class husbands for the daughters of her actress friends. In one case, she arranged a marriage between the daughter of an actress with the stage name of Chrysomallo (Blondie) and the son of a former high official in the civil service. When she heard that the groom had complained after his wedding night that his bride was not a virgin, she ordered him tossed in a blanket. She was no doubt aware that upper-class bridegrooms were rarely virgins, and double standards were not to her liking.

Theodora shared her good fortune with her family. Her sister Komito made a good marriage to a promising young Armenian general, Sittas. What happened to Theodora's mother and her younger sister, Anastasia, is not known, but Theodora's illegitimate daughter had children who moved into the upper crust of Constantinople. Theodora's niece Sophia, probably Komito's daughter, married Justinian's nephew, Justin, who became Emperor Justin II. Theodora also had her own network. Antonina, the wife of the great general Belisarios, was her crony; their relationship must have begun early, for they shared a background in the theater. Their friendship probably helped Belisarios' career. Cronyism was a way of life in the Byzantine administration, and Theodora had her favorites, not all of them as able as Belisarios.

There were also those whom she disliked. Among them was the brilliant general Germanos, who, like Justinian, was a nephew of Emperor Justin. Justin had brought Germanos to Constantinople for an education, and launched him on a military career. He soon made a reputation with a victory in 517 over a horde of barbarians who had crossed the Danube and penetrated as far south as the pass of Thermopylae in Greece. But Theodora feared him. Since her marriage with Justinian was childless, Germanos was the obvious successor, and once he became emperor, she could expect her own power to be eclipsed. Thus Germanos received no major commands. He was sent to Africa to put down a revolt, which he did efficiently, and in 540, he was sent to Antioch with an inadequate force to defend it against an imminent Persian attack. But he soon realized that defense was hopeless. He withdrew, and the shah of Persia, Khusru, took Antioch and destroyed it. Finally, after Theodora's death, Justinian put Germanos in command of the war against the Ostrogoths in Italy. Germanos raised an army, but before he could leave for the Italian front, he took ill and died.

The man whom Theodora was most determined to destroy, however, was the praetorian prefect, John the Cappadocian. John was an efficient administrator, and Justinian appreciated his abilities. But he showed no respect for Theodora. Moreover, he attempted to plant suspicions in Justinian's mind about her, and Theodora recognized danger not only to herself but to the throne as well, for John's power was growing and he was ambitious. With Antonina's help, she set a trap for John. He was overheard plotting against Justinian, who, with some reluctance, dismissed him.

An incident after her death shows how great Theodora's influence at

court had been during her lifetime. In 548, Belisarios, who had been cam-
paigning without success, in Italy for four years against the Ostrogoths,
realized that without reinforcements, there was no chance of victory. His
wife, Antonina, returned to Constantinople to ask for Theodora's help,
relying on their long friendship. When she reached Constantinople and
discovered that Theodora was dead, she realized that the one person who
could induce Justinian to commit more resources to Belisarios' campaign
was gone. With her death, Justinian lost an adviser whose advice he
heeded, even when they disagreed.

THE THEOLOGICAL SCHISM AND THEODORA

The Monophysites were aware very early of Theodora's sympathy for
their cause. Even before she was married to Justinian, hard-pressed anti-
Chalcedonian clergy appealed to her for help. A group of anti-
Chalcedonian monks from near Amida (modern Diyarbakir in Turkey)
were driven from their monastery into the Negev Desert, where they
nearly perished of privation. Desperate, their abbot sent a messenger to
Constantinople to seek out Theodora. She was living with Justinian in
the Palace of Hormisdas and had been raised to the rank of patrician, but
she was not yet Justinian's wife. The year was probably no later than 523.
As soon as she learned of the plight of the refugee monks, she approached
Justinian, who in turn approached Justin, and the monks were allowed
to go to the safe haven of Egypt. When their abbot died, she saw to it
that his body was returned to Amida.

Once Justin was dead and she became empress, Theodora turned the
Palace of Hormisdas into a sanctuary for refugee Monophysite clergy who
fled to Constantinople. Justinian united the palace, which was close to
the shore of the Sea of Marmara, with the imperial palace, so that
Theodora could make frequent visits to the holy men there and receive
their blessings, and upon occasion she brought Justinian with her. Only
one structure of this palace remains today, the Little Ayasofya mosque,
built as the church of Saints Sergius and Bacchus and intended, probably, as a place of worship for the Monophysites. It shared an exonarthex
(a narthex or porch outside the narthex) with a church that no longer
exists, the church of Saints Peter and Paul, built by Justinian in 519 or
520 to mark the end of the Akakian Schism. It was Chalcedonian, and
the outer narthex that it shared with the anti-Chalcedonian church next

door may be symbolic of the sort of modus vivendi which Theodora sought to establish between Chalcedonians and anti-Chalcedonians.

The refuge that Theodora maintained in the Palace of Hormisdas for the anti-Chalcedonians won her their gratitude, but it also served Justinian's purposes. As long as these clergymen remained in the Hormisdas Palace, they were kept in isolation, for though they might receive visitors who came to marvel at their sanctity, they were not living in the cities and villages of the east and making converts. The anti-Chalcedonian clergy who had taken refuge with Severos, the exiled patriarch of Antioch whom the anti-Chalcedonians in the east still regarded as their rightful archbishop, were growing impatient. Their congregations in the east might attend church with the Chalcedonians, but they refused to receive the sacraments from a Chalcedonian priesthood, and thus they were denied the last rites before death as well as the sacraments of communion and baptism. Yet the Monophysite bishops hesitated to ordain a separate priesthood, for that could lead to two separate Christian denominations, and would rouse frantic imperial opposition. Nonetheless, even before Justinian became emperor in 527, a Monophysite bishop named John of Tella had already taken that step with the assent of Severos, if not his blessing. John's success was remarkable. There was clearly a hunger among the Monophysite laity in the east for clergy who shared their anti-Chalcedonian theology.

Justinian recognized the danger. In 530 or 531 the persecution of the Monophysite clergy was relaxed, and Justinian switched to dialogue. He probably made the change of policy at Theodora's urging, for now she began to take an active role in trying to heal the schism between Chalcedonians and anti-Chalcedonians. But Justinian also was aware that the persecution which Emperor Justin had initiated at the urging of the pope was not working. Severos refused the invitation to come to Constantinople for talks, saying he was old and sick, but a group of exiled Monophysite bishops did come, and for more than a year they and the Chalcedonians discussed their differences in the Palace of Hormisdas. Their discussions culminated with a three-day debate in 533.

On the second day of the debate, the Monophysite side made a point that the supporters of the Council of Chalcedon found embarrassing. Both sides agreed that Nestorios, who had argued for two separate natures in Christ, was a heretic. Yet the Council of Chalcedon had rehabilitated two of Nestorios' strongest supporters, Theodoret of Kyrrhos and

Ibas of Edessa. They had, in fact, been returned to their bishoprics. Did that not prove that the Chalcedonians were really Nestorian heretics in disguise? The Chalcedonians replied that before Ibas and Theodoret were returned to their sees, they were made to condemn Nestorios. It was not a completely satisfactory answer, but the anti-Chalcedonians did not press their advantage.

On the third day, Justinian attended the debate and pressed for a formula that he thought would bridge the gap between the two camps. This was the Theopaschite doctrine, and it had a Monophysite flavor. It said that "one of the Holy Trinity suffered in the flesh." Emperor Anastasius had attempted to add these words to the *Trisagion* in the Hagia Sophia liturgy, and the riots that resulted nearly toppled him from the throne. Doctrinal controversy was taken very seriously in the Byzantine world. Justinian's olive branch did not satisfy the Monophysites, however. A bishop and some priests defected from their camp, but by and large both Chalcedonians and anti-Chalcedonians stood firm. Justinian pressed on with his Theopaschite formula, however. The pope assented to it after some hesitation, and Justinian promulgated it as law in time to include it in the second edition of the law code, which appeared in November 534.

Then Severos agreed to come to Constantinople. He had refused Justinian's invitation earlier, but apparently Theodora had used her full powers of persuasion. He may also have had a private reason, for he made the voyage in winter, when ships did not set sail unless there was an urgent motive for it. His brand of Monophysitism was losing ground in Egypt to a more extreme doctrine taught by Julian of Halikarnassos. Severos may have foreseen that he might need Theodora's help against the Julianists, the Aphthartodocetists who taught that decay never touched Christ's body. The patriarch of Alexandria was on his deathbed when Severos set sail for Constantinople, and he must have guessed that his successor would be no easy choice. Whatever the case, Severos' presence in Constantinople gave Theodora her opportunity.

Chance also took a hand. In 535, three patriarchs of the church died: in February, Timothy III of Alexandria; four months later, Pope John II in the west; and a month after him, the patriarch of Constantinople, Epiphanios. Epiphanios' successor was Anthimos, bishop of Trebizond. Theodora engineered his election. It was a violation of canon law for a bishop to move from one bishopric to another, so Anthimos' move from Trebizond to Constantinople was illegal, but Theodora smoothed the way. Anthimos had been a defender of Chalcedon in the debate that took place in the Hormisdas Palace two years earlier, and no one thought that he might have secret Monophysite sympathies. But Theodora probably knew. Once he became patriarch, Theodora introduced him to Severos, and the two churchmen rapidly found themselves in agreement.

It was now Rome's turn. If the see of Rome could be brought into agreement, the schism between the Monophysites and the Chalcedonians might be healed. In Rome, there was a newly elected pope, Agapetus, but Theodora did not know how flexible he would be. She would soon find out, for Agapetus was about to come to Constantinople, dispatched by Theodahad, the king of the Ostrogoths, who was desperate to avert an invasion of Italy. Agapetus achieved nothing for Theodahad, but his arrival in Constantinople demolished Theodora's carefully crafted solution of the Monophysite schism.

Justinian's first instinct was to support his wife, but Pope Agapetus was adamant, and in the end he convinced Justinian that Anthimos was heretical. He and Severos were excommunicated. Severos escaped to Egypt with Theodora's help and died there two years later. Anthimos disappeared. Justinian suspected that Theodora had spirited him away to a safe house somewhere outside Constantinople, but he did not try too hard to find him. Yet he must have been startled to discover, when Theodora died in 548, that she had secreted him in the women's quarters of the imperial palace. He emerged from hiding after her death, and Justinian received him with respect and treated him kindly until his death.

Theodora's plan to mend the schism between Chalcedonians and anti-Chalcedonians had been wrecked by the intransigence of the pope, but all was not lost. Pope Agapetus did not return to Rome. His tongue became swollen, and though the abscess was lanced several times, it gangrened and he died a very painful death. In his entourage was a deacon named Vigilius, who was the papal nuncio in Constantinople. His ambition to ascend the papal throne was known, but whether he approached Theodora first or vice versa is not known. He did intimate to her, however, that he would ease Rome's opposition to compromise with the Monophysites if he became Agapetus' successor. But by the time he could return to Rome, he found the vacancy already filled. Silverius, the son of a previous pope, Hormisdas, had given Theodahad a bribe, and Theodahad had secured his election by ordering the Roman clergy to choose him or be put to death.

Theodora was foiled only for the moment. The military campaign in Italy was already under way, and leading it was Belisarios, whose wife, Antonina, was an old friend from her youth. As the Byzantine army approached Rome from the south, the main Ostrogothic army, led now by Witigis, the king who had replaced the ineffectual Theodahad, withdrew to secure the frontier in the north, where the Franks were threatening an attack. The Romans opened the city gates to the Byzantines, urged on by Silverius even though he had given a pledge of loyalty to Witigis. But the Byzantines had barely occupied Rome when the Ostrogoths, realizing that they had made a strategic error, returned and placed Rome under a siege that lasted over a year. Silverius was shut up in the city with the Byzantine forces, and Theodora seized the chance to unseat him.

Antonina was her agent, and Belisarios cooperated. Rumors that Silverius was plotting treason were circulated. He was summoned before Antonina and Belisarios, and swiftly and efficiently removed from office. The papacy was conferred on Vigilius. Now the way seemed clear. But not quite. Once Vigilius was pope, he became reluctant to rescind the excommunication of Anthimos. Public opinion among the Catholics of the Latin west was solidly opposed to any compromise with the anti-Chalcedonians. Vigilius was caught between his promise to Theodora and political reality. Theodora had to wait.

THE FOUNDATION OF A SEPARATE MONOPHYSITE CHURCH

When Patriarch Timothy III of Alexandria died, the schism in the Egyptian church between the moderate Monophysites (or Miaphysites— single-nature believers) who followed Severos' teachings, and the more extreme Julianists (Aphthartodocetists) burst into the open. Theodora had contrived the election of Theodosios, a follower of Severos, as Timothy's successor, but during his acclamation a mob of Julianists burst into the cathedral and put their own candidate, Gaianas, on the episcopal throne, nearly killing Theodosios in the process. When news of the riot reached Theodora, she got Justinian's consent to send Narses with a detachment of troops to restore order. The rioting, however, could not be quelled, and after seventeen months, Theodosios left Alexandria for

Constantinople and joined the Monophysite exiles there. He resisted Justinian's pressure to join the Chalcedonian camp, and finally Justinian deposed him as patriarch of Alexandria, dispatching a successor who had already been ordained in Constantinople. Henceforth, the patriarchs of Alexandria would be imperial nominees supported by imperial troops, and their congregations were largely urban and Greek-speaking. The Egyptians called them Melchites, after the Syriac word for "imperial." In the villages where most of the native Egyptian populace lived, the religion was Monophysite and the language was Coptic, derived from the language of ancient Egypt spoken by the pharaohs.

Theodosios lived on in Constantinople and enjoyed the hospitality of Theodora in the Palace of Hormisdas. The Monophysites continued to regard him as the legitimate patriarch of Alexandria and looked on him as their spiritual father. In exile from his see, he won the respect that the Alexandrian mob denied him.

In 541 or 542, Theodora had an important visitor: the sheikh of the Ghassanid tribe, al-Harith. The Ghassanids were Monophysite Christians, and they were also important allies. Thus, when al-Harith asked to have a bishop for his tribe (i.e., a Monophysite bishop), Theodora smoothed the way. Theodosios consecrated two monks as bishops: Theodore as metropolitan of Bostra (modern Busra) and Jacob Baradaeus as metropolitan of Edessa. Both bishops traveled with the tribes they served. Jacob proved a tireless missionary who roved throughout the east ordaining clergy, and by his death in 578, he had consecrated twenty-seven metropolitan bishops and some 100,000 clergymen. The imperial authorities tried hard to arrest him at first, but he was never caught, and eventually Justinian conceded toleration in practice if not in theory. The modern Jacobite Church of the east looks back to both Jacob and Empress Theodora as its founders.

THE FINAL YEARS

The year of the plague, 542, must have been a fearful time for Theodora. Justinian fell ill, and she faced the possibility that he would die and all power would be swept away. When she learned that two generals on the eastern front, one of them Belisarios, were discussing the succession, she summoned them to Constantinople and they faced the consequences of her anger. But her last years were taken up supporting

Justinian in his final effort to reconcile the anti-Chalcedonians and the Chalcedonians. (*See* "Theological Controversy," pp. 66–67.) She died of cancer in 548. On her deathbed she made Justinian swear to look after her Monophysite exiles in the Palace of Hormisdas, and he kept his promise.

Theodora's career was remarkable. She was more than an empress; she was truly Justinian's full partner. "Our most pious consort given us by God" Justinian hails her in one of his laws dealing with corrupt provincial governors, in which he acknowledges that he consulted with her. Theodora's first-hand acquaintance with provincial government came from her liaison with Hekebolos, and presumably it gave her some experience with corrupt government. She played the game of politics well. She had no mercy for those who tried to thwart her, as the fate of the powerful praetorian prefect, John the Cappadocian, demonstrated, but neither did she forget her friends. (See biography of John the Cappadocian.) We may suspect Theodora's hand was behind Justinian's measures intended to improve the rights of women, and probably she was the author of the laws that allowed former actresses and their children to marry into the upper class. She was a doughty defender of the Monophysites, and Justinian let her have her way.

One incident that is described by her friend, the Monophysite John of Ephesus, illustrates Theodora's independence. Its exact date is uncertain, but it was about the time that plague was breaking out in Egypt and would soon reach Constantinople. On the Upper Nile south of Aswan, beyond the border of the Roman Empire, lived the Nobadai, whose capital was Dongola. They were still pagans, though the Ethiopians south of them were already Christians. One of Patriarch Theodosios' attendants, an old man named Julian, felt a burning desire to Christianize the Nobadai, and he approached Theodora. No doubt Theodosios backed the project, for he had been replaced as patriarch of Alexandria by a Chalcedonian appointee of Justinian, and the competition between Monophysites and Chalcedonians in Egypt was fierce. Theodora was delighted with the project, and she told Justinian that she intended to send a missionary to the Nobadai.

Justinian was equally happy to propagate Christianity, but when he learned that Theodora planned to send a Monophysite missionary, he was not pleased. He wrote to the Chalcedonian bishops in Upper Egypt, in the Thebais, to prepare a missionary expedition of their own, and he sent ambassadors with gold and baptismal robes to present to Silko, the king of the Nobadai. But Theodora warned the commander of the garrison in the Thebais to make sure that her missionary reached Silko before Justinian's envoys. The commander heeded Theodora. He contrived to delay Justinian's ambassadors long enough for Julian to reach Dongola first, where he gave Silko presents from Theodora, and converted him. Then he warned Silko that missionaries preaching the wicked doctrine of Chalcedon would soon arrive and try to pervert the true Christian message, and he instructed Silko as to what reply he should make. Thus, when Justinian's emissaries arrived, Silko accepted their presents but told them that if the Nobadai accepted Christianity, it would be the doctrine of Theodosios, the exiled patriarch of Alexandria and leader of the anti-Chalcedonians, not the evil faith of the emperor.

The Nobadai, once converted, cooperated with the empire in a campaign against the Blemmyes, nomads who lived between them and Egypt, and forced the Blemmyes to accept Christianity. The spread of Christianity, whether it was Monophysite or Chalcedonian, increased the influence of the empire. As for Justinian, the plague, which reached Constantinople about the time he discovered that his wife had trumped his game plan, must have distracted him from the Nobadai, for he appears to have ignored the matter.

CHAPTER 5

JUSTINIAN'S BUILDING PROGRAM

For the building program of Justinian historians are particularly fortunate, for there is a good literary source that describes it at length in glowing terms. Toward the end of Justinian's reign, probably about 560, the historian Prokopios produced his last work, a long panegyric in six books on the imperial building program. It is, frankly, a work of propaganda, and it reminds us that Roman emperors ever since Augustus, the first of a long line of emperors, constructed monuments, public buildings, temples, and other public works not only for the benefit of the masses but also to advertise themselves and the glories of their reigns. Euergetism had always been a feature of life in Greece and Rome. The donations of the wealthy had financed the public amenities in the cities of the empire, and it befitted an emperor, as the wealthiest patron of all, to show himself a generous benefactor of the people and a supporter of religion.

From Prokopios' *De Aedificiis* (On the Buildings), to give the work its Latin title, it appears that there were four main thrusts to Justinian's building program throughout the empire. The religious aspect was the first and most important. Justinian built, or rebuilt, churches. He constructed and endowed monasteries for men and women, and he built hospices for the sick. Second, there was defense, for it was the duty of a vigilant emperor to safeguard his realm. Justinian rebuilt city walls, and constructed forts and places of refuge for the victims of barbarian raids. The budget for defense works cannot have been much less than the outlay for religious purposes. Then there were the public amenities that Justinian built for his subjects to enjoy, such as colonnaded streets, baths, city squares, roads, and monuments. Prokopios also mentions Justinian's palaces, though they receive no particular emphasis in his *De Aedificiis*. In his *Secret History*, however, he inveighs against Justinian's waste of money on his extravagant palace building. Finally, there was the water supply. Cities in the Roman world had always been lavish in their use of water, none more so than Rome, which was well supplied by sources close by. Constantinople was not so fortunate. Its conduits and aqueducts had to collect water from as far away as the present Bulgarian frontier, and it was by no means the only city where the supply of drinking water could fall short of demand. Sometimes, however, the problem was too much water, especially in the east, where a small stream could turn into a torrent after a rainstorm. Flood control, therefore, was also a concern of this builder-emperor.

Most of Justinian's churches no longer exist. Yet the traveler who approaches Istanbul by ship nowadays can still see the great dome of Hagia Sophia on the skyline. It has been a church, then a mosque, and now is a museum, but anyone who stands under its great dome will still find it a breathtaking experience, for the dome sweeps upward as if suspended in space. The mosque of Little Ayasofya still stands, separated from the shore of the Sea of Marmara by a railway track. Justinian built it early in his reign as the church of Saints Sergius and Bacchus, attached to the Palace of Hormisdas, where Theodora established her refuge for Monophysite clergy who had been ousted from their churches and monasteries by the persecution of emperors Justin I and Justinian. Its twin, the church of Saints Peter and Paul, built by Justinian to celebrate the end of the Akakian Schism, has disappeared without a trace. The church of Hagia Eirene still stands, however, and like Hagia Sophia, it is now a museum. The church of the Holy Apostles with its five domes has been replaced by the Fatih mosque, but it was the inspiration for the cathedral of San Marco in Venice, which gives the visitor a sense of the original. In Ephesus, we can still see the ruins of the church of Saint John the Theologian, and in Jerusalem, archaeologists have explored the foundations of the New Church of the Theotokos, and have vindicated Prokopios' description of it. Not so the monastery of Saint Catherine on Mount Sinai, however. It is still in use, but though Prokopios claims that he saw the buildings he describes, his portrayal of the monastery leads us to suspect that he never laid eyes on it.

JUSTINIAN'S CHURCHES AND MONASTERIES

The original church of Hagia Sophia, built by Constantine's son Constantius II, and rebuilt under Theodosius II, was a basilica because tradition had it that cathedral churches should be basilicas. But the Hagia Sophia that Justinian built after the Theodosian church was burned in the *Nika* riot was a church of a different sort. Less than ten years before, the immensely wealthy noblewoman Anicia Juliana, who must have secretly despised the parvenu Justinian and Theodora, had built a great church dedicated to Saint Polyeuktos. Ostensibly it was her palace chapel, but it was the grandest church in Constantinople. Justinian's church was intended to outclass it, and probably he was planning it before the *Nika* riot, for it was only forty-five days after the riot was suppressed that work began on it. The riot had providentially cleared the site.

The architects were Anthemios of Tralles, a city some thirty miles inland from Ephesus, and Isidore of Miletus, on the coast of southwest Turkey. The ground plan was nearly square, but it preserved the interior layout of a basilica. There was a central nave, and on either side of it were two-story arcades that served as side aisles, one reserved for women and the other for men, for it was the custom for men and women to worship in separate sections in the church. The weight of the great central dome was carried by arches supported on four huge piers, and at the east and west ends of the church were semidomes that served both to lengthen the nave and to buttress the central dome. Prokopios reports that the interior of the dome was overlaid with pure gold. Perhaps it was intended to represent the dome of Heaven, but at least it is clear that it displayed no human figures. It was a low dome, and this was to cause a problem, for its lateral thrust soon began to push the supporting piers and buttresses outward. The problem was made worse by a bed of soft Devonian rock a yard or so below the church floor, which compressed under the weight of the piers. The site was not completely stable.

Yet the building survived an earthquake of 553 and another at the end of 557, but on May 7, 558, as workmen were making repairs in the church, the dome collapsed and had to be rebuilt. The architect for the restoration was Isidore the Younger, the nephew of the original co-architect from Miletus, and he designed a higher dome with less lateral thrust. That change, combined with the fact that the weight of the church had by now compressed the layer of Devonian rock underneath, resulted in a more stable structure. Further repairs were necessary in the tenth century, and again in the fourteenth, but the present dome is essentially the dome that Isidore the Younger designed.

Hagia Eirene was also rebuilt immediately after the *Nika* riot, but it tackled the problem of putting a dome on a basilica by a simpler method. Its nave was remarkably wide, and instead of a timber roof or a barrel vault, it had two domes, end to end. Also rebuilt was the Hospice of Samson, between Hagia Eirene and Hagia Sophia. No trace remains. But the little church of Saints Sergius and Bacchus, which survived the *Nika* riot, is noteworthy because its plan is remarkably similar to the church of San Vitale in Ravenna: in both, the dome is supported by a wall in the shape of an octagon. Yet it is hard to say what Justinian's connection was with San Vitale. It was built at the expense of a local banker, and construction began while Ravenna was still under Ostrogothic control. However, it was dedicated only in 547, and on the sidewalls of its chancel there are two famous mosaics, one showing Justinian with the bishop of Ravenna and attendants, taking part in the dedication of the church, and the other depicting Theodora with her attendants in the atrium of the church. Neither Justinian nor Theodora ever visited Ravenna, but we are probably right to believe that they approved the designs for these mosaics, though the mosaicists themselves may have been Italian.

The church of the Holy Apostles had been built by Constantius II as the last resting place of his father, Emperor Constantine, but the construction was shoddy and the building was in poor repair. Justinian demolished it and rebuilt it to a new design: a cruciform plan with a dome over each of the four arms of the cross, and another in the center. While the construction was taking place, three wooden coffins were dug up, with inscriptions on them revealing that they held the remains of the apostles Timothy, Andrew, and Luke. This church was where the emperors were interred, and Theodora and Justinian were to be laid to rest there, in a special mausoleum built for them.

Then there was a group of churches that Justinian built in Constantinople and its suburbs, which have disappeared. Churches in other cities also were built or restored. Antioch on the Orontes, which had to be completely rebuilt after it was destroyed by the Persian sack of 540, was given a great church dedicated to the Virgin Mary, the Mother of God, and another to the Archangel Michael. At Ephesus, Justinian built a church to Saint John the Theologian that followed the plan of the church of the Holy Apostles in Constantinople. In Jerusalem, his church of Mary, the Mother of God, was a triumph of engineering, for the hill on which it was built did not have enough space for the church's foundation, and part of it had to be supported by a vaulted substructure. But the builders were fortunate. They found suitable building stone that could be quarried from the hills nearby, as well as a forest with trees large enough to provide roof beams, for evidently the church had a timber roof. At Mount Sinai, Justinian built a church and a fortress, but here Prokopios' description is thin and incorrect. The monastery at Mount Sinai still survives, and we can check Prokopios' accuracy. Almost certainly he never visited the monastery of Saint Catherine at Mount Sinai.

PUBLIC AMENITIES

Hagia Sophia stood on the north edge of the main public square in Constantinople, known as the Augustaeum. When Byzantium was founded as a Greek colony more than a thousand years before Justinian's day, this had been the city's marketplace (*agora*), the central feature of every Greek city, and it survived as a monumental square in Constantine's new foundation, taking the name "Augustaeum" from a statue of Constantine's mother, Augusta Helena, that stood on a column in its center. Her column had acquired companions, and one of these was a shaft bearing a silver statue of Theodosius the Great, founder of the Theodosian house, which had left its mark on Constantinople with its monuments. Justinian removed Theodosius' statue and melted it down. In its place he erected a brass equestrian statue of himself that glittered like gold, though it was a good deal less expensive. It commemorated the two victories of the year 530, the victory at Dara won by Belisarios and a second victory won by Moundos over the Bulgars. The statue depicted Justinian as Achilles, the hero of Troy, with breastplate and helmet, facing east, holding an orb surmounted by a cross in his left hand and his right hand stretching toward the rising sun. Prokopios imagines that he was signaling to the Persians to respect the imperial frontiers in the east. He was also sending a message to the upper classes in Constantinople, who remembered the Theodosian house fondly and probably would have preferred to keep the silver statue of Theodosius I that Justinian had removed to make room for his own.

The senate house east of the Augustaeum was also restored, and the *Chalké* (the "Brazen House," so called because of either its great bronze doors or its glittering bronze roof) was rebuilt. Both had been destroyed in the *Nika* riot. Elsewhere in the city the damage caused by the riot was swept away. The Baths of Zeuxippos was rebuilt, though the statues that had once embellished it, borrowed from the cities of Greece, were lost forever. The colonnades were restored that had formerly lined the main street (*Mese*) between the Augustaeum and the Oval Forum of Constantine, still marked in modern Istanbul by the stump of a column that once bore a statue of Emperor Constantine.

Justinian also concerned himself with the city's water supply. At a short distance from Hagia Sophia one may still visit the underground cistern now called Yerebatan Serai, which Justinian built under the law court building known as the *Basiliké*. It stored water gathered in the winter and spring, when rains were abundant, for use in the dry summer months. It is mentioned in Prokopios' *De Aedificiis* as one of Justinian's construction projects. Less fortunate is the Binbirdirik cistern, the "Cistern of One Thousand Columns" (it actually has only 224), which has been dated as early as the fourth century, though the latest view is that it belongs to the sixth century and can be added to Justinian's list of constructions. Like the Yerebatan Serai, it has recently been upgraded with an eye to the tourist trade, but the Binbirdirik has been fitted out with a marble floor so that if it becomes a shopping bazaar, as is planned, the stratigraphy under the floor remains safe for future archaeologists to explore.

Each year during the navigation season, the grain ships from Egypt brought cargoes of wheat to feed Constantinople. But there is a steady north–south current in the Bosporus as water flows from the Black Sea to the Mediterranean, and it was difficult for sailing ships to reach the docks of Constantinople unless there was a fair wind from the south. Ships often had to wait at the mouth of the Hellespont until sailing conditions were favorable. Justinian tried to solve the problem by building granaries on the island of Tenedos (modern Bozcaada) south of the Hellespont, where ships could unload their cargoes if they could not beat their way north to Constantinople. Then they could return to Egypt for a second cargo, and some even made three round trips during the shipping season, before the winter storms shut down navigation. It was a labor-intensive solution, for the sacks of grain would have to be manhandled into the granaries on Tenedos, and then reloaded on boats that would carry them to Constantinople. But feeding the people in the capital city was necessary; emperors who failed to do so would face angry mobs.

Antioch on the Orontes, the chief city of Syria, was destroyed by the Persians in 540, and Justinian restored it after the sack. He gave it all the amenities one could wish for: colonnaded streets, fountains, theaters, and baths. In Africa, he restored 150 cities, according to the historian Evagrios Scholastikos, who exaggerates, but this much is true: there was a last Indian summer of city life in Byzantine Africa. Some of the cities restored by Justinian, such as Leptis Magna and Sabratha in Libya, have left impressive ruins.

In Italy, Justinian did little. By the time the last remnants of the Ostrogothic kingdom were destroyed and Italy was pacified, the empire's financial resources were badly stretched. But across the Adriatic in Epirus, Justinian's birthplace, the village of Tauresium was treated generously by its native son. It was rebuilt as a city named Justiniana Prima, and it became the seat of the archbishop of Dacia. Its archeological remains have been mapped at Cariçin Grad in modern Macedonia.

DEFENSES

An overview can hardly do justice to Justinian's activity as a builder of forts and defensive walls. Prokopios lists over 600 sites in the Balkans where Justinian built or restored forts. Many of them were merely places of refuge where peasants might seek safety for themselves and some of their belongings when barbarian hordes made forays into the region. Still, it is clear that Justinian established a string of forts along the Danube, on both the south and the north banks. In the fifth century, the Huns under Attila as well as the Goths had breached the Danube frontier, but in Anastasius' reign, the Byzantines began to reestablish it. Justinian continued the task. It was impossible to stop the raids; the best that the imperial forces could do was to minimize the damage they did, and to score some victories over the raiders. Somehow, the raids notwithstanding, life in the Balkans went on.

Along the northern segment of the frontier facing Persia, Justinian spent heavily to improve the defenses of the cities. The southern segment, from Rusafa in the north to the Gulf of Aqaba, he entrusted to his Arab allies, the Ghassanid tribe headed by the sheikh al-Harith, whom

Justinian recognized as phylarch, thus giving him virtually the status of a client king. At Callinicum on the Euphrates, which was a customs post for trade with Persia, he entirely rebuilt the wall. At Edessa (modern Urfa), he rerouted the River Skirtos, ordinarily a small stream flowing through the middle of the city that could rise in flood and do great damage, as it did on one occasion. The great fortress city of Dara had its walls strengthened, and there was extensive work done to safeguard it from flooding by the river that ran through it. In Greece, Justinian strengthened the fortifications at the narrow pass of Thermopylae, which Leonidas and his brave Spartans had defended to the death against the Persians in 480 B.C.E. He also established a permanent garrison of 2,000 troops there, and his plan seems to have worked: when the Kutrigurs invaded in 559, none got past Thermopylae. To pay for the garrisons, Justinian confiscated the funds that the Greek cities had set aside to pay for theater productions, a move which did not win him popular acclaim, for it must have meant the end of the long theatrical tradition of Greece. He restored the walls of the cities south of Thermopylae, but he left cities south of the Isthmus of Corinth unwalled, trusting his wall across the isthmus to hold back any invaders.

This is only a sample of Justinian's works aimed at securing the defense of the empire. Wars, raids, and disorder were part of ordinary life in late antiquity. But Byzantine emperors were supposed to be good shepherds of their subjects, and the fortifications that Justinian built across his realm are evidence of the vigor with which he tried to fill that role.

WATER

Most people in the Roman Empire lived in country villages, but nothing symbolizes the importance of city life more than the great aqueducts, the ruins of which still remain to be seen, snaking out into the countryside, gathering the water that might otherwise have been used for agriculture and carrying it into the cities to be used for fountains and public baths. The needs of the cities trumped those of the farmers. Justinian, for whom maintaining the cities was important, took a special interest in water supply, not only because it was a public amenity but also because it was necessary for a city's security. A city without a secure water supply could not be defended.

Thus, at a place called Hemerium near the Euphrates River, Justinian replaced its mud-brick wall with one made of stone, and built a great number of cisterns to store rainwater. At Hierapolis (modern Menbidj), the problem was that a spring-fed lake which could have supplied the need for water in time of siege had become polluted. The fort that Justinian built to guard the pass of Thermopylae in Greece was without a water supply, and a cistern had to be constructed. At Heraclea Pontica, not far from Constantinople, the aqueduct was in disrepair and the city was short of water. Justinian remedied the problem. Helenopolis in Bithynia, named after the mother of Emperor Constantine, suffered from lack of water because it had no aqueduct. Justinian supplied one. At Nicaea he restored the aqueduct, and at Pythia, also in Bithynia, where there were hot springs and a spa favored by Theodora, he built an aqueduct to bring in drinking water from distant cold springs.

Then there was flood control. At Tarsus, the native city of Saint Paul, the Kydnos River, which flowed through the center of the city, flooded on one occasion owing to the spring runoff from the Taurus Mountains where it rose. The *Secret History*[1] reports that the water inundated the city for many days and subsided only after doing enormous damage. Justinian had a new riverbed excavated, so that half the river was diverted from the city, and he replaced and strengthened the bridges that had been swept away. Bridges were vitally important for lines of communication. A bridge over a stream west of Nicaea was in ruins, swept away by floodwaters, and Justinian replaced it with a new bridge built high enough to be out of harm's way whenever the stream became a raging torrent. And over the Sangarios River in northwest Turkey, he built a great bridge that still stands, though it no longer spans the Sangarios, for the river has moved to another channel and left the bridge high and dry.

Finally, in his panegyric, which surveyed the entire empire (Italy excepted) with its description of the benefits that Justinian's building program conferred on his subjects, Prokopios comes to the western limit of the Mediterranean. At the Strait of Gibraltar, in modern Ceuta, which the Romans called Septem, Justinian built a fortress and a church dedicated to the Mother of God. The fortress symbolized imperial power; the

---

1. *Secret History* 18.40.

church, imperial devotion to Christianity. Though the panegyric omits Italy, it is in Ravenna, the capital city in the period of the Ostrogothic kingdom, and later the headquarters of the Byzantine exarchs (the governors of Italy, or at least those parts remaining under Byzantine control after the Lombard invasion of 568), that we can feel the presence of Justinian and Theodora more than in Istanbul itself. The tomb of Theodoric the Ostrogoth is there, and a mosaic portraying Justinian is in the church of Sant' Apollinare Nuovo. Justinian may not have paid the construction cost of the church of San Vitale, where the mosaics of Justinian and of Theodora and their respective retinues face one another across the chancel, but the resemblance of its plan to Saints Sergius and Bacchus in Constantinople, and the imperial mosaics argue for a close connection of some sort. Yet *De Aedificiis* passes over it in silence, either because it was an unfinished work or because Prokopios had little to say, for Justinian's building program left Italy comparatively untouched.

Justinian may have left no great mark in Italy, but elsewhere the remains of his buildings are impressive. Yet they reveal an empire on the defensive. When Prokopios describes the building program in Africa after Justinian recovered it from the Vandals, he stresses his defense works. He mentions only five churches, but thirty-five forts. Archaeology tends to bear out his emphasis: at Timgad (Thamugadi), where there was a flourishing city during the early Roman Empire, spoil from the ruined buildings went to build a huge citadel containing barracks for troops. On the Danube River, Justinian continued the work to secure the frontier that was begun by Emperor Anastasius. The Balkans suffered raid after raid by Slavs and Bulgars, but there were no permanent settlements of Slavs south of the Danube until the end of the sixth century. Justinian's defense works are even to be found in the Crimea, and on the eastern frontier, the great fortress of Dara is still impressive in its ruins. Anastasius built it, but Justinian strengthened it and made it impregnable, or so he supposed (wrongly, for it fell to Persia under Justinian's successor, Justin II). But the most magnificent Justinianic monument of all is Hagia Sophia, whose great dome still impresses the traveler who approaches modern Istanbul by sea and discerns it on the horizon much as a Byzantine mariner sailing into the Golden Horn must have seen it in the sixth century.

CHAPTER 6

CONCLUSION: THE IMPERIAL ACHIEVEMENT

THE BUILDING PROGRAM

In retrospect, under the critical gaze of hindsight, the age of Justinian presents an ambivalent picture. When the great emperor died, the dream of the *renovatio imperii* (renewal of the empire) had become to a large extent a reality. The New Rome on the Bosporus controlled the east as far as Mesopotamia. The frontier along the Danube River in Europe had been secured by a string of forts. The southern half of the Crimea was firmly under Byzantine control, protected by a defensive wall. The Black Sea was a Byzantine lake. North Africa as far west as the Strait of Gibraltar belonged to the Roman Empire again, and even in Spain, there was a Byzantine province. The Mediterranean was firmly under the control of this renewed Roman Empire that Justinian had rebuilt. Italy was in ruins, thanks to the war to wrest it from the Ostrogoths, but when Justinian died, Byzantine control there still seemed secure. Never again would the Byzantine Empire rule over so much territory. But should we count Justinian's reign as a renaissance, or as the end of an era?

Across the empire, Justinian's ambitious building program had left its mark. In modern Istanbul, the museums of Hagia Sophia and Hagia Eirene are mute witnesses to his perception of an imperial capital. We can hardly consider Justinian the catalyst of a Byzantine renaissance, but we should not underestimate his achievement. He knew how to harness the talents of great architects such as Anthemios of Tralles and Isidore of Miletus, and they pushed the technology of the age to its limits. The architecture of the Byzantine Empire would not scale such heights again.

Later Byzantine churches would be more modest in their proportions.

But though nothing was built again that was as large and splendid as Hagia Sophia in Constantinople, it had some influence, particularly in a church like Hagia Sophia in Thessaloniki, which also dates from the sixth century. Like its namesake in Constantinople, the Thessaloniki church tries to capture a large, unified space under its central dome, whereas later churches broke up the space with numerous small chapels and subsidiary structures. Dim, elaborately decorated, quietly glowing interiors became the hallmark of these churches. Yet the influence of Justinian's architects also enjoyed an afterlife in Ottoman Turkey, in the splendid mosques built in Constantinople in the sixteenth and seventeenth centuries, long after the Byzantine Empire had fallen. Begun in 1609, the mosque of Sultan Ahmet, the Blue Mosque, which occupies the site of the imperial loge of the Hippodrome, looks across a corner of *At Meydani*, the "Square of the Horses," at its rival, Hagia Sophia; the sultan commissioned it when he was only nineteen years old, to emulate Justinian's great church. The mosque of Süleymaniye, north of the University of Istanbul, is a masterpiece of Sinan, the great architect of Süleyman the Magnificent. Here the achievement of Anthemios of Tralles and Isidore of Miletos has its last afterglow in the city that was once the center of the Byzantine Empire and the heir of the legacy of Rome.

LITERATURE

Justinian's reign was the last golden age of a literary tradition that stretched back well over a thousand years. It fades a little in comparison with the golden age of the fifth century B.C.E. in Greece, or with the age of Emperor Augustus (r. 31 B.C.E.–14 C.E.) in Rome, but Justinian's reign was a period of reduced circumstances in which the climate of opinion put greater stress on conserving the traditions of the past than on innovation or new ideas. No one wrote classical tragedy or comedy any longer. The pantomime, the staple of the theater in which actors and actresses mimed stories mostly taken from Greek mythology to musical accompaniment, languished under the disapproval of the church. In Greece itself, theaters closed because Justinian confiscated the funds that the cities had set aside to support theatrical productions.

Epic poetry was an unattractive model, though it had one practitioner in Justinian's reign: Corippus, a small-town teacher in Africa and perhaps a wandering poet as well, who came to Carthage in 549 and there recited his *Johannis* before an audience of dignitaries. The subject was the recent victory of John Troglita over the Berbers, which brought peace to the African province. Then, after Justinian's death, Corippus turned up in Constantinople, where he produced a poem on the accession of Emperor Justin II. Authors who wrote in Latin, as Corippus did, had only a tiny audience, and Corippus complains vociferously about his poverty.

But in other areas of literature, the reign of Justinian shone brightly. This was the period of the most brilliant Byzantine hymn writers, Romanos the Melode, a native of Syria who served in the church of the Virgin in the Kyrou district in Constantinople, and composed, it was said, a thousand hymns. Eighty-five have survived, not all of them genuine. But the type of psalmody in which he excelled, the *kontakion*, a sermon in verse chanted antiphonally by a cantor and a choir during matins, fell out of favor after his death. The hymns and theological writings of Severos of Antioch, the leader of the Monophysites, mark him as one of Christianity's great theologians; these have survived only in Syriac translation.

It was in historical writing that the period excelled. Since the second century, writers of history had taken as their models the great classical historians of the fifth century B.C.E., Herodotos and Thucydides—particularly Thucydides, whose austere, detached style had enormous appeal. They belonged to a literary movement called the "Second Sophistic," and its influence continued into the Christian period, even though its guideposts were uniformly pagan. In fact, the veneer of paganism is so marked in the work of Prokopios of Caesarea, the greatest of the historians of Justinian's reign, that at one time, students of the period suspected that he was himself a pagan. But a close reading of his history demonstrates that he shared the beliefs of contemporary Christians, though his passion for theological controversy may have been markedly less fervent than Justinian's. Prokopios followed the conventions of historiography that he had inherited from the "Second Sophistic," and there was a reason for it.

In the two centuries before Justinian, Christianity had developed its own history with its own conventions. The inventor of ecclesiastical history was Eusebios, bishop of Caesarea (elected in 313) and a favorite of the first Christian emperor, Constantine I the Great. Ecclesiastical history is an account of the past in which the Savior is seen as actively leading mankind toward a foreseen future, and victory attends those who follow the Lord's path. One of the great ecclesiastical historians, Evagrios Scholastikos, lived during Justinian's reign, though he wrote his history after Justinian's death. Ecclesiastical history avoids the rhetoric of the classicizing historians, who made a point of ignoring the coming of Christianity and writing, as it were, for a readership of Greeks who might have been living in the Athens of Perikles a thousand years earlier.

The *History of the Wars* by the greatest of the classicizers, Prokopios, which ended with the destruction of the Ostrogoths in 552, was continued by Agathias of Myrina. His five books are in three sections: one dealing mainly with events in Italy, where the defeat of the Ostrogoths was followed by an unsuccessful invasion of Franks led by two adventurers, Butilin and Leutharis; a second dealing with the war against the Persians in what is now northeast Turkey; and a third centering on events in Constantinople, such as the great earthquake of 557, the partial collapse of the dome of Hagia Sophia that followed some six months later, the renewed outbreak of plague, and the restoration of Hagia Sophia. It is from Agathias that we have a description of Belisarios' last campaign that saved Constantinople from the Kutrigurs in 559. Unlike Prokopios, Agathias never experienced war at first hand. He was a lawyer who worked in the *basiliké* stoa (royal stoa) close to Hagia Sophia; the royal stoa was the center of legal activity and the gathering place for lawyers, who made up a large portion of the educated elite. Agathias wrote elegant poetry, and what he considered most important for a writer was to study the great writers of the past and to imitate them. To his mind, Belisarios' rout of the Kutrigurs was comparable with the brave stand of Leonidas, king of the Spartans, against the Persian hosts at Thermopylae in 480 B.C.E.

Agathias' narrative stops in 559, but it was continued by a third historian, Menander Protector, whose work survives only in fragments. Their style indicates that he belonged to the same school as Agathias and Prokopios. These were well-educated historians, soundly grounded in the classics, who wrote for a small audience. They saw themselves as defenders of an educational tradition that was under siege. Their mind-set is well illustrated by a writer who spent forty years laboring in the office of the praetorian prefect, John the Lydian, who wrote a history commissioned by Emperor Justinian. It has not survived, but from his three works that have survived, we can gauge his outlook. It was antiquarian and pedantic. John saw decline all about him. The rot set in when the laws began to be promulgated in Greek, which the populace in the Byzantine Empire could understand, rather than in the Latin demanded by tradition, though fewer and fewer people in the east understood it.

There were other, more popular types of history. There was the chronicle: a year-by-year record of events from Creation, or at least from some recognized starting point. The greatest of these in Justinian's period was the chronicle of John Malalas, who begins with Adam. Adam was, Malalas assures us, six feet tall, lived for 930 years, and had a wife named Eve by whom he had three sons and two daughters. We know nothing about Malalas, except what we can infer from his chronicle and his name: Malalas comes from Syriac *malal* (lawyer). His Greek is close to the Greek spoken on the streets of Constantinople. But chronicles did not have to be written in Greek, nor did ecclesiastical histories. One of the great historians of Justinian's period was the Monophysite bishop John of Ephesus (sometimes called John of Asia). The third part of his *Ecclesiastical History* in Syriac was discovered in 1853, in a Coptic monastery in Egypt. The second part survives in part because it was used by a later Syriac chronicle known as the *Chronicle of Zuqnin*, which was written by an anonymous monk in the monastery of Zuqnin near Amida (modern Diyarbakir in Turkey). The cultures that had been submerged by the spread of Hellenism in the aftermath of Alexander the Great's conquests were surfacing again.

In the field of literature, Justinian's reign marks the end of an era. A number of the poems in the two collections of ancient and Byzantine epigrams that are generally known as the *Greek Anthology* continue a tradition of versification that goes back to the great masters of the classical past, such as Alkaios, Sappho, and Archilochos. The liveliest of them all was Paul the Silentiary, the author of a long poem on the rededication of Hagia Sophia in 562. It is an *ekphrasis*, a poem that describes a work of art or, in this case, a building. Any judgment on the merits of Paul's *ekphrasis* is a matter of taste, though there can be no doubts about the charm of his short poems. In one, he pictures himself in the men's section of a public bath, separated from the women's section only by a wooden door, and he imagines what is to be seen behind that frail barricade. His favorite subject is love and lust, though with a literary flavor. He imagines the softness of a woman's kiss, but the woman is Sappho; he invites a girl to steal kisses and then slip furtively into bed, but the girl's name is Rhodopis, a famous courtesan who was loved by Sappho's brother. Sappho lived in the early sixth century B.C.E. We have a short poem by another contemporary of Paul, Irenaios, a bureaucrat in Justinian's civil service, who also imagines himself in the arms of Rhodopis. This is the Indian summer of classical literature, when educated persons looked back to the past and took as their models authors who wrote a thousand years earlier. The men who wrote these works that have survived from the Justinianic period were lawyers or bureaucrats trying, often with some success, to breathe life into literary forms that they had learned from books.

In 529, Justinian closed down the Neoplatonic Academy in Athens, but before its closure, one of its alumni, Ammonios, had established a school in Alexandria. It was Ammonios who trained the best philosopher of the Justinianic period, John Philoponus. Philoponos means "lover of work," and the *philoponoi* were guilds of church helpers in Alexandria. John was a Christian, a supporter of Monophysitism, and perhaps a member of a guild of *philoponoi*. In any case, he attacked the notions of both Neoplatonism and Aristotelianism; in the process, he adapted them to Christianity and proposed some original theories of his own. But in his later years, he turned to Christian theology. It was a sign of the times. Another writer, who had no use for Aristotle or any Christian adaptation of Arisototle, was Kosmas Indikopleustes, an Alexandrian merchant who traded with Ethiopia and perhaps also India and Sri Lanka. He described his travels in his *Christian Topography*, which tells us a great deal about Byzantine trade, Christianity in Persia, and the flora and fauna of the east, but his central purpose was to show that the Bible is literally true. The world, he argues, resembles the tabernacle of Moses. He had no use at all for John Philoponus.

In Italy, the shadows of the Dark Ages were closing in on the Latin literary tradition. Boethius, the last great name, had been Master of Offices in the service of Theodoric, but he fell under suspicion of treason and was executed. While he was in prison awaiting death, he wrote *On the Consolation of Philosophy*, which became one of the most-read Latin works in the Middle Ages. Another servant of Theodoric, Cassiodorus Senator, who was praetorian prefect for Theodoric and then Amalasuntha and Theodahad, set up a monastery called the Vivarium after the reconquest of Italy, and there monks copied manuscripts, attempting to save the wreckage of Rome's past. "Vivarium" means "fishpond," and evidently Cassiodorus' Vivarium, located on a family estate on the Bay of

Squillace in Calabria, in the toe of Italy, took its name from a fish-farming pond on the estate. The Vivarium, modeled on Byzantine monasticism, did not survive long. All that remains is a sarcophagus found at a church in the region which is identified as belonging to Cassiodorus. The task that Cassiodorus and his monks set for themselves was carried on in the monasteries of the Benedictine order.

THE RESTORATION OF THE EMPIRE

Twenty-first century historians, who have the clarity of hindsight, judge Justinian's attempt to restore the empire harshly. It is argued that he neglected the east while wasting resources in the west, and that somehow this contributed to the weakness of the empire before the onslaught of Islam. The fate of Justinian's conquests seems to validate the judgment. Three years after his death, Italy was invaded by the Lombards, and little by little, Byzantium was driven out of Italy except for Ravenna and Venice in the north and Calabria in the south. Byzantine Africa lasted longer, but seven years after the Arab conquest of Egypt in 640, the Byzantine exarch of Egypt, Gregory, lost his life while fighting Arab invaders. Before the end of the century, the Arabs had captured Carthage and were building ships there with which to attack western Europe. In Spain, the Byzantines held their Spanish province for some seventy years, but it was an insecure conquest.

In the light of history, the reconquest looks like a futile enterprise. But when Justinian launched his offensive in the west, the prospects seemed bright. Peace had been concluded with Persia. The Vandal kingdom in Africa looked vulnerable to a swift, decisive attack, and in any case, Justinian committed only some 15,000 troops to Belisarios' African campaign. He was taking only a limited risk. For the campaign in Italy, Belisarios had only half the number of troops that he had when he set out against the Vandals, because the Ostrogothic kingdom looked like a ripe plum ready to fall into Justinian's hands. He miscalculated; the Ostrogoths put up a stiff fight. But Justinian's gravest miscalculation was one he could not have foreseen: the outbreak of bubonic plague. Tax revenues fell and army recruits became scarce. After the plague, what had seemed to be golden opportunities in the west became more like quagmires.

If we look carefully at Justinian's allocation of resources, Justinian does not seem to have neglected the east in favor of his western enterprise. In

543, one year after the plague epidemic in Constantinople, he managed to muster a force of 30,000 troops for an abortive offensive against Persia. The following year Belisarios was sent back to Italy to continue the struggle against the Ostrogoths with only 4,000 men. The contrast is striking. Justinian's reconquest in the west was motivated as much by opportunism as by ideology.

Justinian was swimming against the tide, and he left the empire overstretched as it faced new enemies. But he could not foresee the future, when the empire would be beset by the Lombards in Italy, the Avars in the Balkans, and the Persians in the east. Nor in his wildest dreams could anyone in Justinian's day have predicted the rise of Islam in the seventh century. When Justinian died in 565, his reconquest of the western empire would have appeared a success to an unbiased observer.

THEOLOGICAL CONTROVERSY

The great controversy of Justinian's reign was the "Three Chapters" dispute, which was part of his continuing effort to reconcile the Chalcedonians and the anti-Chalcedonians (who eventually became known as Monophysites). The Council of Chalcedon had accepted three supporters of the heretic Nestorios into the church, and that, in the eyes of the anti-Chalcedonians, proved that the Chalcedonian Creed was really an expression of the Nestorian heresy. By Justinian's time, these three theologians were long since dead, but Justinian proposed that they should be condemned nonetheless. The Latin church resisted furiously, for Justinian was usurping its right, with the pope at its head, to define church doctrine—that was caesaropapism, which Pope Vigilius was determined to resist. Eventually Justinian had his way. The Fifth Ecumenical Council that gathered in Constantinople in May 553 condemned the "Three Chapters"—and Pope Vigilius into the bargain—and in February of the next year, the pope, already a sick man, gave way. He died on his way back to Rome. Yet Justinian's struggle with the papacy ended in a draw; Vigilius' successor, Pelagius, was as much a defender of the Chalcedonian Creed as Vigilius had been. The aim of the struggle, however, had been to find common ground for the Chalcedonians and the anti-Chalcedonians by making it clear that the Chalcedonian Creed was sharply different from the heretical doctrine of the Nestorians, even though both insisted on two distinct natures in Christ. The anti-

Chalcedonians were not impressed. By this time they were well on their way toward founding their own separate church with its own hierarchy of clergy. The "Three Chapters" dispute solved nothing.

THE HERITAGE OF LAW

Justinian meant well. His edicts betray a real effort to improve the rights of women and of slaves and to bring about a more just society that would give the lower class, the *humiliores*, fairer treatment. He wanted to improve the efficiency of the bureaucracy and to root out corruption. Did he succeed?

The verdict of his contemporaries was that he did not. The *Secret History* of Prokopios passes a harsh judgment on him, even if we discount Prokopios' apocalyptic vision that Justinian was the Antichrist. Evagrios notes his greed. What aborted Justinian's good intentions was his need for money to pay for his wars and his expensive building program. He resorted to dubious methods of raising revenue. Public offices were sold even though Justinian's own laws forbade it. If the plague left a farm vacant with no one to till it, the owner of a neighboring farm would be made responsible for its taxes. To the lower classes, Justinian meant taxes, not fair government.

Yet the corpus of Justinian's laws was a lasting achievement. It provided a foundation for the rule of law in western Europe and Latin America. The *Corpus Iuris Civilis* and his *Novels* form his greatest legacy to the modern world.

THE ART AND ARCHITECTURE OF JUSTINIAN'S EMPIRE

There is a Russian tradition which illustrates the impression that the art and architecture of Justinian's empire still made long after he was dead. In the second half of the tenth century, Grand Prince Vladimir of Kiev united south and central Russia under his rule. Vladimir wanted to found an empire with a distinctive civilization of its own, and he realized that if he was to establish a solid basis for the orderly government of the wild, lawless area that he ruled, he needed an organized religion. There were several that he might choose. There was Islam, which was flourishing south and east of Kiev. There was Judaism, which was an ancient religion and thus deserving respect, and there were also Roman Catholicism and Greek Orthodoxy. An early Slav manuscript called the *Chronicle of Nestor* relates that Vladimir sent out envoys to report on the merits of each religion, and those who came to Constantinople went to a service in Hagia Sophia. The vestments of the priests, the chanting and the incense, but most of all the interior of the great church itself, glittering with mosaics, made an overwhelming impression on Vladimir's envoys, and Russia adopted Greek Orthodoxy as its national faith.

The interior of Hagia Sophia is still breathtaking, but the mosaics that covered its walls in Justinian's day are gone. The best examples of Byzantine mosaics now are found in Ravenna, in the churches of Sant' Apollinare Nuovo, San Vitale, and Sant' Apollinare in Classe, and the Baptistery of the Arians with splendid sixth-century mosaics of the baptism of Christ and of the Apostles in the dome. San Vitale, which was dedicated in 547, a year before Theodora's death, has two famous mosaics of Justinian and Theodora on each side of the chancel. One mosaic shows Justinian with a train of officials, among them Archbishop Maximian of Ravenna and another figure identified as Belisarios (or perhaps Julius Argentarius, the local banker who paid for building the church) and various other figures. On the other side is Theodora with her attendants, none of whom can be identified—in fact, most of them are only faces in a crowd. But two women to Theodora's left are realistic portraits; a middle-aged woman and a girl who bear a strong family resemblance. They must be mother and daughter. Are they perhaps Antonina and Joannina, and does the mosaic commemorate the bethrothal of Joannina to Theodora's grandson, Anastasios?

These mosaics in the chancel of San Vitale are unusual, for they portray a contemporary event, the dedication of the church in 547, at which Justinian and Theodora were present in spirit though not in actuality, for neither of them ever visited Ravenna. Byzantine mosaics generally told stories from the Bible. The church of the Holy Apostles in Constantinople, which was built between 536 and 546, had a series of mosaics that showed scenes from Christ's life. The church of the Holy Apostles has now been replaced by the Fatih mosque, but we can get an idea of what they must have been like from the mosaics in Sant' Apollinare Nuovo in Ravenna, which tell the story of Christ's life. They give the onlooker some idea of the magnificence of Justinian's Constantinople, which we must create in our imagination.

The great church of Hagia Sophia in modern Istanbul. *Photo Jonathan Bardill.*

The church of Hagia Eirene (The Holy Peace) in modern Istanbul. *Photo Jonathan Bardill.*

The church of Saints Sergius and Bacchus, originally part of the Palace of Hormisdas in Constantinople, now the mosque of Little Ayasofya. *Photo Jonathan Bardill.*

The interior of the mosque of Little Ayasofya. *Photo Jonathan Bardill.*

The interior of the church of Hagia Eirene, looking toward the chancel. The church is now a museum. *Photo Jonathan Bardill.*

A modern view of the "Golden Gate," the ceremonial entrance into Constantinople from the west, through the Theodosian Wall. *Photo Jonathan Bardill.*

The church of San Vitale in Ravenna, dedicated in 547 and paid for by a local banker, Julius Argentarius. *Photo Geoffrey Greatrex.*

The ruins of the fortress of Dara, where Belisarios defeated a more numerous Persian army in 530. *Photo Geoffrey Greatrex.*

Mosaic of Justinian and attendants from the chancel wall, San Vitale, Ravenna.
Source: Foto Marburg/Art Resource, New York.

Mosaic of Theodora and attendants from the chancel wall, San Vitale, Ravenna.
Source: Foto Marburg/Art Resource, New York.

The sixth-century cistern of Binbirdirek in Istanbul. The floor is modern. *Photo Jonathan Bardill.*

The tomb of Theodoric the Ostrogoth in Ravenna. *Photo Geoffrey Greatrex.*

The side galleries of Hagia Sophia in Istanbul. *Photo Jonathan Bardill.*

BIOGRAPHIES:
THE PERSONALITIES OF THE BYZANTINE EMPIRE

Amalasuntha, *The Daughter of Theodoric*

Amalasuntha was the daughter of Theodoric the Ostrogoth by his second wife, Audolfleda, who was the sister of Clovis, king of the Franks. After an unsuitable first marriage, Amalasuntha was wed to a Gothic nobleman of royal lineage, Eutharic, and by him had a son, Athalaric, and a daughter, Matasuntha. In 519, Emperor Justin I and Eutharic held the consulship together, Eutharic in Rome and Justin in Constantinople, and Justin adopted Eutharic according to Germanic custom, thereby recognizing his right to succeed Theodoric. However, in 522, Eutharic died, and when Theodoric died (September 30, 526), his heir was the boy Athalaric, with Amalasuntha as regent.

A dispute soon arose over the education of Athalaric, who was no more than nine years old when he became king. Amalasuntha wanted her son to have a Roman education, and she entrusted him to the care of three Goths who admired the humanities and the traditions of the classical world. However, this was a sharp break with Theodoric's policy. He was illiterate himself, and though he had allowed Amalasuntha to have a Roman education, his policy had been to keep his Gothic warriors as a ruling class separate from the Romans and prevent their assimilation. The Gothic nobles protested to Amalasuntha that Athalaric should be brought up as a Gothic warrior, learning the Gothic way of life with Gothic companions his own age. Amalasuntha had to give way, and instead of receiving a liberal education, Athalaric learned to drink and carouse like a good Ostrogothic trooper, and was such an apt pupil that he undermined his health.

Soon Amalasuntha learned of a plot to overthrow her, and she took countermeasures: she dispatched the three ringleaders on military duty to separate posts on the northern frontier. But, finding that they were still conspiring against her, she resolved to have them assassinated. Realizing that if she failed, she would have to flee, she contacted Justinian, who agreed to receive her, and prepared for her flight to Constantinople if it should be necessary. But the assassinations went off as planned, and Amalasuntha remained in Ravenna. Then, in 534, Athalaric died, after a rule of eight years.

Amalasuntha had already anticipated what would happen if her son died, for his death was no surprise, and she had sent Justinian a secret message that she was willing to turn over the rule to him in return for a safe haven in Constantinople. But when Athalaric died, she evidently could not bear to resign her power, and she thought of a maneuver that would allow her to hold on to it. She turned to the one male relative that she had left, Theodahad, the son of Theodoric's sister. Theodahad, far from being a typical Gothic warrior, was a student of philosophy with a special interest in Plato. His overriding interest, however, was the acquisition of wealth, and he had managed to commandeer a large share of the land in Tuscany for himself. The Tuscans had complained to Amalasuntha about his rapacity, and she had forced him to give up some properties that he had appropriated, thereby earning his bitter hatred. Yet now she offered him the title of king on condition that she should continue to hold the reins of government. Theodahad agreed, and Amalasuntha sent letters to the Senate in Rome and to Justinian, announcing what had happened. But once he was king, Theodahad gathered together the relatives of the three Goths whom Amalasuntha had had assassinated, and with their help he arrested her and imprisoned her on an island in Lake Bolsena in Tuscany. He then forced her to write Justinian a letter saying that she had suffered no harm, and he himself sent Justinian a similar message.

Justinian, meanwhile, had already received Amalasuntha's proposal to turn over her rule to him, and sent an agent, Peter the Patrician, to carry on secret negotiations with her. As Peter traveled along the Egnatian Way across northern Greece, he met Amalasuntha's messengers, who told him that Athalaric was dead and Theodahad was king. Then, when he reached the port of Aulon (modern Valona, on the Adriatic Sea), he met Theodahad's messengers, who told him that Amalasuntha was imprisoned. Peter sent a fast messenger to Justinian with the news, and Justinian wrote to Amalasuntha to assure her of his protection; he also instructed Peter to make it clear to Theodahad that he supported the queen. But before Peter reached Theodahad, Amalasuntha had been killed by the relatives of the men she had had slain. Peter told Theodahad that Amalasuntha's murder meant war, and Theodahad pleaded that the deed was done against his will, though he continued to treat her murderers with honor. Her murder gave Justinian a pretext for invading Italy.

But that is not quite the end of the story. Did Peter reach Ravenna before or after Amalasuntha was murdered? The evidence that his arrival was after the murder rests on one ambiguous sentence in Prokopios' *Gothic War*. The question is important, because if Peter arrived before the murder, he might have taken steps to prevent it, had he wished to do so. Moreover, in his *Secret History*, Prokopios adds a sinister gloss. He says that Empress Theodora did not want Amalasuntha at the imperial court, for she feared that she might gain influence over Justinian, and she therefore promised Peter the post of master of offices, and money besides, if he procured Amalasuntha's death. So Peter persuaded Theodahad to get rid of her. Cassiodorus, who was Theodahad's praetorian prefect at this time, has preserved two letters to Theodora, one from Theodahad and one from Theodahad's wife, Gudeliva, that mention Peter's arrival and report that an unspecified event has happened which Theodora should find to her liking. Theodora was evidently taking an active role in negotiations with the Gothic court, and Peter was her loyal henchman. It cannot be proved that Amalasuntha was a victim of Theodora's intrigue. Yet her murder cannot have been unwelcome to Theodora, and it may caused Justinian very little sorrow, for it provided him with a just cause for invading Italy.

Amalasuntha's daughter, Matasuntha, was the last the Amals, the royal house of the Ostrogoths. Theodahad's successor as king, Witigis, attempted to give himself legitimacy by marrying her, much against her will. After Witigis' defeat, we hear of Matasuntha once again when Germanos, a cousin of Justinian, married her in 550. Germanos had just been appointed commander of the Byzantine forces in Italy fighting the Ostrogothic king Totila, and his marriage was politically motivated. He hoped that Matasuntha's royal blood would win some of the Ostrogoths over to the Byzantine side. But before Germanos could reach Italy, he took sick and died. Matasuntha gave birth to a posthumous son, named after his father, but Byzantine foreign policy had no use for him and the Amal royal house dropped out of history.

Antonina

Antonina, wife of Belisarios, Justinian's most famous general, rose from the dregs of society to a position of power and influence. She was the daughter and the granddaughter of charioteers who had competed in the hippodromes of Constantinople and Thessaloniki, and her mother was one of the chorus girls who danced in the orchestras of the theaters. Though she was older than Theodora, it is likely that the two women became friends while they worked in the theater, and it may have been Theodora who introduced her to Belisarios while he was still a member of Justinian's bodyguard. Antonina was by then a widow, having been married to a merchant from Antioch who may have been the father of two of her daughters: one who was the wife of Ildiger, one of Belisarios' officers, and one who was wooed by an officer named Sergius, who, for that reason, enjoyed the favor of Theodora in spite of his manifest in-competence. She also had a young son, Photios. He was a teenager in 533 when he accompanied Belisarios and Antonina on the campaign against the Vandals, and thus he was probably born about 515.

Despite Antonina's past, Belisarios fell deeply in love with her and married her. They had one daughter, Joannina, for whom Theodora tried to arrange a marriage with her grandson so that he would inherit Belisarios' wealth. Unlike Theodora, who was faithful to Justinian after her marriage, Antonina, according to Prokopios, continued to have affairs, though he relates only one in his *Secret History*: her passionate romance with Belisarios' adopted son, Theodosios.

Unlike most military wives, Antonina accompanied her husband on his campaigns. She went with him on his campaign against the Vandal kingdom in 533, and on his campaign against the Ostrogoths in 535–536. Nor was she the sort of wife who took a passive role on campaigns. In Africa, after the battle at the Tenth Milestone outside Carthage, where Belisarios defeated the Vandals with his cavalry, it was Antonina who brought up the infantry to the gates of Carthage, and during the siege of Rome by the Ostrogothic king Witigis in 536–537, it was she, rather than one of his officers, whom Belisarios sent to Naples to get reinforcements. Her relationship with her mentor Theodora remained close: on Theodora's instructions, she deposed Pope Silverius during the siege of Rome and replaced him with Vigilius, and later it was she, acting as Theodora's agent, who trapped John the Cappadocian and brought him down. In 544, Antonina returned to Italy with Belisarios, and in 548, he sent her to Constantinople to use her influence with Theodora to obtain the reinforcements that he desperately needed if he was to recover Italy from the Ostrogoths. When Antonina reached Constantinople, however, she found that Theodora was dead, and she concluded that Belisarios' position in Italy was hopeless, for without Theodora's intervention, Justinian would continue to starve the Italian campaign for troops. She asked Justinian to recall Belisarios, and he complied.

Antonina's relationship with Empress Theodora was not entirely untroubled, though she acted as Theodora's willing agent to depose Pope Silverius and destroy John the Cappadocian. According to Prokopios, Theodora often had harsh words for Antonina, and Antonina feared her. In the *Secret History*[1] he relates how Theodora arranged a betrothal between her grandson Anastasios, the son of her illegitimate daughter, whose name is unknown, and Joannina, the only child of Belisarios and Antonina. Joannina would be a wealthy heiress, which made her an attractive bride. But Antonina kept postponing the marriage, and the empress, suspecting Antonina's intentions and realizing that her own death was near, saw to it that young couple lived together without benefit of clergy. When Antonina arrived in Constantinople from Italy and discovered that cancer had already claimed Theodora's life, she promptly broke up the match, in spite of the fact that the two had lived together as man and wife for eight months and were deeply in love. According to Prokopios, Belisarios was so weak that he backed Antonina's decision when he returned to Constantinople from Italy, even though his daughter's reputation was now ruined. Prokopios leaves the story there, but it is likely that the marriage did eventually take place. As for Belisarios' wealth, Justinian confiscated it when Belisarios died.

The evidence for Antonina's later years is late and not entirely trustworthy, but she seems to have outlived both her husband and Justinian.

---

1. *Secret History* 5.18–5.24.

Antonina spent her last days with Justinian's sister, Vigilantia, the mother of Emperor Justin II. Another tradition suggests that she became a nun. We do not know the year of her death.

Belisarios

The most prominent of Justinian's generals, and the one best known to modern readers, was Belisarios. He was born in present-day western Bulgaria, and as a young man became one of the *bucellarii* (guardsmen) of Justinian. Justinian was not yet emperor, and Belisarios was one of a number of able young men whom he was gathering around him. How he came to Justinian's notice is unknown. However, probably about the time that Justinian married Theodora, Belisarios met and fell deeply in love with Antonina, an older woman who, like Theodora, came from the world of the theater. The two women were friends of long standing, and possibly Theodora used her influence to see to it that the career of the young Belisarios moved forward quickly. At any rate, when war with Persia was renewed in 525, he was assigned to the eastern front, and in 527, while he was still in his mid-twenties, he was appointed duke (commander of the military forces) of Mesopotamia. Two years later, he was given overall command of the Byzantine forces in the east, and in 530, he defeated a more numerous Persian army outside the fortress city of Dara on the eastern frontier. It was the first Byzantine victory over the Persians in over a hundred years, and it gave Belisarios an instant reputation.

He was not so lucky the following year. In 531, he was defeated by the Persians at Callinicum on the Euphrates River, and an official report of the battle faulted Belisarios' leadership. We have two accounts of what happened, one in the *Persian War* of Prokopios, who was Belisarios' *assessor* (legal adviser), that places the blame for the defeat on the insubordination of the Byzantine troops, as well as the unreliability of Byzantium's Arab allies, and the other in the chronicle of John Malalas, which probably reflects the official report and contradicts Prokopios on a number of key points. In particular, Malalas claims that the Arab allies fought courageously. Belisarios was recalled to Constantinople, and his career might have stalled if not for the *Nika* riot the next year.

In early January 532, the Constantinople mob nearly drove Justinian and Theodora into exile. At one point, Justinian lost his nerve and was on the point of fleeing Constantinople, and it was the empress who rallied their forces for a last effort. But what saved the day for Justinian and Theodora was the presence of two loyal generals: Belisarios, who had his own guard of battle-hardened troops from the Persian front, and Moundos, a Gepid officer who headed a detachment of Herulians, a barbarian tribe that was settled in the empire. They led their troops against the mob that was packed into the Hippodrome acclaiming Hypatios, the nephew of Emperor Anastasius, as Justinian's successor. The riot ended in a bloodbath, and Belisarios' reward was the command of an expedition the following year against the Vandal kingdom in North Africa.

Belisarios defeated the Vandals in two pitched battles, and their king, Gelimer, surrendered in late March 534. At this point, some of Belisarios' generals sent a secret warning to Justinian that Belisarios planned to revolt and make himself an independent ruler in Africa. Justinian reacted by offering Belisarios the choice of returning to Constantinople or remaining in Africa. Belisarios was aware of Justinian's suspicions, and chose to demonstrate his loyalty by returning, even though the Berbers were already in revolt. In Constantinople, he was granted the extraordinary honor of a triumph, and a new general took over command in Africa.

Justinian was already planning an attack against the Ostrogoths in Italy, and in 535 he dispatched Belisarios to Sicily, though with a force that numbered only half of that which he had led against the Vandals in Africa. Yet the conquest of Sicily went smoothly; only in Palermo did the Ostrogoths put up a fight. The next year he invaded Italy. The Ostrogothic king, Theodahad, was no warrior, and Belisarios encountered no resistance except at Naples, which withstood a siege. Theodahad made no effort to relieve Naples, and when it fell, the Ostrogoths in disgust dethroned and killed him, replacing him with Witigis, who had a reputation as a good soldier. Nevertheless, Witigis' first move was a tactical error. In northern Italy, the Franks were threatening to invade, and Witigis judged them a greater threat than the Byzantines. He exacted an oath of allegiance from Pope Silverius, and then, leaving Rome with a small force to defend it, he marched north to deal with the Franks. But when Belisarios reached Rome, the Romans opened the city gates for him on the advice of the pope, who, in spite of his oath, felt no loyalty to the Goths, who were Arian heretics.

When Witigis learned that Rome had been captured, he returned quickly and besieged the city for over a year before abandoning it when news reached him that one of Belisarios' generals was threatening his capital of Ravenna. The siege of Rome displayed Belisarios' talents at their best, for he had only 5,000 troops to defend the city against a vastly superior Gothic army. This was the first of three sieges that Rome would endure during the war against the Ostrogoths, and the damage that the city suffered was immense. The Ostrogothic War ushered in the Dark Ages in Italy.

Ravenna fell in 540, and Belisarios returned to a cool welcome in Constantinople. Justinian had wanted to cut his losses, and would have made peace with the Goths, allowing them to keep Ravenna and a small kingdom in northern Italy, but Belisarios was determined to capture Ravenna. To persuade the Goths to surrender it, he tricked them into believing that he intended to rebel against Justinian. Once they realized they had been deceived, they chose an abler king than Witigis. Prokopios calls him Totila, though on his coins, his name is Baduila. The war in Italy was renewed.

The year 540 was a disastrous one: a raid by Huns and Slavs devastated Greece and reached the great walls of Constantinople, while in the east the shah of Persia renewed the war, capturing and destroying Antioch. Belisarios was dispatched to the eastern front in 541 and again in 542, to organize the defense. In the summer of 542, Justinian fell ill with bubonic plague, and after he recovered, two of Belisarios' officers accused him and his second in command of making treasonous remarks about the succession while Justinian's life hung in the balance. The report reached Empress Theodora's ears, and she acted swiftly to nip any sedition in the bud. Belisarios was recalled, his property was confiscated, and he lived in fear of assassination. However, in 544 he was restored to the emperor's good graces thanks to Theodora, who owed Antonina a favor. Much of his property was restored and he was again sent to Italy, most of which Totila had by now reconquered. But his forces were inadequate, and Justinian and Theodora seem still to have suspected his loyalty, for he was not allowed to take his *bucellarii* with him and he was seriously hampered without this crack military unit on whose loyalty he could count. Moreover, Totila was no Witigis; he was a first-rate leader. However, the defense of the eastern frontier, including the eastern approaches of the Black Sea, were more important than Italy in the grand strategy of the empire, and even if Justinian had trusted Belisarios implicitly, he might have decided that the best strategy for the empire was to let Belisarios fight a holding action in Italy while he devoted his scarce military resources to other sectors.

In 548, it was clear that Belisarios could make no headway in Italy with the forces that he had available, and he sent his wife, Antonina, back to Constantinople to beg Theodora to use her influence to get him more troops. But Antonina reached Constantinople to find that Theodora had died and, realizing that there was now no prospect of reinforcements for her husband, she asked Justinian to recall him. Justinian complied, and Belisarios returned to Constantinople. He commanded no more expeditions, but he remained a respected citizen. He had become immensely rich as a result of his campaigns. Belisarios' success at acquiring wealth for himself aroused the suspicions even of Justinian and Theodora, who were willing to tolerate a certain amount of corruption but suspected that Belisarios had helped himself to booty that should rightfully have gone into the imperial treasury.

He had one last victory. In 559, the Kutrigur Huns plundered Thrace and threatened Constantinople. Justinian had no forces to check them, and in this desperate situation, he turned to Belisarios to organize the defense. Belisarios mustered a scratch force of dispossessed peasants with a core of 300 veterans, and routed the Huns. But Justinian recalled him before he could follow up his victory by harassing the Huns on their retreat, allegedly because he was jealous of his old general.

Three years later, Belisarios was put under house arrest after being accused of involvement in a conspiracy against Justinian. In 563, he was cleared of the charges and restored to his dignities. He died in March 565, only a few months before the emperor. His fame lasted long after his death, and a legend arose that in his old age, he was blinded and reduced to begging on the streets of Constantinople. This legend first appears in the twelfth century, and it was further developed by an anonymous poet of the late fourteenth century, who composed a romantic tale of Belisarios, the pitiable victim of envy, who was blinded by the emperor he had served faithfully and left to beg on the streets of Constantinople. The story has no basis, though the theme of envy that brought ruin to Belisarios' career is already evident in the work of Prokopios, to whom we owe most of our information about the great general.

John of Ephesus

John, titular Monophysite bishop of Ephesus and the foremost historian writing in Syriac in Justinian's day, was born about 507 in a village in the province of Mesopotamia, the capital of which was Amida (modern Diyarbakir in eastern Turkey). At an early age he was placed in a neighboring monastery that boasted a stylite saint named Maro. The connection with Maro went back to John's childhood, for while he was still an infant, he fell ill and seemed likely to die; his desperate parents brought him to Maro, who prescribed beans. The beans saved John's life. After Maro's death, John joined a monastery that had been founded at Amida, but at the time John joined it, the monks were living in exile, for they had been expelled from Amida during the persecution of the anti-Chalcedonians initiated by Emperor Justin I after he ended the Akakian Schism and made peace with Rome. John shared the wanderings of these monks, who were not allowed to return to their monastery at Amida until 530, when Justinian relaxed Justin's measures against the anti-Chalcedonian clergy.

John had already been ordained a deacon, and he spent the next few years traveling to visit other monasteries and holy men. He made his first visit to Egypt during this period. This was a time when Empress Theodora was promoting dialogue between the Chalcedonians and anti-Chalcedonians; and Anthimos, the patriarch of Constantinople, and Severos, the exiled patriarch of Antioch, whom the moderate anti-Chalcedonians still regarded as their leader, agreed on a profession of faith. But Pope Agapetus would have none of it, and the Monophysites were finally condemned in a synod held at Constantinople in 536. In 537, the persecution of the Monophysite clergy in the east was renewed. John and his fellow monks fled, and after some years of wandering, he came to Constantinople in 540 and took refuge in the Palace of Hormisdas under Empress Theodora's protection.

The next year John made another visit to Egypt, which was already smitten by the epidemic of bubonic plague that would soon sweep across the empire. Next he journeyed to Palestine, where the plague was just beginning. From there he went to Mesopotamia and then back to Constantinople, and thus he is an important eyewitness of the plague. While the plague was still raging, Justinian sent him to Asia Minor in 542 to convert the remaining pagans, stipulating that he should convert them to the Chalcedonian and not to the Monophysite faith. With the help of four deacons in Asia and ample funds from Justinian, John was able to claim 80,000 converts, each of whom was given a small sum of money, and he reported that he built ninety-two churches and ten monasteries. This is a vivid reminder that paganism was by no means dead, and the plague must have made its annihilation a vital concern for Justinian. To Justinian, who wrote in one of his laws that blasphemy caused earthquakes and other natural disasters, paganism must have seemed a grave danger to the empire in a plague year.

About 558, John was ordained Monophysite bishop of Ephesus by Jacob Baradaeus, though there is no evidence that he ever lived in Ephesus. When the exiled Monophysite patriarch of Egypt, Theodosios, died in Constantinople in 566, John became the leader of the Monophysites there; many anti-Chalcedonians from the east had migrated to Constantinople, seeking Empress Theodora's protection, which Justinian continued to extend to them after her death. John played a role in Justin II's attempt to find a new *Henotikon* that would unite the Monophysites and Chalcedonians. In 571, one was almost found, but it was rejected by the Monophysites in the eastern provinces, and for a few years there was a rift in the Monophysite ranks between those who lived in Constantinople, led by John, and the eastern clergy, led by Jacob Baradaeus. But the new *Henotikon* did not bring theological peace even in Constantinople, and finally Justin II, in exasperation, resorted to persecution. John spent the last year of his life in prison and died there, probably in 586.

John's *Ecclesiastical History* was in three sections. The first, which is lost except for a few citations, started with Julius Caesar and reached the period of Emperor Theodosius II. The second, which reached Justinian's reign, was heavily used in a later chronicle known as *The Chronicle of Zuqnin*, written in the late eighth century by an anonymous monk in the monastery of Zugnin, near Amida. The third part of John's *History* was discovered in the monastery of Saint Mary Deipara in Egypt in the nineteenth century. It reaches the year 585, and the last part was written while John was in prison.

In addition we have John's *Lives of the Eastern Saints*: brief biographies of fifty-eight holy men and women who lived at the same time as John. They give a vivid picture of everyday life in the villages of Syria and Mesopotamia, where the language of the population was Syriac, and the people's reaction to the persecution of the Monophysite clergy. The stories range over a wide field. One tells the tale of the holy brothers Abraham and Maro: Abraham lived for thirty-eight years perched on top of a pillar and died there, sitting with his head between his knees, facing east. Maro carried him down and took his brother's place. A holy man named Paul went to a cave that had been used for pagan worship, expelled the god that occupied it—John calls the god a "fiend"—and lived there for twenty-five years. The holy woman Euphemia and her daughter wove wool, and were paid a small sum for their work by the wealthy women of their town; half of it they gave to the poor. From John's *Lives*, too, we have a picture of what life was like in the Palace of Hormisdas in Constantinople, which Theodora maintained as a refuge for anti-Chalcedonian clergy and monks, for John himself lived there for a brief period.

One other work, John's earliest, written in 537, which told the story of the persecution of the anti-Chalcedonians, has been lost.

John the Cappadocian

John the Cappadocian, praetorian prefect in the early years of Justinian's reign, was a native of Caesarea Mazaca in Cappadocia, a province in Asia Minor notorious for its cold winters. Though he lacked the sort of classical education that ordinarily was needed for appointment to high office in the civil service, he found a job as a clerk during Justin's reign. Probably he served on the personal staff of Justinian, who at this time was master of the soldiers in the presence, that is, commander of the troops in Constantinople. His abilities attracted Justinian's attention, and he rose rapidly through the ranks. Only seven months after Emperor Justin I died, Justinian set up a ten-man commission to produce an updated law code, and John was its chair. John and his commission were efficient: the code was ready the next year. Justinian was impressed by his ability, and in 531, appointed him praetorian prefect of the east.

In the *Nika* riot of January 532, the mob demanded that John be dismissed, and Justinian was too frightened to refuse. But by mid-October of that year, John was back in office again and his advice was highly valued by Justinian. He alone of Justinian's ministers dared openly to oppose the expedition against the Vandal kingdom in 533, and he almost won Justinian over to his view. John's cost-cutting reforms roused hostility in the civil service, and he was a ruthless collector of taxes. The civil service was by this time encrusted with traditional ceremonial, and John had little respect for it. He was an efficiency expert and, like many reformers, he gave offense. His enemies took vengeance by spreading unsavory tales about him—some of them, no doubt, based on fact. But Justinian needed money to finance his wars, to say nothing of his extravagant building program, and he appreciated John's competence.

Empress Theodora hated him, and John made no effort to conciliate her. On the contrary, he began to make accusations against her to Justinian, who continued to esteem John and disregarded his wife's complaints. Theodora was unable to have John assassinated, for he took careful precautions and maintained a large bodyguard. However, in 541, Theodora and her crony Antonina, the wife of Belisarios, devised a snare for John which would convince Justinian that he was not as loyal as Justinian imagined. Antonina, using John's young, naïve daughter as a go-between, intimated to John that Belisarios was seriously disaffected and would support a plot to overthrow Justinian if John were involved as well. John rose to the bait. He agreed to a rendezvous with Antonina at which Narses and the count of the Excubitors, Marcellus, by prearrangement could overhear what was said between them. They heard John agreeing to treasonous proposals that Antonina made to him. Narses and Marcellus immediately tried to arrest him, but John was as usual accompanied by bodyguards, and he managed to escape. But instead of going directly to Justinian with a full confession, he sought asylum in a church, which Justinian took as an admission of guilt.

John was dismissed from office and ordained into the priesthood, much against his will, because priests were disqualified for offices in the civil service, and John hoped to be rehabilitated. His great wealth was confiscated, though shortly afterward Justinian, who still respected his abilities, restored a large portion of it. However, a little while later John was implicated in the murder of the bishop of Cyzicus, and though his guilt was not proved, his wealth was confiscated again and he was exiled to Egypt. After Theodora died, Justinian recalled him to Constantinople but did not restore him to office. Instead, he remained a priest.

John believed in magic and astrology, and Prokopios, who disliked him, implies that he was a secret pagan. Yet no charge of paganism was ever brought against him and he passed for a Christian, even though his faith may have been only skin-deep.

Our sources for John the Cappadocian are uniformly hostile. John the Lydian, who served in the office of the praetorian prefect, hated him and blamed him for the reforms in the bureau of the praetorian prefect that frustrated his efforts to increase his personal wealth. He accuses John of using fellow Cappadocians as his agents, which was no doubt true, since it was common practice for a powerful official to favor his countrymen: John the Lydian had gained his post in the office of the praetorian prefect thanks to the favor of the praetorian prefect, who came from John's hometown. The general view of the Cappadocians was that they were a tough lot: there was a saying that "a viper bit a Cappadocian, and it was the viper that died." Prokopios respected John's ability, but he wasted no affection on him. However, shortly before his fall from favor, John toured the provinces in the east, where he received a warm welcome. The hostile view of John that was held by entrenched bureaucrats in Constantinople may not have been shared by all the taxpayers in the provinces.

John the Lydian

John the Lydian was born in Philadelphia in the province of Lydia in western Asia Minor in 490. He is of interest not only as the author of three surviving works but also for his career in the civil service of Constantinople. He was born into a well-to-do family in Philadelphia and received a good education in classical literature, which was a requisite for entering the imperial bureaucracy. He was evidently a brilliant student with an excellent mastery of Latin, which was the language of Roman law, as well as of Greek, his native language. At age twenty-one, he came to Constantinople to seek a place in the civil service, and while he waited for a vacancy among the *memoriales*, who were secretaries on the staff of the master of offices, he attended lectures on philosophy. However, while he waited, a distant cousin named Zotikus, also from Philadelphia, who was praetorian prefect, brought John into the corps of *praefectiani*, the praetorian prefect's staff, which at the time needed good Latinists.

John's choice of the praetorian prefect's staff rather than that of the master of offices paid handsomely in the short run. In his first year he made 1,000 gold pieces (solidi) from fees and bribes, and at the end of the year he was promoted to an office only three rungs below that of *augustalis* without having to pay a fee for it, which was most unusual. The *augustales* were a corps of thirty senior men of clerical grade within the prefect's office. Two retired every year, and an aspiring bureaucrat who was appointed *augustalis* could look forward to a life of affluence, whereas bureaucrats who failed to make the grade would progress slowly through less lucrative posts. John's future looked bright. His patron Zotikus also found him a wife who brought a dowry of 100 gold pounds. The marriage seems to have been happy, but it did not last long, for John's wife soon died. John did not remarry, preferring to devote himself to his career.

But Emperor Justinian was a reformer and his praetorian prefect, John the Cappadocian, was a new broom that swept clean. Under the new regime, efficiency was preferred to a good command of Latin. John the Lydian's skills were suddenly obsolete, and he nourished an intense hatred for the Cappadocian, whose reforms blighted his career. His hatred was so intense that he made an unwise career move: when Justinian had to appoint the aristocratic Phokas to replace John the Cappadocian as praetorian prefect, to satisfy the mob during the *Nika* riot of 532, John the Lydian attached himself to the new prefect. But once the riot was suppressed, Phokas was soon dropped and John the Cappadocian became prefect again. John the Lydian's career prospects collapsed.

John took comfort in literature. He still had connections with Empress Theodora and with the master of offices, Peter the Patrician; so when the Cappadocian fell in 541, John's connections secured him Justinian's recognition. He retired with honor from the prefecture in 551, but he had acquired none of the wealth he had hoped for, and he was a bitter man. Three of his books have survived. *De Mensibus* (On the Months), on the calendar, shows John's antiquarian interests. A second, *De Portentis* (On Omens), demonstrates that John was a serious student of astrology. It is a historical survey of divination and the art of reading signs and forewarnings, an unexpected interest for a citizen of sixth-century Byzantium. But his most interesting work is *De Magistratibus* (On the Magistracies of the Roman Government), which contains a great deal of information about government officials and the history of their offices. It is a discursive work, but it is John's chief claim to fame both because it reveals the workings of the bureaucracy and because of what it tells us about John's own aspirations and disappointments.

John also produced at least two panegyrics, one on his patron, Zotikus, and the other on Emperor Justinian. Composing panegyrics was a significant part of rhetorical training in late antiquity, and it was an important skill for a man who wanted to advance his career. Panegyrics were written for public delivery in a *theatron*, a chamber large enough to hold an audience of some size; the object of the eulogy sat there quietly, without moving, where all could see him as the panegyric was recited. John's panegyric of Justinian pleased the emperor so much that he commissioned John to write a history of his war against Persia. It no longer survives. Nor does some poetry that John attempted. The exact date of John's death is unknown but it was about 565, the year in which Justinian died.

Emperor Justin I

Justin's Rise to Power

Justin, the brother of Justinian's mother, reigned as emperor from July 10, 518, to August 1, 527, and was followed immediately by Justinian, whom he had made co-emperor four months before his death. He rose from humble origins through the ranks of the army until his unexpected accession to the throne on the death of Emperor Anastasius, and though he has been overshadowed by his nephew Justinian, he was clearly a man of ability who held strong opinions on matters of religion. He was born in the province of Dardania, an enclave of Latin speakers loyal to the pope in Rome and to the Chalcedonian Creed that Rome championed. Justin was virtually illiterate and unsophisticated in matters of theology, but he had no doubts about what creed he should follow.

In the reign of Emperor Leo (457–474), Justin, along with two other young farmers, Zimarchus and Dityvistus, set out to seek his fortune at Constantinople. They left behind a life of grinding poverty, for their homeland had been overrun by Attila and his Huns in 447, then by the Ostrogoths, who ravaged the region until Emperor Leo made peace in 461. The trio traveled with only some dried bread in their pockets for food. Once they reached Constantinople, they found that Leo was creating a new palace guard, the Excubitors, intended to counterbalance the

Germanic troops in the city. The three young farmers had good physiques, and they were enrolled. We hear nothing further of Justin's companions, but Justin rose through the ranks until he became the count of the Excubitors under Emperor Anastasius I.

Anastasius died suddenly in the night of July 9, 518, while a storm raged outside and the palace was struck by lightning. He was without an obvious heir. The senate, the high officials of the bureaucracy, and the patriarch met in the imperial palace to choose a successor, while the people waited with growing impatience in the Hippodrome to learn who he would be. Negotiations dragged on, the people grew impatient, and the high officials became apprehensive. Justin was not an entirely unexpected choice, for as count of the Excubitors, he commanded a corps of soldiers who could fight to keep order if necessary, whereas the palace guard, known as the Scholarians and commanded by the master of offices, was largely ornamental. Justin was taken to the *kathisma*, the imperial box in the Hippodrome, to receive the acclamation of the people, and then went to Hagia Sophia to receive the blessing of the church.

Justin was already elderly and uneducated, and as the years went on and he grew older and ill, power slipped more and more into the hands of his nephew. He had purchased his wife, Lupicina, as a slave from an owner who had tired of her. He then freed her and married her. When she became empress, she abandoned the name Lupicina, which was popular among prostitutes, and became Euphemia. We know little about her, and she was probably dead by 523. However, she seems to have been a strong adherent of the Chalcedonian Creed, and she supported her husband's move to end the Akakian Schism and mend fences with Rome. The marriage was childless, but at some time before Justin became emperor, he adopted his nephew Flavius Petrus Sabbatius, thus conferring on him the agnomen, or surname, "Justinianus" by which he is known. Prokopios reports that Euphemia was very fond of her husband's adopted son. Yet she opposed his marriage to Theodora, who was an ex-actress as well as an anti-Chalcedonian. The wedding of Justinian and Theodora had to wait until after her death.

Justin's Religious Policies

Justin broke sharply with the policy of Anastasius that had favored the anti-Chalcedonians. Vitalian, the champion of the Chalcedonians, who had revolted against Anastasius and been defeated, but was still lurking in Dobruja in his native province of Scythia Minor, was recalled to Constantinople and appointed a master of the soldiers in the presence. Only eleven days after Justin's coronation, a synod was held in Constantinople that pronounced anathema against Severos, the patriarch of Antioch who was the intellectual leader of the Miaphysite anti-Chalcedonians and had been a favorite of Anastasius. John, the patriarch of Constantinople, dispatched letters to all the important bishops to inform them of the decrees of the Constantinople synod, whereupon the patriarch of Jerusalem summoned a synod that followed Constantinople's example. Severos fled from Antioch to Egypt, narrowly escaping arrest. Letters were dispatched as well to Pope Hormisdas in Rome: one from Justin; another, more peremptory in tone, from Justinian; and a third from Patriarch John.

Hormisdas was in no mood to negotiate. He would not come to Constantinople, but he sent legates with the message that if Justin wanted to end the Akakian Schism, he must yield completely to Rome's demands. The papal delegation was instructed simply to set forth Hormisdas' position, and refuse any debate. Akakios, the patriarch of Constantinople who was the author of the *Henotikon* that brought about the schism, was to be condemned. So were the patriarchs who followed him, the prelates who had remained in communion with them, and the emperors Zeno and Anastasius. Patriarch John, of Constantinople was unhappy at the pope's terms for surrender, for they were harsh, but Justin pressured him to yield. In March 519, he signed the papal memorandum in the presence of Justin, the senate, and clergy.

Then, at the pope's insistence, Justin began a persecution of the anti-Chalcedonian clergy. Anti-Chalcedonian bishops in the east were ousted from their churches, and monks from their cells. Even the troops were required to subscribe to the Chalcedonian Creed. Vitalian supported the persecution with enthusiasm; after he was assassinated in 520, Justin relaxed it somewhat. He refused to extend the persecution to Egypt, in spite of the pope's urging, and Egypt became a refuge for dispossessed clergy. Nevertheless, Hormisdas viewed his victory with satisfaction. When he died in 523, his son, Silverius, who would later become pope for a brief, unhappy period, wrote his epitaph, one line of which reads, "Greece, vanquished by pious power, has yielded to you." The *Henotikon* had been destroyed. Though neither Justin nor Hormisdas knew it, Justinian and his successor, Justin II, would spend their reigns trying fruitlessly to find a new *Henotikon* to replace it.

Justin's efforts to enforce orthodoxy extended to the surviving Arians in the east, and in 523–524, he took severe measures against them. This provoked a reaction from Theodoric the Ostrogoth, who ruled Italy though ostensibly he recognized the suzerainty of Constantinople. The Ostrogoths were Arians, and Theodoric was anxious to defend his fellow believers in the east. He dispatched Hormisdas' successor, Pope John I, to Constantinople to remonstrate on behalf of the Arians. John received a warm welcome from Justin and Justinian: so warm that Theodoric became suspicious, and when John returned to Italy, he threw him into prison, where he died. But Justin relaxed his anti-Arian measures, and the Arian churches in the east continued to exist until Justinian closed them in 538, during Belisarios' campaign against the Ostrogoths, and confiscated their property. By then the objections of the Ostrogoths no longer mattered.

Relations with Persia

Lazica (called Colchis by the classical Greeks) lay at the eastern end of the Black Sea between the Rioni and the Chorokhi rivers, and it was a bone of contention between Persia and Byzantium. In 522, Tzath, the Laz king, broke with the custom of going to Persia for his coronation and instead went to Constantinople, where he asked Justin to proclaim him king and baptize him. Tzath was probably already a Christian but not yet baptized, and his trip to Constantinople sent a message to Persia that the Persian king, Kawad, recognized. He got in touch with the Sabiric Huns in the northern Caucasus and made an alliance with their king, Zilbigi, to join in an attack against Lazica. But Zilbigi was too clever for his own good: he negotiated with both sides, and Justin, ostensibly as a friendly gesture, made a point of revealing Zilbigi's treachery to Kawad. Kawad investigated further, verified the intelligence that he had received from Justin, and slew Zilbigi and most of the 20,000 Huns he had brought with him.

Impressed, it seems, by Justin's honorable conduct, Kawad sought his help with a domestic problem. He had four sons, and he wished his third son, Khusru, to succeed him. To secure Khusru's succession, he wanted Justin to adopt him. Justin was willing, but his *quaestor* (legal adviser) pointed out that Khusru would have a claim to be Justin's heir if Justin adopted him according to Roman law. Khusru also would bear the cognomen "Justinianus." Hence Justin offered to make the adoption according to barbarian custom instead, and Kawad was insulted. An opportunity for peace was lost. Kawad moved against Iberia (modern Georgia), a Christian kingdom on the border of the Persian Empire, and demanded that it adopt the rites of Zororastrianism, the state religion of Persia. Justin could do little to help Iberia. The Iberian royal family was forced to flee to Constantinople, Iberia lost its independence, and the Byzantine Empire lost prestige. War followed in 526, though by then Justin was feeble with age, and it was his nephew Justinian who initiated the war.

The Himyarite Affair

Himyar (modern Yemen) was an area where Christianity, Judaism, and paganism vied for allegiance and where Persia, the Christian kingdom of Ethiopia, and the Byzantine Empire competed for political advantage. In 523 (the date is disputed) the Christians in Najran, a center of Christianity in south Arabia, were massacred by a Jew or Jewish convert, Dhu Nuwas, who had seized power in Himyar and undertaken an anti-Christian crusade. The events of this crusade gave rise to a rich martyr literature, and the multiplicity of traditions makes it hard to discern what actually happened. However, a Christian escaped the Najran massacre and reached Ela Atzheba (also called Caleb, the king of Ethiopia). Ela Atzheba had the troops to intervene but lacked ships. He contacted Justin through the patriarch of Alexandria. Justin mustered the necessary ship transports, and in two campaigns, Ela Atzheba took the Himyarite capital and installed a Christian as a client king of Ethiopia. The situation remained unstable, however, and after Justinian's death, Persia occupied Himyar in 570–572.

Conclusion

It is convenient to couple Justin's reign with that of Justinian, but without Justin, there would have been no reign of Justinian. His career is an example of the social mobility that was possible in late antiquity.

He was a poverty-stricken peasant who joined the army and rose through the ranks. As his fortunes improved, so did the fortunes of his family, for he brought family members from Dardania to Constantinople and saw to it they got the education he lacked. When he unexpectedly became emperor, his family entered the ranks of the ruling elite. Justinian was the power behind his throne, but until the later years of his reign, when he was old and ill, Justinian did not completely dominate him. He can easily be underestimated.

Khusru I, *Shah of Persia*

Khusru I Anoushirvan, whose sobriquet, "Anoushirvan," means "with an immortal soul," was the shah of Persia from the death of his father, Kawad, in September 531 until early 579. He was Kawad's third son. The eldest son had evidently become a convert to the Mazdakite movement, which was an offshoot of Zororastrianism with a revolutionary political message, and the second son had lost an eye, which disqualified him, for the shahs of Persia were to be men without physical blemishes. However, Kawad suspected that Khusru's succession might be opposed, and thus he proposed that Emperor Justin I should formally adopt Khusru. But Justin, fearing that adoption according to Roman law would give Khusru a claim to the Byzantine Empire, proposed adoption according to barbarian custom, which he had recently done for Eutharic, the husband of Amalasuntha, the daughter of Theodoric the Ostrogoth. Kawad was insulted at the suggestion, and in 525, war broke out.

However, on his deathbed Kawad named Khusru his successor and the assembled notables accepted his wish. One of Khusru's first acts was to negotiate peace with the Roman Empire, and in early 532, the "Endless Peace" with the Byzantines was signed. Yet Khusru grew uneasy as he learned of the victories of Belisarios in Africa and Italy. The Ostrogothic king Witigis, facing defeat in Italy, sent him two envoys to Khusru disguised as a bishop and his attendant, to warn him of the danger to Persia if the Byzantine Empire consolidated its western conquests. From Roman Armenia, too, where Justinian's reforms had sparked an uprising, envoys came to Khusru to ask for protection and assistance. In 540, Khusru launched an attack upon the eastern provinces of the Byzantine Empire, destroying Antioch on the Orontes, enslaving its inhabitants, and collecting ransom from other cities. Beroea (modern Aleppo, in Syria), which failed to find enough ransom money, was set afire.

The following year Khusru invaded Lazica (modern Georgia), where the Laz king Gubazes had asked for his help. Khusru evidently intended permanent occupation of Lazica, which would give him access to the Black Sea and a back door for attacking Constantinople, but in 547–548, Gubazes, uneasy at Persian intentions, reverted to a pro-Roman policy and asked Justinian for help. The result was that from 548 to 556, war raged in Lazica. Elsewhere, hostilities ended with a five-year truce signed in 545, and when it expired, another five-year truce excluding Lazica was signed in 551. It in turn was followed by long negotiations between Peter the Patrician on the Byzantine side, and Izedh Gushnap for the Persians. The two men met at Dara in the autumn of 561, and hammered out a fifty-year peace. The Persians agreed to evacuate Lazica, and Justinian could claim victory in that sector, though the status of the neighboring kingdom of Suania was left unclear, and would be a future source of friction. Persia would receive an annual subsidy of 420 gold pounds under the terms of the peace, with the first seven years payable immediately. The Christians in Persia would be allowed freedom of religion, including the right to bury their dead, which was considered an abhorrent practice in Zororastrianism, the national religion of Persia.

In 572, in the reign of Emperor Justin II, war broke out again when the Armenians revolted against Persia, which was seeking to impose Zororastrianism, and they sought help from their fellow Christians in the Roman Empire. But the Byzantines were ill-prepared for war, and in 573, the Persians captured the great frontier fortress of Dara, and Justin II's shock when he learned of the loss of Dara seems to have been the cause of his mental breakdown. He went mad, and though he would have brief periods of lucidity thereafter, he remained incapacitated for the rest of his reign. Empress Sophia stepped into the breach and negotiated a one-year truce with Persia that was followed by a three-year truce (575–578) which, however, excluded Armenia, where Khusru was conducting the war in person. Khusru died in early 579, just as peace talks were about to resume.

Khusru was interested in Greek philosophy and had some Greek works translated into Persian. His reputation as a philosopher-king led to a curious adventure after Justinian closed down the Neoplatonic Academy in

Athens in 529.[1] Seven philosophers from the Academy went to Persia, where Khusru welcomed them. But they seem to have been disappointed: Persia was not the ideal society that the philosophers hoped to find, and Khusru turned out to be a superficial philosopher. Although he invited them to remain, they returned home—perhaps they had never seriously intended to stay. But Khusru did them a favor: the "Endless Peace" was being negotiated at the time, and Khusru insisted upon a clause that allowed the philosophers to live in peace and practice their pagan religion. There is some evidence, not altogether convincing, that a few of these philosophers settled in Harran and opened a school there which lasted into the Islamic period. In any case, the philosophers did continue to work and publish, even if, as pagans, they might not teach in Justinian's empire.

Moundos

Moundos, one of the most loyal of Justinian's officers, belonged to a barbarian ethnic group known as the Gepids, and was the son of a Gepid king. When his father died, he went to live with his maternal uncle, who inherited the kingship, and after his uncle's death, he accepted an invitation from Theodoric the Ostrogoth to join him in Italy as an ally. After Theodoric died in 526, Moundos returned to the Danube area, and in 529, offered his allegiance to Justinian. Justinian welcomed him and appointed him *magister militum* (commander of the troops) in Illyricum, whereupon he promptly proved his worth by defeating a raiding party of Slavs and then, in the next year (530), a horde of Bulgars, who in Byzantine sources are always identified as Huns. The following year, after Belisarios' defeat at Callinicum, Moundos briefly replaced Belisarios as the commander of the imperial troops in the east.

In 532, Moundos was reappointed to his former post in Illyricum, but he was still in Constantinople when the *Nika* riot broke out, and commanded a loyal cadre of Herulian troops. His Herulians and Belisarios' bodyguard were the only dependable soldiers in the capital, and hence

---

1. Agathias, *History*, 2.30.3–2.31.3.

he had a vital role in the massacre of the rioters in the Hippodrome that brought the uprising to an end. In 535, when Belisarios launched his Gothic campaign, Justinian sent Moundos to take Dalmatia from the Goths in order to control the Adriatic Sea, and there he lost his life in a skirmish in 536. His death came about when he learned that his son Maurice had been killed. Overcome by grief at the news and bent on revenge, he launched a rash attack on the Goths and was killed. Prokopios reports that the Romans, on hearing of Moundos' death, recalled a Sibylline oracle that said in Latin, "Africa capta, mundus cum nato peribit," which they had translated as "When Africa is taken, the world will perish along with its offspring" (in Latin, *mundus* means "world"). But now they believed they understood the oracle's true meaning to be "Once Africa is taken, Moundos along with his son will perish."

Narses

Narses was a eunuch of Armenian origin who became one of the most able and loyal members of Justinian's militia. Though Roman law prohibited the castration of males, there was nevertheless a demand for eunuch slaves, particularly in the imperial court, and Armenia, partitioned between the Byzantine Empire and Persia, with Persia controlling by far the greater share, was one of the regions beyond the imperial boundaries that supplied the demand for eunuchs. Nothing is known of Narses' youth, but at the time of the *Nika* riot in 532, he was a *koubikoularios* and a *spatharios*. The *koubikoularioi* were palace eunuchs who were in attendance on the emperor or empress, and the *spatharioi* were a corps of the *koubikoularioi* who served as bodyguards. Narses was an invaluable ally of Justinian during the *Nika* riot, for he attempted to sow dissension in the ranks of the mob by bribing rioters who seemed approachable to support the regime. But in the end it was the strong-arm tactics of Belisarios and Moundos that suppressed the uprising.

Narses was a favorite of Empress Theodora, partly, perhaps, because his religious sympathies were with the anti-Chalcedonians, though publicly he maintained a diplomatic neutrality. In the summer of 535, Theodora sent him to Alexandria at the head of a corps of 6,000 troops to support Theodosios, the newly elected patriarch of Alexandria. Theodosios was a moderate Monophysite, a disciple of Severos, the patriarch of Antioch who had been exiled by Emperor Justin I. On the death of Patriarch Timothy III of Alexandria, Theodosios was chosen to succeed him, but as he was being consecrated (February 535), the cathedral was invaded by a mob that supported a rival, Gaianos, a Monophysite extremist whose doctrine, known as Aphthartodocetism, taught that Christ's human body was incorruptible from the moment of birth. Theodosios barely escaped with his life, and once Narses arrived, civil war broke out in the streets of Alexandria. Narses maintained Theodosios on the patriarchal throne for 103 days, after which he admitted defeat and returned with Theodosios to Constantinople.

Narses' next mission was to Italy, to reinforce Belisarios, but the two generals quarreled, and their failure to cooperate led to the fall of Milan to the Goths in 539. The adult males were slaughtered and the women given as slaves to the Burgundians. Justinian assigned fault for the catastrophe to neither general, but he recalled Narses. In 541, Narses helped Theodora and Antonina in their plot to bring about the fall of the praetorian prefect, John the Cappadocian. He then contemplated retiring to a monastery, and in fact, he built a monastery known as Rupis, along with a church and lodgings for pilgrims, in Bithynia in northwest Asia Minor, and gave it a generous endowment. But in 551, Justinian chose Narses to take command of the war in Italy, which had reached desperate straits after Belisarios' recall. Belisarios had been starved for troops, and Narses told the emperor frankly that nothing could be achieved unless he devoted more resources to the war against the Ostrogoths. Justinian listened. Narses got the necessary resources, and in midsummer of 552, he defeated the Goths at Busta Gallorum. Narses' tactics were masterly, but he also commanded an army that outnumbered the Goths.

The Goths chose Teias to replace Totila, who died of his wounds after the battle of Busta Gallorum. The last struggle between the Goths and the Byzantines took place in southern Italy, at the foot of Monte Lattari near Naples. Narses then remained in Italy as its effective ruler until Justinian's successor, Justin II, dismissed him from office. The reason seems to have been a flood of complaints from the Romans to Justin II and his wife, Sophia, that Narses was enriching himself at their expense and was acting as a tyrant. Sophia in particular disliked him, and her enmity made Narses hesitate to return to Constantinople. He remained in Rome and watched from the sidelines when the Lombards invaded Italy in 568, and met only ineffective and disorganized resistance. He died in Rome, aged ninety-five, in 574, and his body was taken to Constantinople in a lead coffin, and then was buried in the monastery that he had founded.

Peter, *also called Barsymes*

Peter was a native of Syria, where he started his career as a banker. His alternative name, "Barsymes," is a Greek form of "Bar Simon," meaning "son of Simon." He found employment on the staff of the praetorian prefect, apparently while John the Cappadocian held the office, and somehow came to the attention of Empress Theodora. This was a period when the empress and John the Cappadocian were bitter enemies, and it is fair to speculate that Theodora recruited Peter as her agent in the prefectural office. In any case, after John fell, his immediate successor was a man named Theodotos, but he lasted only briefly in the office because, Prokopios claims, he was not dishonest enough for Justinian and Theodora. Peter had taken over the office by midsummer of 543.

Prokopios, who is our main source for Peter's career, is completely hostile. Peter sold offices even though Justinian had promulgated a law in 535 banning the practice, and he was a negligent paymaster of the army. The frontier militia (*limitanei*), which was supposed to provide some defense against barbarian raids, had become ineffective, and Peter canceled their pay. The *limitanei* ceased to exist. Provisioning the capital with grain was another drain on the treasury, and it was Peter's effort to cut costs in that department which brought him down. One year, when the state granaries had an oversupply that was in danger of spoiling, he forced the cities of the east to buy the surplus. Prokopios claimed it was already beginning to rot, and the cities that had been forced to purchase it had to dump it. Then, when Peter was faced with a grain shortage the next year, he made purchases in Bithynia, Phrygia, and Thrace, the provinces nearest Constantinople, and assigned the transportation costs to the provinces supplying the grain. Still the supply was not enough, and the Constantinople mob was angry at the high price of grain. That, added to the protests of the soldiers who went unpaid, was too much for Justinian. Peter Barsymes was dismissed from the office that he had held for three years, less two and a half months.

He had been made a scapegoat for a situation that he did not create, and Theodora in particular did not forget him. Soon after his dismissal as praetorian prefect, Peter was appointed count of the sacred largesses, with jurisdiction over imperial revenues and expenses. He continued to find new ways of raising money. The empire was still feeling the loss of tax revenues resulting from the plague, and Justinian valued a man who could balance the books. One of Peter's schemes was to issue a light-weight gold *nomisma*, the standard gold coin known as the *solidus*, which was ordinarily minted at seventy-two to a pound of gold. Some of these coins have been found, and there is no doubt that they were issued along-side the coins of normal weight. They were probably used to pay the sol-diers and perhaps the civil servants; if so, they were a relatively painless way of making a pay cut.

Another of Peter's schemes was to establish a state monopoly over the silk trade. Silk came from China, and though some was shipped directly overland via a caravan route that terminated in the Crimea, most of it was handled by Persian middlemen who sold the silk to private weaving houses in Berytus (Beirut) and Tyre. The war with Persia that broke out in 540 disrupted the trade, and Justinian's efforts to deal with the silk shortage made it worse. Peter took advantage of the crisis to make silk manufacture a state monopoly, which enriched the treasury and, inci-dentally, Peter himself. The monopoly, however, ruined the private weav-ing establishments. Ten years later, Byzantium would obtain some silkworm eggs that were smuggled out of China, and soon the produc-tion of silk fabrics became an important Byzantine industry. But the im-port of raw silk from China remained significant.

Peter was reappointed praetorian prefect in 555 and lasted in the of-fice until 562. In that year, a mob burned his house in Constantinople, which was not a mark of popularity. However, he replaced it with a splen-did new residence. Years later, Emperor Maurice (r. 582–602) gave it to his sister; apparently at some previous point in time it had come under imperial ownership. We know no more of Peter. Prokopios claims that he was fascinated by sorcery and magic, and this was one reason why Theodora favored him, for she, also, was thought to have had an inter-est in sorcery. Accusations of sorcery, however, were a common method of blackening the character of one's enemies.

Peter *the Patrician*

Peter the Patrician held the powerful position of master of offices from 539 to 565, and though Prokopios[1] assails him for his avarice and his clever thievery, he was an inoffensive man who seems to have been a fair-minded administrator of justice. Among his duties was court ceremonial, which became increasingly elaborate during Justinian's reign, and Peter can take credit for some of this development. He wrote a book on the post of master of offices from Emperor Constantine to Justinian, which listed all the holders of the position and cited many documents that illustrated the ceremonies surrounding the accession of a new emperor as well as other ceremonies. In addition, he wrote a history of the Roman Empire, and finally, toward the end of his life, he produced an account of his diplomatic mission to Persia in 561 and 562, which resulted in the Fifty-Year Peace. None of these works has survived, though his account of his diplomatic mission was used as a source by Menander Protector, whose history continued from where Agathias of Myrina broke off in 559, and his book on ceremonies was used in a tenth-century work titled *On Ceremonies* (*De Caerimoniis*), attributed to Emperor Constantine VII Porphyrogenitus (r. 945–959), who collaborated in its composition.

Peter was one of a number of men who during Justinian's reign rose from obscure backgrounds to positions of influence. He was born near Dara in the province of Mesopotamia, pursued legal studies as a young man, and then practiced law in Constantinople. In late 534, he was sent to the Ostrogothic court in Italy. His ostensible mission was to discuss the status of Lilybaeum (modern Marsala in Sicily), which both the emperor and the Goths claimed, but he had secret instructions to discuss the future of Italy with Amalasuntha, the regent for her son Athalaric. On his way, he met envoys from Amalasuntha who told him that Athalaric had died and Theodahad was king; and then, before he crossed the Adriatic into Italy, he met envoys from Theodahad who told him that Theodahad had imprisoned Amalasuntha. He reported the news to Justinian, who instructed him to make it known among the Goths that Amalasuntha had the emperor's support, but when Peter reached Italy,

---

1. *Secret History* 24.22–23.

he found that Amalasuntha had been murdered. He protested, threatening war, and returned to Constantinople with letters from Theodahad
claiming his innocence. A few months later, with war imminent, he returned to Ravenna to put pressure on Theodahad, who agreed to surrender Sicily and acknowledge Justinian as his overlord. Then, after Peter
had left, Theodahad recalled him and offered to hand over all of Italy in
return for sanctuary in Constantinople, all expenses paid. But when Peter
returned again with instructions from Justinian to accept the offer, Theodahad had recovered his courage. The Goths had won a victory in Dalmatia, where the Byzantine commander, Moundos, had lost his life in a
skirmish, and Theodahad, now overconfident, put Peter under arrest. He
remained under arrest until 539, when Belisarios negotiated his release.

Prokopios' *Gothic Wars* is our source for this account, but in his unpublished *Secret History*[2] he reveals a cloak-and-dagger story that is quite
different. Peter carried secret instructions from Theodora that urged
Theodahad to murder Amalasuntha, for she feared that the beautiful, cul-
tured Gothic princess would challenge her influence at court. Peter was
promised the post of master of offices for carrying out his mission. The
two stories cannot be reconciled, and historians generally reject the *Secret
History*'s tale. However, among Cassiodorus' *Variae*,[3] a collection of documents written while Cassiodorus was Theodahad's praetorian prefect,
there is one from Theodahad and another from Theodahad's queen,
Gudeliva, that refer mysteriously to a deed that had evidently been carried out, and Theodora should find its result pleasing. Theodora was
clearly carrying out negotiations with the Gothic court, but it is not clear
what they involved. However, it is clear from Theodahad's letter that
Peter enjoyed Theodora's favor.

On Peter's return to Constantinople in 539, he was appointed master
of offices, and soon after had the honor of *patricius* conferred on him. He
was involved in all the important diplomatic negotiations with the Persians during the rest of Justinian's reign. He was also involved peripher-
ally in the "Three Chapters" dispute as a go-between for Justinian and
Pope Vigilius and his party. At the end of his career, he was the imperial representative who negotiated the Fifty-Year Peace with the Persian

---

2. *Secret History* 16.5.
3. *Variae* 10.21.

envoy Izedh Gushnap. He died shortly afterward, leaving behind him a good reputation as a reliable bureaucrat. Prokopios alone struck a sour note.

Prokopios of Caesarea

The historian Prokopios of Caesarea is our major source for Justinian's reign. His birthplace was Caesarea in Palestine, but our knowledge of his early life is very sketchy. It is clear that he received a good education in the Greek classics, particularly the historians Herodotos and Thucydides. Latin was also an important part of the curriculum, for it was still the language of law, and a legal education was a prerequisite for entry into the imperial civil service. Prokopios became a *rhetor* (a lawyer), and in 527, he was attached to the staff of Belisarios as his *assessor*, a combination of legal adviser and secretary. He accompanied Belisarios on his campaigns against the Vandals and the Goths, and presumably returned with Belisarios to Constantinople after the capture of Ravenna in 540. However, in 542 Belisarios fell from favor and his friends were forbidden to visit him. Prokopios must have been affected by this ban, and it is not clear what contacts the two men may have had afterward. Belisarios was reappointed to the command of the war against the Ostrogoths in 544, and Prokopios had good sources for Belisarios' conduct of the war in Italy. There is no solid evidence that he witnessed it personally.

However, Prokopios was growing increasingly disillusioned with Belisarios and hostile toward Belisarios' wife, Antonina. There may have been private reasons for this that we cannot know, but one remark in his *Secret History* seems significant. He wrote there that when Belisarios was reappointed to the command of the war against the Ostrogoths in 544, his friends believed that when he was back in Italy, he would seize the opportunity to rebel against Justinian, and were bitterly disillusioned when he did not. Prokopios may have been among this circle of friends who looked to Belisarios as the savior who would deliver them from Justinian and Theodora, and turned against him when he did not. Probably Prokopios blamed Antonina, who was the friend and ally of the empress and whose infidelity to her husband disgusted him. He could not understand the bond that tied Belisarios to her, and imagined that Antonina must have used sorcery to keep Belisarios her faithful slave.

Prokopios published his history of Justinian's wars, which is his major work, no earlier than 551. It consists of seven books, the first two dealing with the war against the Persians; the next two with the wars in Africa against the Vandals and then against the Moors (the Berbers), who revolted against Byzantine rule; and the last three with the war against the Ostrogoths in Italy. Prokopios belonged to a school of historians who modeled their works on the classical historians Herodotos and Thucydides (fifth century B.C.E.). These historians appeared to be writing for a readership that lived a thousand years before their own time. Terms that a pagan Greek of the classical period would not understand were used with an apologetic "so-called" attached, or explained with a gloss. Christianity was treated as if it were an alien religion with which readers would be unfamiliar. As a result, many modern readers have speculated that Prokopios was a pagan, but there can be little doubt that his supposed paganism was nothing more than a literary pose which he shared with other historians of his school. He mentions at one point that he intended to write an ecclesiastical history of the theological disputes which split the Christian Church. As far as we know, he never did, but his mention of it shows that, like his contemporaries, he took an interest in theological disputes. One gets the impression from Prokopios' *Wars*, however, that he regarded Justinian's obsession with theology as a distraction from the more important business of ruling the empire justly and efficiently.

At the same time as Prokopios published *Wars*, he was finishing his *Anekdota* (never published), more commonly known as the *Secret History*, which reveals not only scandalous information about Belisarios, Antonina, Justinian, and Theodora that he could not include in his *Wars*, but also a darker, more superstitious side to Prokopios' mind-set. We do not know how the *Secret History* survived, for Prokopios did not dare to publish it. The first mention of its existence is in a late Byzantine lexicon dating to about 1000, called the *Suda*, which treats it as the final book of Prokopios' history of Justinian's wars and refers to it as a "comedy" or "burlesque," a work intended to make its readers laugh, even though the laughter might be bitter. The *Secret History* reveals that Prokopios had become an embittered man, hostile to his old general and particularly hostile to Justinian, whom he regards as the Antichrist. When he wrote it, Theodora was only recently dead—she died in 548—and Prokopios looked forward to Justinian following her to the grave in the near future. He would wait a long time.

Prokopios wrote two more works. One was an eighth book of his *History*. It brings the war against the Ostrogoths in Italy to an end, and deals summarily with the wars on the Persian and African fronts. The date commonly assigned for its composition is 554, though there is some evidence that would date it as late as 557. Its introduction echoes the *Secret History*, and must be a covert reference to it by Prokopios himself. The other work is the *Peri Ktismaton* (its more common Latin title is *De Aedificiis*, On the Buildings). An uneven work in six books, it is a panegyric on Justinian's building program. The first book, which deals with buildings in Constantinople, is written in polished prose, and must date before the first collapse of the dome of Hagia Sophia in 557, for it describes the church as if it were still intact. However, there is internal evidence that the rest of the panegyric was written later, in the early 560s. It covers the whole empire except Italy, where Justinian built little: for example, the church of San Vitale in Ravenna with its splendid mosaics in the chancel showing Justinian and Theodora was begun while the Goths still controlled Ravenna and was paid for by a local banker. The *De Aedificiis* concentrates on churches, aqueducts, and defense works and presents Justinian as a pious servant of God, a benefactor of the cities, and a protector of his subjects. Prokopios must have had access to official records to write this work, and it is generally reliable, though the claim that he makes in his conclusion that he has seen everything he describes is clearly untrue.

De Aedificiis is the last work that Prokopios wrote, and the uneven style may indicate that it is unfinished. If so, Prokopios may have been interrupted by death while he was working on it. In 562, however, Belisarios was implicated in a conspiracy and brought before the court of the urban prefect, whose name was Prokopios. It would be ironic if the urban prefect was Belisarios' old *assessor*. However, the name Prokopios was not uncommon, and no ancient source connects the urban prefect of 562 with the historian Prokopios.

Vigilius

Vigilius, who was Justinian's antagonist in the "Three Chapters" dispute, was pope and bishop of Rome from 537 until his death in 555. He belonged to a Roman senatorial family and was the son of a consul, and like many members of the Roman aristocracy he opted for a career in the church. He became a deacon, the lowest of the three orders of clergy. Vigilius was a favorite of Pope Boniface II (d. 532), who tried to designate him as his successor, but he had to yield to the resistance of the Roman clergy and the Roman senate. When Pope Agapetus (535–536) journeyed to Constantinople on the orders of the Ostrogothic king Theodahad, who hoped that the pope's intercession would avert the Byzantine invasion of Italy, Vigilius went with him as *apokrisarios* or nuncio (representative) of the Roman see in Constantinople. After Agapetus died in Constantinople, Empress Theodora conspired with Vigilius to elevate him to the papacy.

We do not know which of the two took the initiative, but Theodora was well aware of Vigilius' ambition, and believed he would be a useful ally. She had Anthimos, the dethroned patriarch of Constantinople whom Pope Agapetus had excommunicated, hidden in the women's quarters of the imperial palace, and she wanted the excommunication lifted and Anthimos rehabilitated. She promised Vigilius 200 gold pounds and gave him letters to take to Belisarios and Antonina, instructing them to give Vigilius their support. Vigilius in turn promised to reestablish Anthimos as patriarch of Constantinople.

Vigilius headed for Rome, and Pelagius, who would later succeed him as pope, assumed the office of nuncio in Constantinople. But before Vigilius could reach Rome to claim the papacy, Theodahad engineered the election of his own candidate, Silverius, son of the Hormisdas who had been pope in Justin I's reign. Silverius had purchased Theodahad's support with a large bribe, and Theodahad had pressured the Roman clergy to support his candidacy by threatening them with death. Theodora made an attempt to win over Silverius, but when he refused to restore Anthimos, she sent secret instructions to Antonina to replace him with Vigilius. Rome was under siege by the Ostrogoths at the time, and Silverius had good reason to hope that the siege would not be successful, for he had taken an oath of fidelity to the Gothic king Witigis, and then, when Belisarios and his army reached Rome, he urged the Romans to open the city gates to them. Antonina trumped up a charge of treason against Silverius, who was accused of planning to betray Rome to the Ostrogoths. He was deposed swiftly and efficiently, and Vigilius was chosen in his place. Silverius was dealt with pitilessly. He died of starvation on a small island in the Tyrrhenian Sea, where Vigilius sent him into exile.

Vigilius proved as inflexible as Silverius, however. He did not deny that he had promised Theodora that he would rehabilitate Anthimos, but he claimed that now he was pope, the situation had changed. He could not revoke the anathema that both Silverius and Agapetus had upheld. Rome was solidly Chalcedonian, and Vigilius realized that it was politically impossible for him to make any compromise with the anti-Chalcedonians, whatever his private inclinations might be. Theodora was foiled for the moment.

But Vigilius was soon caught in the next theological upheaval to roil the church, the "Three Chapters" dispute. The "Three Chapters" referred to the writings of three theologians who had lived a century earlier and had been supporters of the heresy of Nestorios, who had held that Christ had two distinct natures, one human and the other divine. The Council of Chalcedon, held in 451, which had drawn up the Chalcedonian Creed, had rehabilitated these theologians and their writings, thus giving some credibility to the anti-Chalcedonian charge that orthodoxy as defined by Chalcedon was no different from Nestorianism, which everyone agreed was heretical. Justinian hoped that by undercutting this argument, he could reconcile the Chalcedonians and the anti-Chalcedonians. In 544, he issued a long edict under three headings or "chapters" that condemned these three theologians, and he expected the patriarchs to countersign it. Vigilius refused. Like most of the Latin bishops, he could not read Greek and hence could not read the writings that Justinian had condemned. But he did know that his bishops considered Justinian's edict an attack on Rome's supremacy, and he could not ignore their opposition.

Vigilius was arrested in Rome in November 545, but he made his way slowly to Constantinople and did not reach it until the spring of 547. Once there, he continued to oppose Justinian's edict. What was at stake, as he saw it, was the right of the Roman Church to define orthodox belief, which Justinian had usurped. There is some irony to the fact that the patriarch of Constantinople, Menas, had excerpts from the writings which Justinian condemned, translated into Latin so that Vigilius could read them, and when he did, he quickly realized that they were in fact heretical. But he could not ignore the bitter opposition to Justinian's edict among the Latin clergy in Italy, Gaul, and, in particular, Africa, nor could he agree that Justinian had any right to define what Christians should believe. In the end, though, Vigilius had to give way. When the Fifth Ecumenical Council opened in Constantinople in May 553, he absented himself, but his resistance was weakening. The council condemned him, and finally, in February 554, he capitulated and gave his unqualified consent to the "Three Chapters" edict. A broken man suffering from kidney stones, Vigilius died at Syracuse (in Sicily) on his way back to Rome. Yet the Latin bishops did not forgive his surrender, and he was denied burial in St. Peter's Basilica. It remained for his successor, Pope Pelagius, to heal the rift in the church.

Pelagius had been a strong supporter of Vigilius' refusal to countersign Justinian's "Three Chapters" edict, but when Justinian offered him the papacy, he accepted. There was a condition, however: Justinian insisted that Pelagius accept the condemnation of the "Three Chapters." Pelagius had just written a defense of them, but nonetheless he accepted the papacy with the condition attached, and he returned to a hostile reception in Rome. However, Narses and his soldiers maintained firm control, and on Easter Sunday, he was ordained bishop of Rome in the cathedral of St. John Lateran. Once the ceremony was done, he was escorted by troops to St. Peter's, where from the pulpit he declared his support of the Council of Chalcedon and the "Three Chapters" that the Fifth Ecumenical Council had condemned. Justinian had been outwitted after all.

PRIMARY DOCUMENTS OF THE BYZANTINE EMPIRE

THE LEGAL REFORMS OF JUSTINIAN

DOCUMENT 1
The *Institutes* of Justinian

Justinian came to the throne determined to reform legal procedure. Barely seven months after Justin I died, he appointed a ten-man commission under John the Cappadocian to update the law codes, and the result was a new code that came into effect in April of the next year. This was the Codex Vetus (Old Code), which is now lost. Twenty months later Justinian set up another commission under the senior law minister (quaestor sacri cubiculi), Tribonian, to examine legal precedents and opinions from the first to the fourth centuries, and codify them. This task took three years and resulted in a massive work known as the Digest of Roman law (the Pandects, in Greek). At the same time it became clear that law students needed a new textbook, and one was drawn up by the legal experts Dorotheos and Theophilos under Tribonian's general supervision. Known as the Institutes, it was given the validity of an imperial statute and could be cited in court. The Institutes was promulgated on November 21, 533, by the constitution (i.e., imperial decision) titled "Imperatoriam," the first word of the preamble to the constitution that is quoted as follows. The work of the commission was not yet finished, however, for it had become clear that the Codex Vetus was already obsolete. Thus Justinian gave the commission the task of producing a new code. This was the Codex Repetitae Praelectionis, which means literally a code resulting from a second reading, or, as we would put it, a second edition. This is the law code that survived.

In the section of the "Imperatoriam" quoted below, Justinian gives us some insight into the preparation of the Digest and the Code. "Imperatoriam" introduced the Institutes, and was intended for the enlightenment of young law students who would use the Institutes as a textbook.

Preamble to the *Institutes* of Justinian

IN THE NAME OF OUR LORD JESUS CHRIST.

THE EMPEROR CAESAR FLAVIUS JUSTINIANUS, CONQUEROR OF THE ALA-MANNI, GOTHS, FRANKS, GERMANS, ANTES, ALANI, VANDALS AND AFRICANS, DUTIFUL, FORTUNATE AND RENOWNED, VICTORIOUS AND TRIUMPHANT, TO YOUNG MEN WISHING TO LEARN THE LAW, GREETING.

Imperial majesty should not only be adorned with arms but also graced by laws, so that in times of peace and war alike the state may be governed aright and so that the Emperor of Rome may not only emerge victorious on the battlefield, but may also by operation of justice cast out the evil of wrongdoers, and thus at one and the same time prove as anxious to uphold the law as he is triumphant over his vanquished foes.

Each of these aims we have achieved through our utmost watchfulness and foresight with the consent of God. The barbarian races brought under our rule know well our military achievements; and not only Africa but other provinces, too, beyond number, that have been restored to the dominion of Rome and to our Empire bear witness to our power, for they have been brought back under our sway after so long a time by our victories which we have won with the approval of Heaven. Moreover, all these peoples are now governed by laws that we ourselves have made or compiled.

When we had clarified and brought into perfect harmony the hallowed imperial constitutions which hitherto were in disorder, we turned our attention to the vast bulk of ancient jurisprudence. Now, with Heaven's favor, we have . . . concluded this task which, like voyagers venturing on the open sea, we once despaired of achieving.

When this task was achieved with God's blessing, we summoned Tribonian, a distinguished master and former quaestor of our sacred Palace, and along with him, the professors of law, Theophilos and Dorotheos, men with the rank of *illustris*, all of whom have on numerous occasions proved to us their acumen, legal skill and obedience to our orders. We gave them special mandate to compose these our *Institutes* under our authority and guidance, so that you may no longer learn the first principles of law from out-dated stories, but grasp them in the bright illumination of our imperial wisdom, and both your ears and minds shall receive only what obtains in current practice and nothing that is useless or erroneous. Accordingly, the study of the imperial constitutions which hitherto appeared on the curriculum only after four[1] years, you may now undertake at the very start of your legal studies, and you may rejoice that you merit such an honor that both your first lessons and the completion of your legal studies proceed from the very mouth of the Emperor himself.

Therefore, when we had compiled the Fifty Books titled the *Digest* or *Pandects* where all the ancient law was gathered, a work we achieved through the same eminent Tribonian we mentioned before, and the other illustrious and learned men, we directed that these our *Institutes* should be divided into four books so that they might be a primer of the whole science of law. In these books the law that was previously in force is briefly described as well as the law that had fallen into disuse but now has been remedied by the emperor and clarified. These three learned men we have referred to above have compiled these our *Institutes* from all the ordinances left by the ancient authorities—especially from the commentaries of our Gaius, particularly his *Institutes* and his work *On Daily Business*, but from many other commentaries also. We have read their work and understood it and have accorded it the full force of law.

Therefore with all your heart and soul receive these our laws and study them with cheerful diligence, and prove yourselves persons of such learning that you may fulfil the splendid aspiration of being able to help govern our Empire in the spheres allotted to you when you complete your legal studies.

Given at Constantinople 21 November 533, in the third consulate of the Emperor Justinian, ever Augustus.

Source: Trans. James Allan Evans.

---

1. *Quadrennium* (a period of four years) is the manuscript reading. One editor has emended *quadrennium* to *triennium* (a period of three years) because four years of study in the pre-Justinianic law curriculum seems too long before students began to read the imperial constitutions.

JUSTINIAN'S *NOVELS*: A TASTE OF HIS LEGISLATION

DOCUMENT 2
Novel 38, Preface (535 C.E.)

After the Digest was complete, it was clear that the Codex Vetus of 529 was already obsolete; so Justinian gave Tribonian's commission, which had produced the Digest, a fresh mandate to produce a new edition of the code. The new code, the Codex Repetitae Praelectionis, was published on November 16, 534; this is the law code that has survived. It contains twelve books, and its regulations reflect the social, ecclesiastical, and economic problems of the day. Justinian continued to issue laws, most of them now in Greek rather than Latin, unless they were directed specifically to a Latin-speaking part of the empire such as Italy (once it had been recovered from the Ostrogoths). These were the Novels (Novellae Constitutiones), collected after Justinian's death. One of Justinian's concerns was the decay of the town councils or "senates" (curiae; boulai in Greek) in the cities of the empire. Decurions, men of the curial class, were required to serve on these councils, but it was a burdensome and expensive duty, and they tried to avoid it. One change made under Emperor Anastasius saw the appointment of watchdogs in each city (vindices) who were to supervise the town councils and see to it that the decurions were honest and that wealthy decurions were not treated too leniently. In many of the cities, the vindices seem to have shoved the councils aside. The Novel below is one of Justinian's efforts to attack this problem.

Justinian to John [the Cappadocian], the most glorious Praetorian Prefect of the East: Those who of old established our form of government thought [it] right that following the precedent of the capital city, they should form in each city an assembly of the well-born and give it a senate through which public business should be conducted and everything be done in proper order. The scheme so prospered and gained such reputation that the greatest and most numerous families had members in the senates, the senators forming a large body, and what were regarded as the burdens of the service being by no means insupportable to any of them. For through being distributed amongst a large number the burden was almost imperceptible to those who shouldered it. But when gradually certain individuals began to get their names removed from the senatorial lists and to discover pretexts why they should be exempt, then little by little the senates shrank, since countless pretexts were devised, the result of which was that private interests were likely to prosper but the general weal of the community to suffer. The public services devolved on a small body of men, and this state of things undermined their fortunes and did such injury to the cities that they fell into the clutches of those pernicious hirelings who are known as *vindices*. The state system had become a sink of all iniquity.

This condition of things we have been constantly investigating and we have decided that we must apply a remedy. But the more we labored at this problem, the more the senators devised every trick to thwart our just and right enactments and the public interest. When they saw that they were being forced by every possible means to reserve a fourth part of their estate for the senate and that this provision had with great difficulty been entered among our laws, they started dissipating their property so as to die in poverty and to leave the senate not the quarter that was due to it but a property completely bankrupt; next, having decided to deprive the senate even of their persons, they formed the most impious plot of all, abstaining from lawful marriage and choosing rather to die childless from the legal point of view than to prove themselves useful to their race and to their senate.

Source: Trans. Percy Neville Ure, *Justinian and His Age* (London: Penguin Books, 1951), p. 111. © Percy Neville Ure, 1951. Reproduced by permission of Penguin Books Ltd.

DOCUMENT 3
Novel 45, Preface (537 C.E.)

Two years after Novel 38 (previous document), Justinian gives a response in Novel 45 (as follows) to a memorandum from John the Cappadocian about a petition he has received from the decurions who are Jews, Samaritans, Montanists, and others whom Justinian considered heretics. They have made the ingenious argument that since they are heretics and Justinian is on record as hating heretics, they should be excused from serving on the town councils of their municipalities. John the Cappadocian apparently thought their argument was not completely unsound. Justinian replies that not only should these groups not be excused, but that they should bear

all the burdens of service on the town councils and receive none of the priv-
ileges. There were, in fact, few privileges left; even their exemption from
flogging was not always granted now to decurions when they claimed it.

This excerpt also shows Justinian's attitude toward Jews and Samari-
tans, both of whom belonged to "permitted religions" (religiones licitae)
in Roman law. The Samaritans were the remnant of the northern king-
dom of Israel, and relations between them and the Jews were chilly. The
Samaritans twice rose in revolt in Justinian's reign and were suppressed
cruelly. Justinian lumped Jews and Samaritans together with Christian
heretics, though in practice his treatment of the Jews did not differ greatly
from that of his predecessors.

Justinian to John, praetorian prefect, ex-consul and patrician: Your emi-
nence recently sent us a memorandum stating that certain amongst the
senators are Jews, Samaritans or Montanists or men of some other de-
testable sort who are not even now illumined by the true faith. . . . And
since we hate heretics, they think that they are for that reason exempt
from service in the senate, and you submit that a decision should be pronounced on these questions. We were astonished that your intelligence
and acumen could listen to such arguments and did not straightway tear
in pieces those who talked like this. If there are certain men who think
that their extreme perversity constitutes a claim to privileges which we
have reserved for the highest dignities, who will not detest their miserable folly? Let such men serve on the senates and let them be sorry that
they have to.

Source: Trans. Percy Neville Ure, *Justinian and His Age* (London: Penguin Books,
1951), pp. 112–113. © Percy Neville Ure, 1951. Reproduced by permission of
Penguin Books Ltd.

THE POSITION OF THE EMPEROR

DOCUMENT 4
Justinian on the Relationship between the
Empire and the Church

The following document is part of the preface to one of Justinian's laws,
Novel 6, which defined the qualifications necessary for appointment to

the priesthood. It is important because it sets forth for the first time the distinction between imperium (*imperial rule*) and sacerdotium (*the priesthood*). In pagan Rome there was no need for a distinction between church and state—nor, for that matter, any concept that a distinction might exist. The emperor was himself a god, and received worship. Once the emperors were Christian, the situation changed: emperors were no longer gods themselves, but they were the vicars of God, that is, viceroys who received their authority from God to rule on Earth. The idea that the secular realm might be separated from the ecclesiastical realm did not occur to Emperor Constantine I and his immediate successors. The emperor was ex officio a priest (sacerdos) and archbishop (archiereus), and he was a friend of the Logos, the Divine Word. He was a sacred being.

In Novel 6, for the first time Justinian draws a distinction between imperial authority and the Christian priesthood, though he also emphasizes a connection between the two that was mutually beneficial. This is the first recognition in Roman law of a distinction between the ecclesiastical sphere and the secular one. Novel 6 does not imply any separation between church and state, a concept that was entirely foreign to the Byzantine mind-set. In fact, historians have frequently accused Justinian of caesaropapism, whereby the caesar (the emperor) assumes the right of the head of the church to define Christian dogma, and the charge is well founded. Yet Justinian did recognize that imperial authority and the Christian priesthood were distinct entities, and he was the first emperor to express the distinction in law.

Novel 6 was addressed to the patriarch of Constantinople. Justinian was concerned that unsuitable men were entering the ranks of the clergy, and he was determined to remedy this defect.

The greatest blessings of mankind are the gifts of God which have been granted us by the mercy on high—the priesthood and the imperial authority. The priesthood ministers to things divine: the imperial authority is set over, and shows diligence in, things human; but both proceed from one and the same source, and both adorn the life of man. Nothing, therefore, will be a greater amount of concern to the emperor than the dignity and honor of the clergy; the more so as they offer prayers to God without ceasing on his behalf. For if the priesthood be in all respects without blame, and full of faith before God, and if the imperial authority rightly and duly adorn the commonwealth committed to its charge, there will ensue a happy concord which will bring forth all good things for mankind. We therefore have the greatest concern for true doctrines of the Godhead and the dignity and honor of the clergy; and we believe that if they maintain that dignity and honor, we shall gain thereby the greatest of gifts, holding fast to what we already have and laying hold on what is yet to come. "All things," it is said, "are done well and truly if they start from a beginning that is worthy and pleasing in the sight of God." We believe that this will come to pass if observance be paid to the holy rules which have been handed down by the Apostles—those righteous guardians and ministers of the Word of God, who are ever to be praised and adored—and have since been preserved and interpreted by the Holy Fathers.

Source: Trans. Ernest Barker. Ernest Barker, *Social and Political Thought in Byzantium* (Oxford: Oxford University Press, 1957), pp. 75–76. Reprinted by permission of Oxford University Press.

THE IDEAL EMPEROR: THE COUNSEL OF AGAPETOS

DOCUMENT 5
A Mirror for Justinian

When Justinian became emperor or shortly afterward, a deacon of the church of Hagia Sophia named Agapetos addressed an exposition of advice to him on his duties as emperor. This little work set forth Agapetos' counsel in seventy-two short chapters, fifteen of which are quoted below. It belongs to a type of literature known as the "mirror for princes," which has antecedents in classical literature, where we find a number of essays on ideal kingship. It takes on a new shape in the medieval world and early modern world, where we find many examples in various languages, including Persian and Arabic. Agapetos assumed without question that the emperor was the source of all power, and that his dominion on Earth was analogous to God's position in Heaven. His exposition addressed to Justinian proved popular: in the sixteenth century twenty editions of it were printed.

The standard that Agapetos sets for an ideal emperor is high. God has given the emperor his authority, and hence the emperor should imitate God; and since God is merciful, so also should the emperor be merciful. Kingship has been entrusted to the emperor by God, and hence he should never employ corrupt officials, for God will require an account from the emperor for the wrongs his corrupt officials have done. The true emperor rules with the consent of his subjects even though his authority comes from God. There is a practical reason for this rule: subjects who do not accept their sovereign willingly are prone to revolt. Yet the true emperor must never forget that he is the servant of God.

Chapter 1. Having a dignity which is set above all other honors, Sire, you render honor above all to God, who gave you that dignity; inasmuch as He gave you the sceptre of earthly power after the likeness of the heavenly kingdom, to the end that you should instruct men to hold fast the cause of justice, and should punish the howling of those who rage against that cause; being yourself under the kingship of the law of justice and lawfully king of those who are subject to you.

Chapter 2. Like the man at the helm of a ship, the mind of the king, with its many eyes, is always on the watch, keeping a firm hold on the rudder of enforcement of the law and sweeping away by its might the currents of lawlessness, to the end that the ship of the State of the world may not run into the waves of injustice.

Chapter 3. The divine lesson which we first learn, O men, is that a man should know himself. For he who knows himself will know God; he who knows God will become like God; a man will become like God when he becomes worthy of Him; and a man becomes worthy of God when he does nothing unworthy of Him, but thinks the things that are God's, speaks what he thinks, and does what he speaks.

Chapter 5. Know this, thou divinely made image of piety [the writer here addresses the emperor], that the more God deems thee worthy of His great gifts, the greater is the return which thou owest Him. Pay, therefore, thy debt of gratitude to thy Benefactor, who receives the debt paid as a grace, and gives grace in return for grace. For He is always in Himself the first author of grace, and repays grace done as if it were a debt. He asks for gratitude from us—not in the proffering of good words, but in the offering of pious works.

Chapter 9. The soul of the king, full of many cares, must be wiped clean like a mirror, that it may always shine with divine illumination, and attain thereby to knowledge of affairs. For there is nothing which has such power to make a man see what is right, as to keep the soul always pure and clean.

Chapter 15. It is the crown of piety that adorns the king above all the ornaments of kingship. Wealth vanishes; glory perishes. But the glory of Godlike government is prolonged for eternal ages, and it sees its possessors beyond the reach of oblivion.

Chapter 18. I reckon you as indeed a king because you have the strength to be king and master of your passions, and because you wear the crown of temperance and are clothed with the purple of justice. Other sorts of authority have death for their heir; but kingship such as this endures for ever and ever. Other sorts of authority end with this life; but this is saved from the pains of eternal punishment.

Chapter 19. If you wish to reap the harvest of being honored by all men, become the common benefactor of all. For there is nothing that moves men to feel goodwill to their ruler so much as the grace of [his] goodwill bestowed on the needy. For obedience which arises from fear is only a simulated adulation, which cheats with the fictitious name of honor those who pay heed thereto.

Chapter 21. In the nature of his body, the king is on a level with all other men, but in the authority attached to his dignity he is like God Who rules over all; for he has no man on Earth who is higher than he. Therefore, like God, he must never be angry, yet as a mortal man he must never be lifted up in conceit, for if he be honored by being in the divine image, he is also involved in the earthly image whereby he is taught his equality with other men.

Chapter 27. Impose on yourself the compulsion of observing the laws, since you have no man on Earth who is able to apply compulsion to you. Thus you will testify to the majesty of the laws by reverencing them above all else; and thus, too, it will be clear to your subjects that any breach of the laws is not free from peril.

Chapter 35. Consider yourself to be surely and truly a king when you rule with the consent of your subjects. For a subject people which is unconsenting revolts when it finds an opportunity; but a people which is attached to its sovereign by the bonds of goodwill keeps firm and true in its obedience to him.

Chapter 37. He who has attained to great authority should imitate, so far as he can, the Giver of that authority. If in any way he bears the image of God, Who is over all, and if through Him he holds rule over all, he will imitate God best if he thinks that nothing is more precious than mercy.

Chapter 40. Kingship is the most honored of all things: and it is so most especially, when the person who is vested with this authority does not incline to self-will, but keeps his mind fixed on equity; turning away from inhumanity as a thing that is bestial, and showing forth humanity as a quality that is Godlike.

Chapter 59. Guide your kingdom aright here below, that it may become for you a ladder to the glory above. Those who govern well an earthly kingdom are deemed worthy also of the heavenly; and they are good governors of the earthly kingdom who show a paternal affection to their subjects and receive from them in return the awe which is proper to rulers—preventing them by threats from stumbling, and not bringing trials upon them by punishments.

Chapter 72. Strive for ever, unconquered king, and even as those who begin to climb a ladder do not halt in their upward movement till they reach the topmost rungs, so do you persevere in your climbing upward to what is good, that you may also enjoy the kingdom which is above. May Christ grant you that kingdom, along with the empress your wife; Who is King of kings and of the subjects of kings, for ever and ever. Amen.

Source: Trans. Ernest Barker. Ernest Barker, *Social and Political Thought in Byzantium* (Oxford: Oxford University Press, 1957), pp. 54–61. Reprinted by permission of Oxford University Press.

HAGIA SOPHIA

Modern Istanbul bears the scars of a turbulent history, yet three churches built by Justinian survive, though none of them is used for Christian worship. Hagia Sophia (Holy Wisdom), Hagia Eirene (Holy Peace), and the church of Saints Sergius and Bacchus still await the modern visitor. Hagia Sophia and Hagia Eirene are now museums, and Saints Sergius and Bacchus is Little Ayasofya mosque. Hagia Sophia and Hagia Eirene, patriarchal churches served by the same clergy, were burned in the Nika riot and were rebuilt as basilicas roofed with domes.

The churches were built at the same time, but the plan of Hagia Eirene seems less adventuresome. Basilicas up to this time were usually timber-roofed. The central nave was separated from the side aisles by rows of columns that supported a clerestory, and the roof was upheld by wooden beams. Alternatively, instead of a wooden roof, there might be a barrel vault over the nave. The architects of Hagia Eirene and Hagia Sophia, however, chose to roof them with domes. In Hagia Eirene there were two domes, end to end, each supported by great transverse arches. This plan allowed the central nave to be unusually wide. In Hagia Sophia, the nave is even wider, but instead of two domes, there is a great, single dome; in order to support the dome, as well as to add length to the nave, it is buttressed at the eastern and the western ends by large semidomes. This was an original solution to the problem of putting a dome over a basilica church, and it makes Hagia Sophia unique. Nothing quite like it was built again, though we can trace its influence in later churches, to say nothing of the mosques built in Constantinople by the Turkish sultans.

The first dome was damaged in an earthquake of 557, though it did not immediately collapse. However, on May 7 of the next year, while workmen were repairing the damage caused by the quake, the eastern semidome and perhaps part of the main dome collapsed. The dome was redesigned and made higher, so that there was less outward thrust on the piers that held it in position, and the rebuilt church was rededicated in 562.

DOCUMENT 6
Prokopios on the Construction of Hagia Sophia

The following passage comes from the Buildings of Prokopios. The long description is abbreviated here. Although the Buildings cannot have been completed in its present form until after the earthquake that damaged the first dome and led to its fall a few months later, Prokopios ignores the collapse and writes as if the dome were intact. Probably this passage was written before the collapse, and was never revised.

So the whole church at that time lay a charred mass of ruins. But the Emperor Justinian built not long afterwards a church so finely shaped that if anyone had enquired of the Christians before the burning if it would be their wish that the church should be destroyed, and one like this should take its place, showing them some sort of model of the building we now see, it seems to me that they would have prayed that they might see their church destroyed forthwith, in order that the building might be converted into its present form. At any rate, the Emperor, disregarding all questions of expense, eagerly pressed on to begin the work of construction, and began to gather all the artisans from the whole world. And Anthemios of Tralles, the most learned man in the skilled craft which is known as the art of building . . . ministered to the Emperor's enthusiasm . . . and associated with him was another master builder, Isidore by name, a Milesian by birth. . . .

So the church has become a spectacle of marvellous beauty, overwhelming to those who see it, but to those who know it by hearsay altogether incredible. For it soars to a height to match the sky, and as if surging up from amongst the other buildings it stands on high and looks down upon the remainder of the city. . . . Both its breadth and its length have been so carefully proportioned, that it may not be improperly said to be exceedingly long and at the same time unusually broad. . . . Indeed one might say that its interior is not illuminated from without by the sun, but that the radiance comes into being within it, such an abundance of light bathes this shrine. [There follows a technical description of the building of the dome of Hagia Sophia. Then Prokopios describes the aisles on either side of the nave, separated from it by colonnades and reserved for laymen and women.] And there are two stoa-like colonnades, one on each side. . . . And they, too, have vaulted ceilings and decorations of gold. One of these two colonnaded stoas has been assigned to men worshippers, while the other is reserved for women engaged in the same exercise.

Source: Trans. H. B. Dewing with Glanville Downey. *Procopius, Volume VII*, Loeb Classical Library Vol. 343 (Cambridge, MA: Harvard University Press, 1940). Reprinted by permission of the publishers and the trustees of the Loeb Classical Library. The Loeb Classical Library® is a registered trademark of the President and Fellows of Harvard College.

DOCUMENT 7
Agathias on the Rebuilding of Hagia Sophia

> In the following passage, Agathias of Myrina, who continued Proko-
> pios' History of the Wars of Justinian from where Prokopios left off in
> 552 to 559, describes the collapse of the dome of Hagia Sophia in 558
> and its rebuilding with a new, less daring design.

During that winter, then, the city was afflicted by these calamities. For several days everyone had the impression that the ground was shaking even though the tremors had ceased and it was already quite firm and motionless. People had not yet recovered from the shock of their recent experience and their minds were clouded by nagging doubts and persist-ent fears. The Emperor tried to restore a large number of public build-ings affected by the disaster. Some of them were insecure and unsound; others had already tumbled down. He was particularly concerned about the Great Church [Hagia Sophia]. Previously burned by the mob, he had built it up anew from its foundations, creating a church of amazing beauty which was further enhanced by its vastly increased dimensions, its ma-jestic proportions and . . . a lavish profusion of ornamental marble. It was built of baked brick and lime on a structure of iron girders, the use of wood being avoided to prevent its ever being set on fire again. The ar-chitect was the celebrated Anthemios of Tralles, whom I have already had cause to mention. On this occasion, however, the church had lost the top of its dome as a result of the earthquake. The Emperor, therefore, had it repaired, reinforced and raised to a greater height. Anthemios, however, was by then a long time dead. Consequently Isidore the Younger and the other architects, after studying the original form of the structure and observing by a comparison of what was still intact the nature of the part affected and the extent to which the construction had been faulty, left the arches on the east and west side exactly as they were, but extended the [curve of the arches supporting the dome on the north and south, so that they made a broader arc]. . . . They then replaced the dome. But despite the fact that it is straighter, despite its balanced curves and regular outline, it has become narrower, its lines have hardened and it has lost something of its old power to inspire awe and wonder in the beholder. It is, however, more firmly and securely fixed.

Source: Trans. Joseph D. Frendo. *Agathias, The Histories* (Berlin: De Gruyter, 1975), 5.9.1–5.9.5. Reprinted by permission of Verlag Walter de Gruyter, Berlin.

THEODORA'S EFFORT TO END PROSTITUTION

Putting an end to prostitution was a concern of both Theodora and Justinian. "It is Our wish that everyone lead chaste lives, so far as is possible," Justinian wrote in the preface of a law of 535 that outlawed procurers and panderers who exploited women for prostitution.[1] *But if we are to believe Prokopios, it was Theodora who took the lead. Perhaps it was her early experience on the stage, where actress and courtesan were virtually synonymous, that gave her an understanding of the commerce in women's bodies that went on in Constantinople and in other cities of the empire. Procurers would visit country villages, buy young girls from their fathers, and bring them into the city, where they hired them out as prostitutes. The girls were promised a glamorous life, and the fathers, who were dirt-poor and could not afford dowries for their daughters, were easily persuaded to sell them to the procurers, who, according to the report of John Malalas, would pay five nomismata for each girl. For a poor peasant, whether a tenant farmer or a freeholder, this was an enormous amount of money, and there must have been many fathers who yielded to the temptation to sell their daughters.*

Sentiment against prostitution had been growing in the previous century. Constantine I, the first Christian emperor, accepted it as a fact of life and made prostitutes subject to the sales tax that he levied on other businesses. But with the final victory of Christianity, the official attitude toward prostitution became chillier. Theodosius II prohibited fathers from making a profit from their daughters, and slave owners from prostituting their slaves. Emperor Leo I banned prostitution outright, but it continued nonetheless. Theodora attempted to put a stop to it almost as soon as she became empress.

---

1. *Novel* 14.1.

Yet the demand for prostitutes continued, and entrepreneurs were always ready to satisfy it, given the fact that enforcement of the laws was generally uneven. Add to that the root problem of poverty. A poor girl without a dowry had few options in Justinian's empire. The strategy that Theodora adopted to end prostitution did not succeed; in fact, the panderers to whom she refunded what they had paid for their prostitutes probably took the money and then toured the country villages to purchase more victims to replace those whom Theodora had freed. Yet contemporaries noted the zeal with which she attacked the problem.

The first passage quoted below comes from Prokopios' Secret History, written about 550, and reports how Theodora had the prostitutes removed from the main square of Constantinople (one favorite place for them to ply their trade was in front of the imperial palace) and sent to the Metanoia (Repentance) convent on the Asian side of the Bosporus, which she had founded by converting an old palace to a new function. The change of life was not at all welcome for some of the women, he reports. The second passage, from the Buildings, written about ten years later and intended as a panegyric, gives a much more flattering picture of the same episode. The final passage, from John Malalas, does not mention the Metanoia convent, but it does report an effort by Theodora to end prostitution by buying out the panderers.

DOCUMENT 8
Prokopios, *Secret History* (17.5–17.6)

Theodora also made it her business to think up penalties for women convicted of carnal sin. She arrested prostitutes up to the number of more than five hundred, who earned barely enough to live by selling themselves at the rate of three obols, and sent them off to the mainland across the Bosporus, where they were incarcerated in the monastery that went by the name "Penitence" and there compelled to convert to a new way of life. However some of them threw themselves down from the lofty walls of the monastery at night, and thus freed themselves from a conversion that they did not welcome.

Source: Trans. James Allan Evans.

DOCUMENT 9
Prokopios, *On the Buildings* (1.9.2–1.9.10)

There was a great number of women in Constantinople who took part in the business of prostitution in brothels, not because they wanted it, but because the lechery of men compelled them. For they were supported by brothel-keepers because they were extremely poor and they were forced to practice their lewd trade whenever there was a demand for it, and without a moment's notice receive men they did not know who happened to appear, and submit to their lust. But the Emperor Justinian and the Empress Theodora—for they forever shared a common religious zeal in everything they did—thought up the following plan. They purged the state of the pollution of the whorehouses, erasing even the name of brothel-keepers, and liberated those women who were struggling with destitution from a licentious behavior fit only for slaves, providing them with an independent livelihood where they might be free to live a life of virtue. This is how they did it. On the right-hand shore of the strait by which one sails north to the sea called the Euxine (Black Sea), they remodeled what had once been an imperial palace into a splendid convent that was intended as a lodging for women who repented of their former lives. Wherefore they called this dwelling-place for women the "Penitentiary" which was a name suitable for its purpose. These Sovereigns too have endowed this convent with a generous income of money, and have constructed many additional buildings of extraordinary beauty and costliness which are intended as a consolation for these women, so that none of them should ever be forced to lapse in any way from the practice of virtue.

Source: Trans. James Allan Evans.

DOCUMENT 10
John Malalas, *Chronicle* (18.24)

At that time the pious Theodora added the following to her other good works. Those known as brothel-keepers used to go about in every district on the look-out for poor men who had daughters, and giving them, it is said, their oath and a few *nomismata*, they used to take the girls as though under a contract; they used to make them into public prostitutes, dressing them up as their wretched lot required and, receiving from them the miserable price of their bodies, they forced them into prostitution. She ordered that all such brothel-keepers should be arrested as a matter of urgency. When they had been brought in with the girls, she ordered each of them to declare on oath what they had paid the girls' parents. They said they had given them five *nomismata* each. When they had all given information on oath, the pious empress returned the money and freed the girls from the yoke of their wretched slavery, ordering that henceforth there should be no brothel-keepers. She presented the girls with a set of clothes and dismissed them with one *nomisma* each.

Source: Trans. Elizabeth Jeffreys, Michael Jeffreys, and Roger Scott, with Brian Croke, Jenny Farber, Simon Franklin, Alan James, Douglas Kelly, Ann Moffatt, and Ann Nixon. *The Chronicle of John Malalas: A Translation*. Byzantina Australiensia IV (Melbourne: Australian Association of Byzantine Studies, 1986; rep. 2004). Reprinted by permission of the Australian Association of Byzantine Studies.

BUBONIC PLAGUE IN THE EMPIRE

In 542, bubonic plague arrived in Europe. It had appeared the year before in Egypt and, according to Prokopios, the first cases were at Pelusium at the mouth of the Nile, the terminus of one of the trading routes with the east. Its introduction seems to have coincided with the arrival of the rat. The ancient world had known mice, but there is no good evidence that it knew rats. But at some point in late antiquity, the rat reached Europe, possibly coming from India along the trade route to the Red Sea. The carrier of the Black Death in the fourteenth century, which was an equally devastating epidemic of plague, was the black rat, which has now been driven almost to extinction by the later-arriving brown rat. Dead or dying rodents on the streets have been one of the first signs of the epidemic in modern times, and contemporary accounts of the Justinianic plague report the death of dogs, mice, and even snakes. Pseudo-Dionysius of Tell-Mahre, quoted below, includes rats among the dead rodents.

We now know that the bacterium which causes plague, Yersinia pestis, is carried by a flea that lives on infected rodents. The flea contracted the plague, then bit human victims and thus transmitted the bacteria. Without the presence of fleas, a caregiver could nurse a plague victim without fear of infection, and this accounts for one of Prokopios' observations: that doctors who attended the sick did not ordinarily contract the disease.

*However, if the plague bacteria invade the lungs and cause plague pneu-
monia, the result is pulmonary plague, which is directly communicable to
another person by airborne bacteria and is always fatal unless it is treated
with antibiotics. Bubonic plague is about 60 percent fatal without treatment.*

*The plague was devastating. It probably destroyed no less than half the
population of Constantinople in 542, and it returned in 558. No part of
the empire was exempt from its ravages. Moreover, since pregnant women
were particularly vulnerable, the population did not recover as quickly as
it usually does from other types of epidemic. It has been estimated that the
total population of the empire in 600 was only about 60 percent of what
it was in 500.*

The first excerpt below is taken from the History of the Wars *by
Prokopios of Caesarea. His account is modeled on the great description of
the plague that Thucydides gave of the plague which struck Athens in 430
B.C.E. The second comes from John of Ephesus, whose* Chronicle *of this
period is lost. Fortunately, his description of the plague was copied by an
anonymous chronicler who lived in the monastery at Zuqnin in northern
Mesopotamia at the end of the eighth century. Both are contemporary accounts. The* Chronicle, *which is written in Syriac, is known either as the*
Chronicle of Zugnin *or the* Chronicle of Pseudo-Dionysios of Tell-
Mahre, *for at one time Dionysios of Tell-Mahre, the Jacobite (Monophysite) patriarch of Antioch from 818 until his death in 845, was thought
to be its author.*

DOCUMENT 11
Prokopios on the Plague

It started from the Egyptians who dwell in Pelusium. Then it divided
and moved in one direction towards Alexandria and the rest of Egypt, and
in the other direction it came to Palestine on the borders of Egypt; and
from there it spread over the whole world, always moving forward and traveling at times favorable to it. For it seemed to move by fixed arrangement,
and to tarry for a specified time in each country, casting its blight slight-
ingly upon some, but spreading in either direction right out of the ends of
the world, as if fearing lest some corner of the earth might escape it. For
it left neither island nor cave nor mountain ridge which had human inhabitants; and if it had passed by any land, either not affecting the men

there or touching them in indifferent fashion, still at a later time it came back; then those who dwelt round about this land, whom formerly it had afflicted most sorely, it did not touch at all, but it did not remove from the place in question until it had given up its just and proper tale of dead, so as to correspond exactly to the number destroyed at the earlier time among those who dwelt round about. And this disease always took its start from the coast, and from there went up to the interior.

And in the second year [542] it reached Byzantium [Constantinople] in the middle of the spring, where it happened that I was staying at the time. And it came as follows. Apparitions of supernatural beings in human guise of every description were seen by many persons, and those who encountered them thought that they were struck by the man they had met in this or that part of the body, as it happened, and immediately upon seeing this apparition they were seized also by the disease. Now at first those who met these creatures tried to turn them aside by uttering the holiest of names and exorcising them in other ways as well as each one could, but they accomplished absolutely nothing, for even in the sanctuaries where most of them fled for refuge they were dying constantly. But later on they were unwilling to give heed to their friends when they called to them, and they shut themselves up in their rooms and pretended that they did not hear, although their doors were being beaten down, fearing, obviously, that he who was calling was one of those demons. But in the case of some, the pestilence did not come on in this way, but they saw a vision in a dream and seemed to suffer the very same thing at the hands of the creature who stood over them, or else heard a voice foretelling to them that they were written down in the number of those who were to die. But with the majority it came about that they were seized by the disease without becoming aware of what was coming either through a waking vision or a dream. And they were taken in the following manner. They had a sudden fever, some when just roused from sleep, others while walking about, and others while otherwise engaged, without any regard to what they were doing. And the body showed no change from its previous color, nor was it hot as might be expected when attacked by a fever, nor indeed did any inflammation set in, but the fever was of such a languid sort from its commencement and up till evening that neither to the sick themselves nor to a physician who touched them would it afford any suspicion of danger. It was natural, therefore, that not one of those who had contracted the disease expected to die from it. But on the same day in some cases, in others on the following day, and in the rest not many days later, a bubonic swelling developed; and this took place not only in the particular part of the body which is called "boubon" [the groin], that is, below the abdomen, but also inside the armpit, and in some cases also beside the ears, and at different points on the thighs.

Up to this point, then, everything went in about the same way with all who had taken the disease. But from then on very marked differences developed; and I am unable to say whether the cause of this diversity of symptoms was to be found in the difference in bodies, or in the fact that it followed the wish of Him who brought the disease into the world. For there ensued with some a deep coma, with others a violent delirium, and in either case they suffered the characteristic symptoms of the disease. For those who were under the spell of the coma forgot all those who were familiar to them and seemed to be sleeping constantly. And if someone cared for them, they would eat without waking, but some also were neglected, and these would die directly through lack of sustenance. But those who were seized with delirium suffered from insomnia and were victims of a distorted imagination; for they suspected that men were coming upon them to destroy them, and they would become excited and rush off in flight, crying out at the top of their voices. And those who were attending them were in a state of constant exhaustion and had a most difficult time of it throughout. For this reason everybody pitied them no less than the sufferers, not because they were threatened by the pestilence in going near it (for neither physicians nor other persons were found to contract this malady through contact with the sick or with the dead, for many who were constantly engaged either in burying or attending those in no way connected with them held out in the performance of this service beyond all expectation, while with many others the disease came on without warning and they died straightway); but they pitied them because of the great hardships which they were undergoing. For when the patients fell from their beds and lay rolling upon the floor, they kept putting them back in place, and when they were struggling to rush headlong out of their houses, they would force them back by shoving and pulling against them. And when water chanced to be near, they wished to fall into it, not so much because of a desire to drink (for most of them rushed into the sea), but the cause was to be found chiefly in the diseased state of their minds.

They also had great difficulty in the matter of eating, for they could not easily take food. And many perished through lack of any man to care for them, for they were either overcome by hunger, or threw themselves down from a height. And in those cases where neither coma nor delirium came on, the bubonic swelling became mortified and the sufferer, no longer able to endure the pain, died. And one would suppose that in all cases the same thing would have been true, but since they were not at all in their senses, some were quite unable to feel pain; for owing to the troubled condition of their minds they lost all sense of feeling.

Death came in some cases immediately, in others after many days; and with some the body broke out with black pustules about as large as a lentil, and these did not survive even one day, but all succumbed immediately. With many also a vomiting of blood ensued without visible cause, and straightway brought death.

And in the case of women who were pregnant, death could be certainly foreseen if they were taken with the disease. For some died through miscarriage, but others perished immediately at the time of birth with the infants they bore. However, they say that three women in confinement survived though their children perished, and that one woman died at the very time of childbirth but that the child was born and survived.

Now in those cases where the swelling rose to an unusual size and a discharge of pus had set in, it came about that they escaped from the disease and survived for clearly the acute condition of the carbuncle had found relief in this direction, and this proved to be in general an indication of returning health; but in cases where the swelling preserved its former appearance there ensued those troubles which I have just mentioned. And with some of them it came about that the thigh was withered, in which case, though the swelling was there, it did not develop the least suppuration. With others who survived, the tongue did not remain unaffected, and they lived on either lisping or speaking incoherently and with difficulty.

Source: Trans. H. B. Dewing. *Procopius*, Volume 1: *History of the Wars, Books I and II.* Loeb Classical Library Vol. 48 (Cambridge, MA: Harvard University Press, 1914). Reprinted by permission of the publishers and the trustees of the

DOCUMENT 12
Chronicle of Zugnin (Part III)

John of Ephesus, like Prokopios, witnessed the plague firsthand and described it in the second part of his History. *The second part of his* History *is lost, but his description of the plague was copied by the monk who wrote the* Chronicle of Zugnin. *John mentions the effect of the plague on animals, including rats—which were, it is believed, the main carriers of the plague.*

When thus the scourge weighed heavy upon this city, first it eagerly began [to assault] the class of the poor, who lay in the streets. It happened that 5000 and 7000, or even 12,000 and as many as 16,000 of them departed [this world] in a single day. Since thus far it was [only] the beginning, men were standing by the harbors, at the crossroads and at the gates, counting [the dead]. Thus having perished, they were shrouded with great diligence and buried; they departed [this life] being clothed and followed [to the grave] by everybody.

Thus the [people of Constantinople] reached the point of disappearing, only a few remaining, whereas [of] those only who had died on the streets—if anyone wants us to name their number, for in fact, they were counted—over 300,000 were taken off the streets. Those who counted, having reached [the number of] 230,000 and seeing that [the dead] were innumerable, gave up [reckoning] and from then on [the corpses] were brought out without being counted.

Also we saw that this great plague showed its effect on animals as well, not only on the domesticated but also on the wild, and even on the reptiles of the earth. One could see cattle, dogs and other animals, even rats, with swollen tumors, struck down and dying. Likewise wild animals could be found smitten by the same sentence, struck down and dying.

Standing on the seashore, one could see litters colliding with each other and coming back to carry and to throw upon the earth two or three [corpses], to go back again and to bring [further corpses]. Others carried [the corpses] on boards and carrying poles, bringing and piling them up one upon another. For other [corpses], since they had rotted and putrefied, matting was sewn together. People bore them on carrying poles and coming [to the shore] threw them [down], with pus running out of them. And they would return, bringing [corpses] again. Others who were standing on the seashore dragged them and threw them down upon boats, piling them in heaps of two or three and [even] of five thousand [each]. Innumerable corpses piled up on the entire seashore, like flotsam on great rivers, and the pus flowed, discharging itself down into the sea.

Source: Trans. Witold Witakowski. *The Pseudo-Dionysius of Tel-Mahre Chronicle,* Translated Texts for Historians XXII (Liverpool: Liverpool University Press, 1996). Reprinted by permission of Liverpool University Press.

DOCUMENT 13
Agathias, *The Histories*

> *Agathias of Myrina, who continued the* History of Prokopios of Cae-*sarea from 552, where Prokopios left off, until 559, records here a re-currence of the plague in 558. Those who had survived the plague of 542 had built up some immunity to it, and hence were less likely to contract it a second time. But those who were not yet born in 542 were fresh fodder for the pestilence. Whereas Prokopios mentions the vulnerability of pregnant women, Agathias notes that young men were more susceptible than women, and does not mention pregnant women.*

During that year at the beginning of spring, a second outbreak of plague swept the capital, destroying a vast number of people. From the fifteenth year of the reign of the Emperor Justinian when the plague first spread to our part of the world it had never really stopped, but had simply moved from one place to another, giving in this way something of a respite to those who had survived its ravages. It now returned to Constantinople almost as though it had been cheated on the first occasion into a needlessly hasty departure.

People died in great numbers as though seized by a violent and sudden attack of apoplexy. Those who stood up to the disease longest barely lasted five days. The form the epidemic took was not unlike the earlier outbreak. A swelling in the glands of the groin was accompanied by a high non-intermittent fever which raged night and day with unabated intensity and never left its victim until the moment of death. Some experienced no pain or fever or any of the initial symptoms but simply dropped dead while about their normal business at home or in the street or wherever they happened to be. People of all ages were struck down indiscriminately, but the heaviest toll was among the young and vigorous and especially among the men, women being on the whole much less affected.

Source: Trans. Joseph D. Frendo. *Agathias, The Histories* (Berlin: De Gruyter, 1975). Reprinted by permission of Verlag Walter de Gruyter, Berlin.

JOHN THE CAPPADOCIAN AS DESCRIBED BY JOHN LYDOS AND PROKOPIOS

DOCUMENT 14
John Lydos Denounces John the Cappadocian

John Lydos (John the Lydian), from whose work On the Magistracies *the following passage is excerpted, was a scholar, an author, and a bureaucrat who was born in the city of Philadelphia in Lydia (Asia Minor) in 490. He received the standard education for a youth who hoped for a government career, and he was proud of his mastery of Latin and his acquaintance with the Greek classics. As a young hopeful, he came to Constantinople, where, by a stroke of luck, a countryman of his, Zotikos, was praetorian prefect. Zotikos' tenure of the office was brief, but he found John a post in his bureau* gratis—*other, older men in the bureau had had to pay for theirs—and the extra fees that Lydos could charge for his services were so profitable that he made 1,000 gold pieces (solidi) over and above his salary in his first year.*

John Lydos spent forty years in the civil service, but he retired a disappointed man, much less rich than he had hoped. For that he clearly blamed John the Cappadocian, who valued efficiency much more than the traditional ways of doing things, and allowed Latin to fall into disuse. After retirement, Lydos devoted himself to writing, and three works of his have survived: On the Magistracies, *a history and description of the late*

Roman *bureaucracy;* On the Months, *a history of calendars and festi-*
vals; and On Omens, *a historical survey of divination. Clearly astrology*
was among John's interests though Justinian tried to suppress it. His On
the Magistracies *contains a bitter attack on John the Cappadocian. We*
lack the conclusion of the work, however, and though John mentions Em-
press Theodora's enmity for the Cappadocian, we do not have a descrip-
tion of his downfall.

It was in this fashion, then, as I have just said, that the villainous John
the Cappadocian won power. He then proceeded to cause misfortunes
that were felt by the general public. First, he set out chains and shack-
les, stocks and irons. Within the praetor's court he established a private
prison there in the darkness for punishments that were inflicted upon
those who came under his authority—like a Phalaris[1]—craven coward
and only to his slaves a man of very great power. There he shut in those
who were being subjected to constraint. He exempted no one, whatever
his station, from torture. He had no compunction about stringing up,
without holding an enquiry, those among whom the only information
that had been laid was that they possessed gold, and they were either
stripped of all they possessed or dead when he let them go. To this the
population is witness, but I personally have knowledge of it because I was
an eye-witness and was present at what was done. And I will tell you the
ins and outs of it. A certain Antiochus, who was advanced in years at
the time when this happened, was named by an informer who told a tale
to John that he possessed some gold. So John arrested him and hung him
up by the hands, which were fastened by strong, fine cords, until the old
man, who denied the charge, was a corpse. Then he was freed from the
ropes which bound him. Of this murder I was an eye-witness, for I had
known Antiochus.

Well, now, as a deed, this one was, for the Cappadocian, the most moderate of all his doings—and would that he had at least been on his own
in his tireless preoccupation with wrong-doing! But just as Briareus of
mythology is said by the poets to have innumerable hands, so this infa-
mous scourge had countless ministers of evil. It was not merely in the
imperial city [Constantinople] that he operated; no, to every place and

---

1. An early tyrant of Akragas (modern Agrigento in Sicily), who ruled about
570–555 B.C.E. and was famous for his cruelty.

land he sent off men like himself, raising as if from a well with a bucket and a windlass, the small coins that had escaped notice up to this time. I shall recall one out of the swarm of these agents to illustrate the bestiality of the rest. He was a man with the same name as the Cappadocian, closely related to him, a man whose evilness with its dire consequences surpassed anything you could imagine.

John the Lydian goes on to describe at length the depredations of John the Cappadocian's agent, and the hardships they inflicted on the taxpayers. Finally he mentions the hatred of Empress Theodora for John.

Because of the Cappadocian's unrestricted power everyone, although subject to his injustices, spoke highly of the scoundrel, and their praises of him were loudest of all when they were in the emperor's presence— for who would have ventured to bring up his mere name without a word of praise? Only the emperor's wife, the superior in intelligence of any man ever, who was maintaining a vigilant watch out of sympathy for those to whom injustice was being done, finding it intolerable to watch any longer without doing something while the state foundered, armed with accounts that told no ordinary tale, went to the emperor and informed him of everything that he had failed to notice up to this time. She told him that not merely was the citizenry at risk of ruin from the wrongs that were being done, but also that the empire itself was near to being brought down.

Source: Trans. T. F. Carney. T. F. Carney, *Bureaucracy in Traditional Society*, Book Three: *John the Lydian: On the Magistracies of the Roman Constitution* (Lawrence, KS: Coronado Press, 1971), 57.3–58.3, 69.2. Reprinted by permission of Barbara Carney.

DOCUMENT 15
Prokopios Recognizes John's Ability

Prokopios of Caesarea is kinder to John the Cappadocian. In the passage quoted below, from his Vandalic War (Book 3 *of his* History of the Wars), *he describes the apprehension of Justinian's ministers when he revealed that he was mustering an expeditionary force against the Vandal*

> kingdom. *The generals were reluctant, morale among the troops was low, and the treasury officials were anxious, for they knew they would be expected to raise the money to finance the war. Yet only John dared speak up and oppose the emperor.*

But as for saying anything to the emperor to prevent the expedition, no one dared to do this except John the Cappadocian, the praetorian prefect, a man of the greatest daring, and the cleverest of all men of his time. For this John, while all others were bewailing in silence the fortune which was upon them, came before the emperor and spoke as follows, "O Emperor, the good faith which thou dost shew in dealing with thy subjects enables us to speak frankly regarding anything which will be of advantage to thy government, even though what is said and done may not be agreeable to thee. For thus does thy wisdom temper thy authority with justice. . . . Led by these considerations, O Emperor, I have come to offer this advice, knowing that, though I shall give perhaps offence at the moment, if it so chance, yet in the future the loyalty which I bear you will be made clear, and that for this I shall be able to shew thee as a witness.

Source: Trans. H. B. Dewing. *Procopius*, Volume II: *History of the Wars*, Loeb Classical Library Vol. 81 (Cambridge, MA: Harvard University Press, 1916). Reprinted by permission of the publishers and the trustees of the Loeb Classical Library. The Loeb Classical Library® is a registered trademark of the President and Fellows of Harvard College.

DOCUMENT 16
Prokopios, *Secret History* (17.35)

> *Justinian listened to John's advice and would have canceled the expedition, except that a bishop arrived from one of the eastern provinces and told Justinian that God had instructed him in a dream to go and rebuke the emperor for fearing to undertake the task of protecting the orthodox Christians in Africa from their oppressors, because the Vandals were Arians and persecuted the Catholics.*
>
> *In his* Secret History, *Prokopios refers to his account of how Empress Theodora plotted John's downfall with the help of Belisarios' wife, Antonina, and argues that her motive was spite, for John did not hesitate to oppose her.*

John's Fall is Due to Theodora's Hatred

These things [her maltreatment of John] Theodora inflicted on the fellow because she was furious at him, not because of his offences against the State—what proves that is the fact that when men at a later time committed worse crimes against her subjects, she gave none of them similar punishment—but because he opposed her boldly in a number of matters, and particularly because he would vilify her to the Emperor, so that she came close to finding herself at war with her husband.

Prokopios goes on to describe how Theodora pursued John even in exile and attempted to destroy him. All the while, Justinian pretended not to know what was going on.

Source: Trans. James Allan Evans.

THE DESTRUCTION OF THE OSTROGOTHIC KINGDOM

The decisive battle between the Byzantines, led by Narses, and the Ostrogoths, led by Totila, took place in 552 at Busta Gallorum. The exact site is unknown, but Prokopios claims that it took its name from an ancient battle fought there between the Romans and the Gauls, though his knowledge of the history of the Roman Republic fails him at this point and he imagines that it was where the Roman Camillus defeated the Gauls after their sack of Rome in 387 B.C.E. He must be wrong, but Busta Gallorum may have been the site of the battle of Sentinum (modern Sassoferrato) in 280 B.C.E., which was equally famous. The battle of Busta Gallorum ended with the defeat of the Ostrogoths and the death of Totila. Although there was one more battle in southern Italy before the Goths were destroyed, Busta Gallorum was the battle that decided their fate.

The passage quoted below comes from Prokopios' description of the preliminaries to the battle. Totila wanted to delay the action until a detachment of 2,000 Goths could arrive and join him. So as the two armies stood in their battle lines, in the space between them he put on a magnificent display of his physical prowess. It was, in fact, a kind of war dance.

DOCUMENT 17
The Battle of Busta Gallorum

But Totila now went alone into the space between the armies, not in order to engage in single combat, but in order to prevent his opponents from using the present opportunity. For he had learned that the two thousand Goths who had been missing were now drawing near, and so he sought to put off the engagement until their arrival by doing as follows. First of all, he was not at all reluctant to make an exhibition to the enemy of what manner of man he was. For the armor in which he was clad was abundantly plated with gold and the ample adornments which hung from his cheek-plates as well as from his helmet and spear were not only of purple, but in other respects befitting a king, marvelous in their abundance. And he himself, sitting upon a very large horse, began to perform the dance under arms skillfully between the armies. For he wheeled his horse round in a circle and then turned him again to the other side and so he made him run round and round. And as he rode, he hurled his javelin into the air and caught it again as it quivered above him, then passed it rapidly from hand to hand, shifting it with consummate skill, and he gloried in his practice in such matters, falling back on his shoulders, spreading his legs and leaning from side to side, like one who has been instructed with precision in the art of dancing from childhood. By these tactics he wore away the whole early part of the day. And wishing to prolong indefinitely the postponement of the battle, he sent to the Roman army saying that he wished to confer with them. But Narses declared that he must be trifling.

In the following passage, Prokopios remarks on the inflexibility of the Gothic tactics. The Gothic cavalry and infantry relied on their long spears, whereas the Byzantines used bows, spears, and swords.

Now orders had been given to the entire Gothic army that they should use neither bow nor any other weapon in this battle except their spears. Consequently it came about that Totila was outgeneralled by his own folly; for in entering this battle he was led, by what I do not know, to throw against his opponents his own army with inadequate equipment, and outflanked and in no respect a match for their antagonists. For the

Romans,[1] on the one hand, made use of each weapon in the fighting according to the particular need of the moment, shooting with bows or thrusting with spears or wielding swords, or using any other weapon which was convenient and suitable at a given point, some of them mounted on horses and others entering the combat on foot, their numbers proportioned to the needs of the situation, so that at one point they could carry out an encircling movement around the enemy, and at another receive a charge and with their shields stop short an attack. The cavalry of the Goths, on the other hand, leaving their infantry behind, and trusting only to their spears, made their charge with reckless impetuosity; and once in the midst of the fray they suffered for their own folly. For in making their charge against their enemy's center they had, before they realized it, placed themselves in between the eight thousand infantry, and being raked by their bow-shots from either side they gave up immediately, since the bow-men kept gradually turning both the wings of their front to form the crescent which I mentioned above. Consequently the Goths lost many men as well as many horses in this phase of the encounter before they had ever engaged with their opponents, and only after they had experienced very heavy losses did they with difficulty finally reach the ranks of the enemy.

Totila fled from the battle accompanied by no more than five men, and he was mortally wounded by one of his pursuers. The Byzantines did not know of his death until a Gothic woman pointed out his grave, whereupon they exhumed the body and satisfied themselves that it was Totila.

Source: Trans. H. B. Dewing. *Procopius*, Volume V: *History of the Wars*, Loeb Classical Library Vol. 217 (Cambridge, MA: Harvard University Press, 1925). Reprinted by permission of the publishers and the trustees of the Loeb Classical Library. The Loeb Classical Library® is a registered trademark of the President and Fellows of Harvard College.

---

1. Byzantines. The Greeks called themselves *Romaioi* until the nineteenth century.

POSSIBLE EVIDENCE FOR THEODORA'S IMPLICATION IN AMALASUNTHA'S MURDER

DOCUMENT 18
Theodahad to Theodora

Flavius Magnus Aurelius Cassiodorus Senator was the son of a praetorian prefect of Italy under Theodoric the Ostrogoth, and himself served as quaestor from about 507 to 511, master of offices from 523 to 527, and as praetorian prefect from 533 to approximately 540, under the Gothic king Theodahad and his successor Witigis. Thus he served the Ostrogothic rulers during the years of Justinian's war of reconquest that demolished the Ostrogothic kingdom. His Variae (Miscellanies) in twelve books contains official correspondence of the Gothic regime, and includes a letter from Theodahad to Empress Theodora written in 535, perhaps in May, while Peter the Patrician was in Italy carrying on negotiations prior to Belisarios' invasion. This letter makes an ambiguous reference to a person "about whom a delicate hint has reached me": Theodahad trusts that the action he has ordered against this person will please Theodora. Is this a reference to the murder of Amalasuntha? If so, it may corroborate Prokopios' claim in his Secret History *that Theodora brought about Amalasuntha's murder. It is, however, quite possible that Theodahad refers to something else. A new pope named Agapetus had been elected, and Theodora must have been anxious to make contact with him and discover how flexible he was prepared to be on the burning theological question of the day: how to heal the split between the Chalcedonians and the anti-Chalcedonians. At the same time as Theodahad sent this letter to Theodora, his queen, Gudeliva, sent her a fulsome letter, which shows how much influence Theodora had, and how anxious Theodahad was to please her.*

I have received your piety's letters with the gratitude always due to things we long for, and have gained, with the most reverent joy, your verbal message, more exalted than any gift. I promise myself everything from so serene a soul, since, in such kindly discourse, I have received whatever I could hope for. For you exhort me to bring first to your attention anything I decide to ask from the triumphal prince, your husband. Who can now doubt that what so great a power deigns to advocate will attain its object? Previously, indeed, I relied on the justice of my cause, but now I have more happiness in your promise. For my pleas cannot be adjourned when they involve her who has a right to an audience. Now fulfill your promises, that you may cause the man to whom you gave a sure hope to hold his own.

It also adds to my joy that your serenity had dispatched such a man as so much glory should send, and your service should retain. For inevitably, she in whom it is constantly observed chooses a man of good character, since a mind formed by worthy precepts is clearly purified.

Hence it is that, advised by your reverence, I ordained that both the most blessed Pope [probably Agapetus] and the most noble Senate should reply without any delay to what you saw fit to request from them: thus, your glory will lose no reverence because a spirit of delay opposed it; but rather, speed of action will increase your favor that we pray for. For in the case of that person, too, about whom a delicate hint has reached me, know that I have ordered what I trust will agree with your intention. For it is my desire that you should command no less in my realm than in your empire, through the medium of your influence. Now, I inform you that I made the venerable Pope issue the afore-mentioned reply before your envoy, the bearer of this letter, could leave the city of Rome, lest anything might happen to oppose your intention.

Source: Trans. S.J.B. Barnish. *The "Variae" of Magnus Aurelius Cassiodorus Senator*, Translated Texts for Historians XII (Liverpool: Liverpool University Press, 1992). Reprinted by permission of Liverpool University Press.

THE *NIKA* REVOLT

DOCUMENT 19
John Malalas Describes the Riot

The Nika revolt broke out in January 532, and it very nearly unseated Justinian and Theodora. The immediate cause was Justinian's crackdown on gangs of hooligans: fans of the Blue and Green factions in the Hippodrome who carried their partisanship out to the streets. Justinian himself was well known to be a fan of the Blues, and so was his wife, Theodora,

for when she was a little girl, the Blues has given her stepfather employ-
ment as their bearkeeper, thereby saving Theodora's family from destitu-
tion. Before Justinian became emperor, Blues in trouble with the law could
count on him for support. But once Justinian became emperor, he was de-
termined to maintain law and order, and the city prefect of Constantino-
ple, who was in charge of policing the streets, took a hard line against
malefactors. Once the riot got under way, however, and seemed to have
a chance of success, a number of the senators gave it support. The old
ruling class in Constantinople regarded Justinian and Theodora as up-
starts, and they did not like their reforms. The suppression of the revolt
meant that the opposition to Justinian was silenced.

   The chief source for the Nika revolt is Prokopios of Caesarea, but there
are other sources as well, among them the chronicler John Malalas.
Malalas is an unknown: he was evidently born about 490 and was edu-
cated in Antioch. Sometime after 535 he moved to Constantinople, per-
haps in the wake of the Persian sack of Antioch in 540. He was probably
a bureaucrat (the name "Malalas" comes from the Syriac malal, *mean-*
ing "lawyer"; the equivalent in Latin was rhetor, *and in Greek,*
scholastikos). He seems to have had good sources for information in Con-
stantinople and was a loyal supporter of Justinian, to judge from his
Chronicle.

In that year of the 10th indiction, a pretext for rioting occurred in
Byzantion caused by some avenging demons when Eudaimon was city prefect and was holding in custody trouble-makers from both factions. When
he had examined various persons, he found seven of them guilty of murder and sentenced four of them to be beheaded and three to be impaled.
After they had been paraded through the whole city and had crossed to
the other side,[1] some of them were hanged. But two of them, one a Blue
and the other a Green, fell as the scaffold broke. The people who were
standing around saw what happened and acclaimed the emperor. When
the monks near St. Konon's had heard this and came out, they found two
of those who had been hanged lying on the ground, still alive. Taking
them down by the sea and putting them in a boat, they sent them to St.
Lawrence's [church] to a place of sanctuary. On learning of this, the city
prefect sent a military force and kept guard over them where they were.

---

1. That is, had crossed the Golden Horn to Sycai (now Galata).

Three days later the chariot-races known as those of the Ides were held. They are known as the Ides because the Roman emperor entertains at banquets in his palace all those who are being promoted in the service, bestowing on each the office of *primicerius*. While the chariot-racing was being held on the 13th January, both factions began to call upon the emperor to show mercy. They continued chanting until the 22nd race, and they were not granted an answer. Then the devil prompted evil counsels in them, and they chanted to one another, "Long live the merciful Blues and Greens!" After the races, the crowds went off united, having given themselves a watch-word with the word "Conquer" (*Nika*), so as not to be infiltrated by soldiers or *excubitores*. And so they charged on. Towards evening they went to the city prefect's *praetorium*, demanding an answer about the fugitives at St. Lawrence. Not receiving an answer, they set fire to the *praetorium*. This fire destroyed the *praetorium*, the *Khalké* Gate of the palace as far as the Scholae,[2] the Great Church and the public colonnade.[3] The people continued to charge on their disorderly way. At daybreak, the emperor ordered the races to be held and after the customary flag had been hoisted the faction members now set fire to the tiers of the Hippodrome. Part of the public colonnade as far as the Zeuxippon [Baths of Zeuxippos] was burnt. Moundos, Constantinolus and Basilides went out with a force at the emperor's command, intending to silence the rioting mob which by then was chanting against John, nicknamed the Cappadocian, the *quaestor* Tribonian and the city prefect Eudaimon. The senators who had not been sent out heard this chanting from them and reported it to the emperor. Immediately John, Tribonian and Eudaimon were dismissed. Belisarios went out with a troop of Goths; there was fighting and many of the faction members were cut down. The mob was incensed and started fires in other places and began killing indiscriminately.

On the 18th of the same month, the emperor went up to the Hippodrome, carrying the Holy Gospels. On learning of this, the crowds came

---

2. The Scholae were the barracks for the Scholarians, palace guards who were more ornamental than useful. The Excubitors were a more effective corps of guardsmen who kept law and order in the capital.

3. The "Great Church" was Hagia Sophia, the predecessor of Justinian's Hagia Sophia, which still stands in Istanbul. The "colonnade" was the porticoes that lined either side of the main street of Constantinople, the *Mese* (the modern name is Divanyolu).

in, too, and he made a proclamation on oath. Many of the people chanted for him as emperor, but others rioted, chanting for Hypatios. The people took Hypatios and led him off to the place known as the Forum of Constantine. Setting him on high on the steps and bringing regalia and a golden collar out of the palace, they put these on his head. Then they took him and led him off to the Hippodrome, intending to take him up into the imperial *kathisma*, for the crowd was eager to throw imperial robes for him out from the palace. Hypatios had learnt that the emperor had left, and, seating himself in the *kathisma*, he boldly came out for rebellion.

When Moundos, Constantinolus, Belisarios, other senators and an armed force had come up through the *kathisma* from behind, Narses, the *cubicularius* and *spatharius* slipped out without being noticed and beguiled some of the Blue faction by distributing money. Some of the mob started a disturbance and chanted for Justinian as emperor for the city. The mob as divided and set upon one another. The *magistri militum* entered the Hippodrome with a force and began to cut down the crowds from both entrances, some with arrows, others with swords. Belisarios went off unnoticed, seized hold of Hypatios and Pompeios and brought them before the emperor Justinian. They fell down at the emperor's feet, saying in their defence, "Lord, it was a great effort for us to assemble the enemies of your majesty in the Hippodrome." The emperor answered them, "You have done well. But if they were obeying your authority, why did you not do this before the whole city was burnt?" At an order from the emperor, the *spatharii* arrested Hypatios and Pompeios and put them in prison. Those slaughtered in the Hippodrome amounted to 35,000, more or less. On the next day, Hypatios and Pompeios were put to death and their bodies were thrown into the sea. The emperor announced his victory and the rebels' destruction to all the city, and he undertook to rebuild the places that had been burnt. He built a granary and reservoirs near the palace so as to have supplies in times of crisis.

Source: Trans. Elizabeth Jeffreys, Michael Jeffreys, and Roger Scott, with Brian Croke, Jenny Ferber, Simon Franklin, Alan James, Douglas Kelly, Ann Moffatt, and Ann Nixon. *The Chronicle of John Malalas.* Byzantina Australiensia IV (Melbourne: Australian Association for Byzantine Studies, 1986; repr. 2004). Reprinted by kind permission of the Australian Association for Byzantine Studies.

THE CONVERSION OF THE NOBADAI

DOCUMENT 20
John of Ephesus on How Theodora Won the Nobadai for the Anti-Chalcedonian Faith

In Egypt, south of the First Cataract, lived the Nobadai, whose capital was at Dongola. The Nobadai, were pagans until they were converted to Christianity about 540 or shortly thereafter. By this time, the leader of the anti-Chalcedonians was Theodosios, who had been chosen as patriarch of Alexandria in 535. But Theodosios faced an insurrection by the supporters of a rival, Gaianos, who accepted an extreme form of Monophysitism called Aphthartodocetism, which taught that Christ's body was incorruptible. Though Empress Theodora sent Narses with 6,000 troops to support Theodosios, he left Egypt for Constantinople after hanging on to the patriarchal throne for sixteen months. Once he was in Constantinople, Justinian tried to persuade Theodosios to support the Chalcedonian Creed, and when he failed, he appointed a tough supporter of the Chalcedonians to Alexandria, to take over the patriarchal see. Thus in Egypt, the patriarch was a Chalcedonian imperial appointee—"Melchite," he was called, after the Syriac word for "imperial"—and the Monophysites were divided into two factions. Theodosios in exile, however, gained the respect and loyalty of the moderate Monophysites and was recognized unofficially as their leader.

The passage below, which describes how Theodosios' missionary, Julianus, reached the king of the Nobadai, Silko, is taken from the Ecclesiastical History of John of Ephesus, who was a Monophysite. John's sympathies were with Theodora and her determination to win over the Nobadai for Monophysitism. This passage is a remarkable illustration of how independently Theodora could act, and how much she was respected and feared within the power structure of the empire. With Theodora's help, the Monophysite emissary of Theodosios reached Silko before Justinian's Chalcedonian missionary, who arrived to find that Silko was primed and ready. Silko took the presents that Justinian sent him, but he announced that if the Nobadai accepted Christianity, it would be the faith of Theodosios, the rightful patriarch of Alexandria, and not the wicked doctrine of Justinian.

Among the clergy in attendance on the Patriarch Theodosios was a proselyte named Julian, an old man of great worth, who conceived an earnest spiritual desire to christianise the wandering people who dwell on the eastern borders of the Thebais beyond Egypt, and who are not only not subject to the authority of the Roman Empire, but even receive a subsidy on condition that they do not enter nor pillage Egypt. The blessed Julianus, therefore, being full of anxiety for this people, went and spoke about them to the late queen Theodora, in the hope of awakening in her a similar desire for their conversion; and as the queen was fervent in zeal for God, she received the proposal with joy, and promised to do everything in her power for the conversion of these tribes from the errors of idolatry. In her joy, therefore, she informed the victorious King Justinian of the purposed undertaking, and promised and anxiously desired to send the blessed Julian thither. But when the king [emperor] heard that the person she intended to send was opposed to the council of Chalcedon, he was not pleased, and determined to write to the bishops of his own side in the Thebais, with orders for them to proceed thither and instruct the Nobadai, and plant among them the name of the synod. And as he entered upon the matter with great zeal, he sent thither, without a moment's delay, ambassadors with gold and baptismal robes, and gifts of honor for the king of that people, and letters for the duke of the Thebais,[1] enjoining him to take every care of the embassy, and escort them to the territories of the Nobadai. When, however, the queen [Theodora] learnt these things, she quickly, with much cunning, wrote letters to the duke of the Thebais, and sent a mandatory of her court to carry them to him; and which were as follows: "Inasmuch as both his majesty and myself have purposed to send an embassy to the people of the Nobadai, and I am now dispatching a blessed man named Julian; and further my will is that my ambassador should arrive at the aforesaid people before his majesty's; be warned, that if you permit his ambassador to arrive there before mine, and do not hinder him by various pretexts until mine shall have reached you and shall have passed through your province and arrived at his destination, your life shall answer for it; for I shall immediately send and take off your head."

Soon after the receipt of this letter the king's ambassador also came, and the duke said to him, "You must wait a little while we look out and

---

1. The duke (*dux*) of the Thebais was the commander of the military force stationed in upper Egypt.

procure beasts of burden and men who know the deserts, and then you will be able to proceed." And thus he delayed him until the arrival of the merciful queen's embassy, who found horses and guides waiting, and the same day, without loss of time, under a show of doing it by violence, they laid hands upon him, and were the first to proceed. As for the duke, he made his excuses to the king's ambassador, saying, "Lo! When I had made my preparations and was desirous of sending you onward, ambassadors from the queen arrived and fell upon me with violence, and took away the beasts of burden I had got ready, and have passed onward; and I am too well acquainted with the fear in which the queen is held to venture to oppose them. But abide still with me until I can make fresh preparations for you, and then you also shall go in peace." And when [Justinian's envoy] heard these things, he rent his garments, and threatened him terribly and reviled him; and after some time he also was able to proceed, and followed the other's track without being aware of the fraud which had been practised upon him.

The blessed Julian meanwhile and the ambassadors who accompanied him had arrived at the confines of the Nobadai, whence they sent to the king and his princes informing him of their coming; upon which an armed escort set out, who received them joyfully, and brought them into their land unto the king. And he, too, received them with pleasure, and her majesty's letter was presented and read to him, and the purport of it explained. They accepted also the magnificent honors sent them, and the numerous baptismal robes, and everything else richly provided for their use. And immediately with joy they yielded themselves up and utterly abjured the errors of their forefathers, and confessed the God of the Christians, saying, "He is the one true God, and there is no other beside Him." And after Julian had given them much instruction, and taught them, he further told them about the Council of Chalcedon, saying that "inasmuch as certain disputes had sprung up among the Christians touching the faith, and the blessed Theodosios being required to receive the council and having refused was ejected by the king [emperor] from his throne, whereas the queen received him and rejoiced in him because he stood firm in the right faith and left his throne for its sake, on this account her majesty has sent us to you, that you also may walk in the ways of Pope Theodosios, and stand in his faith and imitate his constancy. And moreover the king has sent unto you ambassadors who are already on their way, in our footsteps."

They then instructed them how they should receive them, and what answer they should give, and when everything was fully settled, the king's ambassador arrived. And when he had obtained an audience, he also gave the king the letters, and began to inform and tell him, according to his instructions, as follows: "The king of the Romans has sent us to you, that in case of your becoming Christians, you may cleave to the church and those who govern it, and not be led astray after those who have been expelled from it." And when the king of the Nobadai and his princes heard these things, they answered them, saying, "The honorable present which the king of the Romans has sent us we accept, and will also ourselves send him a present. But his faith we will not accept."

Source: Trans. R. Payne Smith. *The Third Part of the Ecclesiastical History of John, Bishop of Ephesus*, 4.6–4.7 (Oxford: Oxford University Press, 1860).

GLOSSARY

Acolyte: A member of the inferior order of clergy who assisted at the altar, lighting the candles and making preparations for Holy Communion.

Adsessor (assessor): A legal adviser on the staff of an official such as a master of soldiers.

Akakian Schism: Dispute (484–518) that separated Rome from the churches of the east, because of Emperor Zeno's compromise profession of faith known as the *Henotikon*, which Akakios, the patriarch of Constantinople, had devised and Rome rejected.

Alexandrian theology/Christology: Alexandrian Christology emphasized the divine nature of Christ and the unity of His person. Its most important exponent was Cyril, patriarch of Alexandria (412–444).

Ambo: Pulpit in a basilica; there were two of them, one on each side of the church, one for the reading of the Epistle and the other for the reading of the Gospel.

Anathema: A declaration of expulsion from the church, somewhat stronger than excommunication.

Aphthartodocetism: A doctrine propagated by Julian of Halicarnassus, an anti-Chalcedonian opponent of Severos who, like Severos, fled to Egypt to escape the persecution initiated by Justin I. Julian taught that Christ's body was not susceptible to corruption or to suffering, but that, in order to save humanity, Christ had voluntarily accepted suffering and death on the cross. This position was not completely incompatible with Chalcedonian doctrine, and at the end of his life, Justinian adopted it and attempted to impose it on the church by imperial edict. He died before a new controversy erupted, and his successor, Justin II, immediately revoked his edict.

Apokrisarios: Representative of the bishop of a particular church; also known as a "nuncio."

Archimandrite: Abbot or head of a monastery.

Arian: Follower of Arius, a deacon of the church at Alexandria, who taught that Christ the Son was created by God the Father out of nothing, and thus Christ was less than fully God.

Augusta: Title of the wife of a reigning emperor.

Augustus: Title of a reigning emperor.

Basileus: Greek term meaning "emperor."

Basilica: A type of building developed in Rome, or perhaps in the Hellenistic world, for secular uses (for example, a law court) that was adapted for Christian usage in the early fourth century. The characteristic basilica had a central nave and two or more side aisles, with an apse at the rear for the bishop's throne and, at the front, a long, narrow vestibule called a narthex stretching across the full width of the building. In front of the narthex there might be a colonnaded courtyard called an atrium. By the fifth century, the apse was sited at the east, and the entrance at the west, end of the basilica.

Boulé: Greek term for the "senate" or town council of a municipality. *See also* **Curia.**

Bucellarii: Originally official bodyguards and irregular retainers used by public officials or wealthy private citizens. In Justinian's day they were crack mobile units of the regular army, but still were often maintained by a levy on the estates of wealthy persons (e.g., Belisarios, who kept 7,000 *bucellarii*), and thus the distinction between a private guard and a unit of the regular army became blurred.

Caesaropapism: The doctrine that the emperor had the right to make rulings on matters of concern to the church, including theological questions.

Candidatus: An imperial guardsman who wore a white (*candidus*) uniform.

Cenobitic: A type of monastery where monks shared a life together, governed by a rule that set forth a code of conduct and the order of each day.

Chalcedonians: Adherents of the Chalcedonian Creed which was formulated by the Council of Chalcedon in 451. The Creed defined Christ as one person in two natures, one divine and consubstantial with the Father, and the other human and consubstantial with ourselves.

Clarissimi: "Celebrated persons": senators of the lowest rank who entered the senate by right of birth. During the fifth century their rank was downgraded, and, by Justinian's reign, they no longer had the right to the title of senator. *See also* **Illustres; Spectabilis.**

Clergy: A designation at first of the whole Christian community, but by the third century restricted to the ministers of worship within the Christian community. There were three major orders of clergy: first, bishops; second, priests; third, deacons. Below them were various minor orders.

Cognomen: Among the Romans, an added third name or epithet that may be used as a surname; for instance, in the case of Marcus Tullius Cicero, Cicero is a cognomen used as a surname. When a

Roman adopted a man as his son, the adoptee took the family name of his adoptive father in adjectival form as his cognomen; if he already had a third name, then as his agnomen or fourth name. Thus Justin's nephew, Flavius Petrus Sabbatius, took Justinianus as his agnomen when Justin adopted him.

Colonnade: A row of columns.

Comes (plural, *comites*): The title of a holder of a civil or imperial office. Usually translated as "count," though the literal meaning is "companion."

Comes domesticorum: Commander of a unit of troops attached to the imperial household.

Comes excubitorum: Commander of the imperial bodyguard known as the *excubitores*.

Comes foederatorum: Commander of the federate troops who, in the sixth century, were no longer exclusively barbarians. *See also* **Federate troops.**

Comitatenses: Mobile field army, as opposed to the frontier troops (*see also* **Limitanei**). In the eastern empire there were five armies of *comitatenses*, each under a master of the soldiers. Two armies were attached to the court, and Oriens (the east), Thrace, and Illyricum were assigned one army each. *See also* **Master of the soldiers.**

Consistorium: The consistory, the imperial advisory council probably instituted by Emperor Constantine I, replaced the *consilium principis* (emperor's council) that advised the emperors in the earlier period. The consistory took its name from the hall where it met, not because participants had to stand during a session (*silentium*), as was once believed. For practical purposes Justinian merged the senate in Constantinople with the consistory. *See also* **Silentium.**

Constitutio: A "constitution," a decision of the emperor that had the force of law.

Consulship: An office that survived from the Roman Republic into late antiquity. Two consuls continued to be appointed each year, one in the western empire at Rome, and the other in Constantinople. The consulship conferred great prestige but no political power. Justinian abolished the office in 541, and after that date no further consuls were appointed until after his death.

Coptic: The language of the native Egyptians in late antiquity. It was derived from ancient Egyptian, although it contained large numbers of Greek words.

Cruciform: In the shape of a cross.

Cubicularius: Chamberlain, normally a eunuch, who was an attendant of the emperor's bedchamber.

Curia: A senate or town council of a municipality. *See also* **Boulé.**

Curial class: Citizens of a municipality who possessed enough property to allow them to sit on the *curiae* (town councils), which were responsible for the collection of taxes.

Deacon: The lowest of the three major orders of the clergy. Deacons assisted at baptism and served at the celebration and distribution of the Eucharist (though they could not perform the rite), supervised charities and church properties, and acted as bishops' secretaries.

Deaconess: A female deacon; her chief function was to assist at the baptism of women.

Decurions: Members of the town council of a municipality.

Demes: The word *demos* in classical Greek referred to the people as a whole (as in the word *demokratia*, meaning "rule by the people"). The meaning of the word in the Justinianic period has been a matter of controversy, but it seems clear that it continued to mean the people as a whole, whether used in the singular or the plural. Thus "demes" (*demoi*) in Justinian's day can often be translated as "the masses." The term was applied to the fans of the Blue and Green factions in the Hippodrome.

Diadem: A ribbon worn around the head and tied at the back. Emperor Constantine I wore a diadem encrusted with pearls as a symbol of the imperial office, and his successors followed his example.

Diocese: In the reorganization of the empire by Diocletian (r. 284–305), the provinces were made into smaller units and grouped into twelve large administrative units, called dioceses, that were headed by vicars representing the praetorian prefects. Dioceses were abolished by Justinian. *See also* **Vicar**.

Diphysite: The opposite of Monophysite. This was a term used by Severos of Antioch to describe the Chalcedonians, and was thus in usage among the anti-Chalcedonians before the term "Monophysite" was coined. It derives from the Greek *diphyes* (bipartite, or of a double nature).

Diptychs: Lists of persons for whom prayers were offered, which were read aloud during the liturgy. The removal of a person's name from the diptychs indicated that he was no longer considered orthodox.

Dobruja: In modern Romania, the region at the mouth of the Danube River where the Danube twists north and creates a finger of land between the river and the Black Sea.

Dromos: System of imperial post and transportation. The regular *dromos* for transporting goods was served by oxen harnessed to carts; the "swift" *dromos*, for imperial officials and their baggage, was served by horses and mules. There were posting stations along the roads where draft animals could be changed and travelers could rest. Only the praetorian prefect could issue a permit allowing a person to use the *dromos*.

Duke: In Latin, *dux*. The commander of the military forces in a province.

Ecumenical: Universal, taking in the whole inhabited world.

Edict: An order or command of an emperor that had the force of law.

Eparch: Greek term for the urban prefect. *See also* **Prefect of the city**.

Eremite: A hermit or religious recluse, from the Greek *eremos*, meaning "lonely" or "solitary."

Eremitic: Like a hermit. Eremitic monks lived alone in cells or caves, though their lonely dwellings were connected by paths known as *lauras*. The eremitic monks living in one area might have an archimandrite, and might gather every Sunday for religious services. *See also* **Archimandrite**.

Eucharist: The sacrament of the church also known as Holy Communion.

Euergetism: Generosity to the public manifested by pious donations of churches or public buildings, for which the donor receives honor and recognition in return.

Excommunication: Expulsion from communion with the church. Excommunicated persons are denied the sacraments.

Excubitors: A corps of guardsmen recruited by Emperor Leo I (r. 457–474) to counterbalance the power of the German federate troops in Constantinople. *See also* **Federate troops**.

Factions: Companies responsible for staging chariot races in the Hippodrome and for productions in the theaters and amphitheaters. The colors of the factions (Red, White, Green, and Blue) were inherited from the Circus Maximus in Rome. Contemporaries blamed the rivalry between Blue and Green fans for the increased urban violence from the late fifth to the early seventh century, but there may have been economic and social roots for it as well. The theory that the Green fans were Monophysites, and the Blue fans, Chalcedonians, has been abandoned.

Federate troops: Barbarian troops fighting under their own leaders who made a treaty (*foedus*) with the emperor. Theodosius I, desperate for troops after the disaster of Adrianople (378), began the practice of recruiting barbarians under treaty, as separate units that were not integrated into the Roman army. By the time of Justinian, however, federate units were made up of citizen troops as well as noncitizens.

Hellene: In the classical period, the word for "Greek." In the sixth century, it meant "pagan."

Hellenistic: Term applied to the period after Alexander the Great's death (323 B.C.E.) when Greek culture spread into Egypt and the Middle East, and assimilated many non-Greeks.

Henotikon: Statement of doctrinal unity (*henosis*). It was devised by Akakios, the patriarch of Constantinople, and issued by Emperor Zeno in 482. Because it failed to endorse the Chalcedonian Creed, it was condemned by Rome and gave rise to the Akakian Schism between Rome and Constantinople.

Heresy: From the Greek meaning "choice" (that is, something one chooses for himself or herself). A doctrine devised by a theologian or religious teacher that is condemned by the church.

Heterodoxy: A doctrine that is not approved by a Christian Church council.

Hippodrome: Track for chariot races with bleachers for spectators. *See also* **Spina**.

Homoiousios: Meaning "of similar substance." It was used by the moderate followers of Arius, sometimes known as semi-Arians, who rejected the dogma of the Nicene Creed that God the Son was of the same substance as God the Father.

Homoousios: Meaning "of the same substance." Used in the Nicene Creed to define the relationship between God the Father and God the Son, it excluded the definition of Arius and his followers, who subordinated God the Son to God the Father.

Hospice: A charitable institution, often well endowed, intended for the care of the sick.

Huns: An Asian people from the Russian steppes, possibly Turkic, who were known in Chinese sources as the Hsiung-nu. They invaded Roman Gaul in 451, led by Attila, and were defeated at the Catalaunian Fields. In 452, Attila invaded Italy but withdrew after negotiations with Pope Leo I, and the next year died in his camp of a hemorrhage. After his death, his horde broke up, but the Byzantines continued to apply the label "Hun" to various peoples, such as the Kutrigurs and Utigurs, who may have been related to Attila's Huns, as well as to others who were not, such as the Bulgarians and the Hungarians.

Hypostasis: A state of being. The term was used in theological debates about the essence of God.

Illustres: "Illustrious persons," senators of the highest rank. By Justinian's reign only *illustres* had the right to speak in the senate, and the title "senator" was reserved for them. The other two senatorial ranks that existed earlier, the *clarissimi* and the *spectabiles*, had been downgraded to the point that they were no longer senators. Entry into the class of *illustres* was by virtue of holding high office or by the pleasure of the emperor. The rank was not hereditary; sons of *illustres* were only *clarissimi*. *See also* **Clarissimi; Spectabilis.**

Julianists: Aphthartodocetists. *See* **Aphthartodocetism.**

Jurisprudence: The science or philosophy of law; also a system of law.

Kathisma: The emperor's loge or viewing stand on the eastern side of the Constantinople Hippodrome. It was connected by a private passage to the Great Palace.

Khalké Gate: Translated as "the Brazen House." This monumental entrance to the imperial palace compound took its name either from its bronze roof or from its great bronze doors. It was burned during the *Nika* riot and rebuilt splendidly by Justinian.

Lazica: Country of the Lazi, on the isthmus between the Black and the Caspian seas. In the classical period it was known as Colchis.

Legate: A deputy or representative.

Limes: The frontier.

Limitanei: Soldiers who defended the frontiers (*limites*) as opposed to the mobile army (*comitatenses*). They were peasant soldiers and enrollment was hereditary, from father to son. *See also* **Comitatenses**.

Magistrianus: A member of the staff of the *magister officiorum*.

Manumission: Granting freedom to a slave.

Master of offices (*magister officiorum*): The head of the imperial chanceries and the most powerful man at court and in the administration. He selected the bureaucrats who ran the empire and was in charge of foreign affairs. He was also master of ceremonies at court, and commanded the imperial bodyguard known as the Scholarians. He maintained a corps of spies to keep himself informed and to protect the emperor. *See also* **Scholarians**.

Master of the soldiers (*magister utriusque militiae*): A commander of a force of *comitatenses*. He was called a "master of both services" because, following a reform of Emperor Theodosius I, the cavalry and infantry operated together under a single commander. Two masters, titled "masters of the soldiers in the presence," were stationed in Constantinople. The "master of the soldiers in the east," in charge of the defenses of the eastern provinces, was stationed in Antioch; the master of the soldiers in Illyricum was stationed in Thessaloniki; and the headquarters of the master of the soldiers in Thrace was Constantinople. At the start of his reign, Justinian created a master of soldiers in Armenia, and after the conquest of North Africa, a master of soldiers in Africa, which was, however, soon combined with the office of praetorian prefect of Africa. *See also* **Comitatenses**.

Melchite: The word derives from the Syriac *málkâyâ* (imperial), and refers to members of the Chalcedonian Church in Syria and Egypt, where the majority of the populace was Monophysite. The Melchite clergy were supported by imperial troops and ministered to Greek-speaking congregations in the cities. The countryside was generally Monophysite.

Mesé: The main street of Constantinople, now the Divanyolu in Istanbul.

Metropolis: The capital city of a province.

Metropolitan bishop: The bishop of a metropolis, with jurisdiction over the other bishops of the province.

Miaphysites: The "one-nature believers." The Miaphysites held to the doctrine enunciated by Cyril, the great patriarch of Alexandria in the early fifth century, that even though Christ was the "Word" (*Logos*) made flesh, and thus possessed a human nature, after the incarnation, His human and divine natures fused to form one nature (*mia physis*). Thus the Miaphysites, who included among their number Severos and Empress Theodora, never denied Christ's human nature, as the real Monophysites did, but claimed that it united with his divine nature to form a single Godhead.

Monophysite: Anti-Chalcedonians who rejected the Creed enunciated at the Council of Chalcedon (451) that stated that Christ had two distinct natures, one human and the other divine. "Monophysite" is a pejorative term coined by the Melchites in the eighth century, and strictly-speaking, it is anachronistic in the Justinianic period, though it is commonly used as a label for the various sects, from Miaphysites to Julianists, who rejected the Chalcedonian Creed.

Narthex: The vestibule of a basilica.

Nave: The central aisle of a basilica, reserved for the clergy.

Nestorians: Followers of Nestorios, the patriarch of Constantinople who was deposed by the First Council of Ephesus (431). He insisted that Christ possessed both a human and a divine nature, while at the same time accepting the unity of Christ's person. He also rejected the epithet "Mother of God" (*Theotokos*) for the Virgin Mary.

Nika: The imperative of the Greek verb meaning "to win." It was the watchword for the *Nika* riots of 532.

Nomisma (plural, nomismata): The standard gold coin, known in Latin as the *solidus*, minted at seventy-two to the pound.

Numerus: A contingent of troops.

Orthodoxy: Correct belief; doctrine approved by the church councils.

Panegyric: A formal speech praising an important person.

Passion: In Christian theology, the suffering of Christ on the cross.

Patriarch: A term that was originally used for a prominent and respected bishop. The title acquired its precise canonical sense in a law of Justinian that applied particularly to the bishops of the five major sees or patriarchates: Rome, Constantinople, Alexamdria, Antioch, and Jerusalem, thereby recognizing in law what was already popular usage. *See also* **Patriarchate**.

Patriarchate: One of the five great sees of the Christian Church. Three claimed to be apostolic foundations: Antioch, founded by Saint Peter; Alexandria, founded by Saint Mark; and Rome, founded by Saint Peter. Byzantium had been a suffragan bishopric before the city was refounded by Emperor Constantine as Constantinople, but in 381, the Council of Constantinople recognized it as second only to Rome. The bishopric of Jerusalem was raised to a patriarchate by the Second Council of Ephesus in 449, and its status was confirmed by the Council of Chalcedon (451). *See also* **Patriarch; Suffragan bishop.**

Patrician: This title, which had once belonged to a select group of families in the early Roman Republic that formed the ruling class, was revived as an honorary title by Emperor Constantine I. The emperor conferred it on a citizen in a ceremony at which the empress was not present. Thus, when the title was conferred on Theodora, Empress Euphemia would have taken no part in the ceremony.

Praefectus vigilum: "Prefect of the watch" (chief of police), subject to the urban prefect. In 538, the office was abolished and was replaced by the "*praetor* of the demes." *See also* **Prefect of the city.**

Praepositus: A military officer—the word means "officer commanding (a given unit)."

Praetorian prefect: A regional civil official responsible for a praetorian prefecture. There were two of these when Justinian came to the throne: the prefecture of the east (Oriens) with headquarters in Constantinople, and the prefecture of Illyricum, with headquarters in Thessaloniki. The prefect's responsibilities included taxation, justice, public construction, trade, prices, higher education, and the public post. *See also* **Dromos**.

Prefect of the city: The city prefect, or urban prefect, who governed Constantinople and its territory up to 100 miles from the city. *See also* **Eparch.**

Quaestor: Chief legal minister.

Ravenna: The capital of the western Roman Empire after 402, when Emperor Honorius moved there from Milan because it occupied a secure position, surrounded by a marsh and with easy access by river channels to the Po River and to the Adriatic Sea. It became the capital of Ostrogothic Italy and, after its capture by Belisarios in 540, the capital of Byzantine Italy.

Responsum: A legal opinion given by an expert, or a ruling by the emperor himself, in reply to a question that was put to him.

Rex: Title borne by the early kings of Rome, the last of whom, Tarquin the Proud, was expelled in 510 B.C.E. In late antiquity, the Romans applied the title *rex* to barbarian kings such as the rulers of the Vandal kingdom and the Ostrogothic kingdom, reserving the term *basileus* for the emperor.

Rhetor: A lawyer.

Rhomaioi: "Romans"; the name the Byzantines applied to themselves.

Schism: A rupture or split. Schisms in the church occurred when sees disagreed about doctrine to the point that they no longer remained in communion.

Scholai: The barracks of the Scholarians in the monumental vestibule to the imperial palace known as the "Brazen House." *See also* **Scholarians**.

Scholarians: Imperial guard that dated back to Emperor Constantine. By the time of Justinian they had ceased to be a crack regiment and had become largely ornamental.

Scholastikos: A lawyer; the Greek translation of the Latin *rhetor*.

See: The authority or jurisdiction of a bishop.

Senate: Constantinople's senate was founded by Emperor Constantius II, the son of Constantine, after the model of the senate in Rome. In 357 it numbered barely 300 members, but thirty years later, its numbers had ballooned to 2,000. The prefect of the city presided over it, wearing the traditional garb of a Roman citizen, the toga, which by the time of Justinian was worn by no other official of the state. In theory the senate conferred power on the emperor, and in fact, when Emperor Anastasius died, it fell to the senate, along with other high officers of state and the patriarch, to choose the new emperor. *See also* **Boulé; Curia; Patriarch; Prefect of the city**.

Shah: Persian for "king." The title "shahanshah" borne by the Persian monarchs means "king of kings."

Silentarius: An usher for the *silentium*; an imperial administrative official.

Silentium: A session of the imperial advisory council known as the consistory. *See also* **Consistorium**.

Solidus: Standard gold coin first minted by Emperor Constantine at seventy-two coins to one pound of gold.

Spatharios: A bodyguard.

Spectabilis: "Notable person"; senatorial rank above that of *clarissimus* and below that of *illustris*. By the time of Justinian, the privileges enjoyed by the *spectabiles* had been largely whittled away. *See also* **Clarissimi; Illustres**.

Spina: A low wall down the center of a hippodrome race track, dividing the track into two, so that the chariots could gallop down one side, wheel round and gallop up the other side, thus completing one full lap. The chariots had to complete seven laps.

Sportulae: Fees or bribes paid to officials for services rendered.

Stoa: A covered colonnade. In the sixth century, the term might be applied to any building with columns.

Stylite saint: A pillar saint, who mortified the flesh by passing his life perched on top of a column. The first stylite saint was Saint Simeon the Elder (c. 389–459), who lived out his life on a column at Qal'at Sem'an near Antioch, and was visited by pilgrims from as far away as Spain and Britain. Simeon had many imitators among the Christians in the east; Saint Simeon the Stylite the Younger (521–592), who lived during Justinian's reign, followed Saint Simeon the Elder's example and was almost as famous.

Suffragan bishop: Assistant bishop; consecrated to assist a bishop in a portion of his diocese.

Synod: In late antiquity, a "synod" of the church was usually an assembly of the clergy of a patriarchate.

Syriac: The language of the non-Greek Christians of the Middle East, derived from Aramaic.

Thebais: The province of Upper Egypt, stretching from the First Cataract in the south about halfway north to the Nile mouth. The military forces in the Thebais were under the command of a duke.

Tribune: A common title for a military officer, used loosely for all commanding officers.

Tribuni vacantes: Tribunes temporarily without a unit, who served on the staff of the emperor or of a general and were assigned special duties. *See also* **Tribune**.

Trisagion: Literally, "thrice-holy hymn." The *Sanctus* sung at the beginning of eastern and some western Eucharists: "Holy God, holy and mighty, holy and immortal: Have mercy upon us!"

Triumph: In Republican Rome, a celebration of victory by a general who paraded his captives and loot through the streets of Rome, along the Sacred Way, across the Roman Forum, and up the Capitoline Hill, where he formally laid down his command (*imperium*). In the imperial period, triumphs were reserved for the emperor. In the fifth through seventh centuries, the triumph moved to the Hippodrome, where successful generals and vanquished enemies paraded and honored the emperor seated in the imperial loge.

Vicar: Translation of the Latin *vicarius*, "representative."

ANNOTATED BIBLIOGRAPHY

Reference

Late Antiquity: A Guide to the Postclassical World, ed. by G. W. Bowersock, Peter Brown, and Oleg Grabar. Cambridge, MA, and London: Belknap Press of Harvard University Press, 1999. A series of essays including "Barbarians and Ethnicity," "War and Violence," "Islam," and "Christian Triumph and Controversy," followed by an alphabetical guide to a number of short entries.

The Oxford Dictionary of Byzantium, ed. by Alexander P. Kazhdan et al. 3 vols. New York and Oxford: Oxford University Press, 1991. The *ODB* contains short entries on the figures and events of Justinian's reign.

Prosography of the Later Roman Empire, ed. by A.H.M. Jones, J. R. Martindale, and J. Morris. Vol. 1. Cambridge: Cambridge University Press, 1971. This massive work was begun by Jones before his death in 1970, and has been continued by J. R. Martindale. It lists the important figures in the secular world of late antiquity and gives the important events of their lives, along with references to primary sources. Volume 3B (published 1992) contains biographies of the important figures of Justinian's reign.

Translated Sources

Agathias, *The Histories*, trans. with introduction and notes by Joseph D. Frendo. Berlin and New York: Walter de Gruyter, 1975. Agathias continues Prokopios' *History of the Wars* until 559, when he breaks off, evidently interrupted by illness or death.

Chronichon Paschale 284–628 AD, trans. by Michael Whitby and Mary Whitby as *Chronichon Paschale 284–628 AD*. Translated Texts for Historians no. 7.

Liverpool: Liverpool University Press, 1989. A universal chronicle probably written in the 630s. It was given the title *Chronichon Paschale* (The
Easter Chronicle) by its first editor, because it presents methods of deter-
mining the date of Easter.

Chronicle of Pseudo-Dionysius of Tel-Mahre, part 3 trans. by Witold Witakowski
in Translated Texts for Historians no. 22. Liverpool: Liverpool University
Press, 1996. Also known as *The Chronicle of Zuqnin*, this is a chronicle of
world history that was written by an anonymous monk in the northern
Mesopotamian monastery of Zuqnin at the end of the eighth century. It
contains the longest description we have of the great plague of Justinian's
reign, which the chronicler has taken from John of Ephesus, who wrote a
history in Syriac. The third part of John's work has survived, but the part
dealing with the plague is lost, and we have the description thanks to
Pseudo-Dionysius.

Corpus Iuris Civilis, ed. by P. Krueger. Weidmann, Berlin, 1954–1959; repr.
Dublin and Zurich: Weidmann, 1967–1973, 3 vols. This contains the
Codex of Justinian, the *Institutes,* the *Digest,* and the *Novels.* Trans. by S. P.
Scott as *The Civil Law, Including the Twelve Tables.* New York: AMS Press,
1973.

The Digest of Justinian, Latin text ed. by Theodor Mommsen with the aid of Paul
Krueger; English trans. ed. by Alan Watson, 4 vols. Philadelphia: University of Pennsylvania Press, 1985.

Evagrios Scholastikos, *The Ecclesiastical History,* trans. by Michael Whitby.
Translated Texts for Historians no. 33. Liverpool: Liverpool University
Press, 2000.

The Institutes of Justinian, text, trans., and commentary by J.A.C. Thomas. Am-
sterdam: North Holland, 1975. The *Institutes* was the textbook for law students produced by the same team, headed by Tribonian, that produced the
Digest.

Justinian, *The Digest of Roman Law: Theft, Rapine, Damage and Insult,* trans. by
C. F. Kolbert. Harmondsworth: Penguin, 1979. This is a translation of a
small portion of the *Digest,* with a general introduction and an essay on
the legal background.

John Malalas, *The Chronicle,* trans. by Elizabeth Jeffreys, Michael Jeffreys, and
Roger Scott. Byzantina Australiensia 4. Melbourne: Australian Association for Byzantine Studies, 1986. This is a chronicle of world history that
begins with Adam. The eighteenth book is devoted to Justinian's reign.

We do not know John's identity, though the word *malalas* is Syriac for *rhetor* (in Greek, *scholastikos* "lawyer"). He seems to have been able to tap official sources for Justinian's reign.

Prokopios of Caesarea, *History of the Wars*, trans. by H. B. Dewing. Loeb Classical Library, 5 vols. London: William Heinemann; Cambridge, MA: Harvard University Press, 1914–1928. The first volume contains the Greek text and English translation of the Persian War. The second volume deals with the Vandal War, and the third, fourth, and part of the fifth volumes deal with the war against the Ostrogoths. The eighth book, which takes up the remainder of the fifth volume, was written after the previous books were published.

Prokopios of Caesarea, *The Anecdota or Secret History*, trans. by H. B. Dewing. Loeb Classical Library. London: William Heinemann; Cambridge, MA: Harvard University Press, 1935. The Greek text and an English trans. of Prokopios famous *Secret History*, which he wrote to supplement his *History of the Wars* with information that he alleged he was unable to include in his published work. There is also a translation of the *Secret History* in the Penguin Classics series, by G. A. Williamson. Harmondsworth: Penguin, 1966.

Prokopios of Caesarea, *Buildings*, trans. by H. B. Dewing and Glanville Downey. Loeb Classical Library. London: William Heinemann; Cambridge, MA: Harvard University Press, 1949. The date of this last work is disputed, with some scholars putting it as early as 554. However, it seems most likely that it was written around 560, and that if Justinian did not commission it, at least he encouraged Prokopios to write it. The first book deals with buildings in Constantinople, and the remaining five books deal with the rest of the empire. Italy is omitted, which has led to the suspicion that the work is unfinished. However, Justinian did little building in Italy, and that may be the reason for Italy's omission.

The Variae of Magnus Aurelius Cassiodorus Senator, the Right Honourable and Illustrious ex-Quaestor of the Palace, ex-Ordinary Consul, ex-Master of the Offices, Praetorian Prefect and Patrician, trans. by S.J.B. Barnish. Translated Texts for Historians 12. Liverpool: Liverpool University Press, 1992. Cassiodorus, who served as praetorian prefect for Theodoric the Ostrogoth, for his daughter Amalasuntha, and for Theodahad, the last of the Amal kings, was in Constantinople for unknown reasons about 550, and when he returned to Italy, he founded a monastery called the Vivarium, where he lived until his death about 580. The *Variae* are twelve books of official correspondence of the Gothic court, written in ornate Latin; Barnish has published a selection of them in translation in this volume.

General

Allen, Pauline. "The 'Justinianic' Plague." *Byzantion* 49 (1979): 5–20. The Justinianic plague has attracted less scholarly attention than the Black Death in fourteenth-century Europe, but there have been a number of recent studies, of which this is one of the best.

Allen, Pauline. "Contemporary Portrayals of the Byzantine Empress Theodora (A.D. 527–548)." In Barbara Garlick, Suzanne Dixon, and Pauline Allen, eds., *Stereotypes of Women in Power*. Westport, CT: Greenwood Press, 1992, pp. 93–103. An examination of how Theodora was portrayed by contemporaries, particularly in Prokopios' *Secret History*. Evidence provided by sources other than Prokopios is largely ignored.

Barker, John E. *Justinian and the Later Roman Empire*. Madison: University of Wisconsin Press, 1979. A compact history of the period.

Bridge, Anthony. *Theodora: Portrait in a Byzantine Landscape*. London: Cassell, 1978. This is a readable book aimed at the general public.

Browning, Robert. *Justinian and Theodora*. London: Thames and Hudson, 1971; 2nd ed., 1987. A readable account by a first-rate scholar, with many illustrations.

Bury, J. B. "The *Nika* Riot." *Journal of Hellenic Studies* 17 (1897): 92–119. This is a classic study of the *Nika* riot of 532, which nearly toppled Justinian's regime. It has been brought up to date by Geoffrey Greatrex (see below).

Bury, J. B. *History of the Later Roman Empire from the Death of Theodosius I to the Death of Justinian II*. New York: St. Martin's Press, 1923; repr. New York: Dover, 1958. This is still the standard account of Justinian's reign against which later works must be measured. It includes an excellent bibliography of the primary sources.

Cameron, Alan. *Circus Factions: Blues and Greens at Rome and Byzantium*. Oxford: Oxford University Press, 1976. The standard study of the role of the factions in the production of spectacles in Rome and Constantinople.

Cameron, Averil. *The Mediterranean World in Late Antiquity, AD 395–600*. London and New York: Routledge, 1993. A good general account with emphasis on the changes taking place in the army, the church and its role in society, social and economic transformation, and the mentality of the age.

Chuvin, Pierre. *A Chronicle of the Last Pagans*. Translated by B. A. Archer. Cambridge, MA: Harvard University Press, 1990. A succinct and readable account of the end of paganism in the period of Justinian.

Croke, Brian, and A. Emmett, eds. *History and Historians in Late Antiquity.* Sydney, Oxford, and New York: Oxford University Press, 1983. Essays on how historians viewed history, and the historian's craft in late antiquity.

Downey, Glanville. "Justinian as Builder." *Art Bulletin* 32 (1950): 262–266. A brief account of Justinian's building program.

Downey, Glanville. *Constantinople in the Age of Justinian.* Norman: University of Oklahoma Press, 1960. This book is still the best brief account available in English of what life was like in Constantinople during Justinian's reign.

Evans, J.A.S. *The Age of Justinian: The Circumstances of Imperial Power.* London: Routledge, 1996. Contains much background information on the structure of society in the sixth century.

Evans, James Allan. *The Empress Theodora: Partner of Justinian.* Austin: University of Texas Press, 2002. A brief account of Empress Theodora and the role that she played in Justinian's empire, particularly in the controversy between the Monophysites and the Chalcedonians.

Fisher, E. A. "Theodora and Antonina in the *Historia Arcana*: History and/or Fiction?" In J. Peradotto and J. P. Sullivan, eds., *Women in the Ancient World.* Albany: State University of New York Press, 1984.

Foss, C. "The Empress Theodora." *Byzantion* 72 (2002): 141–176. Foss compares the picture we have of Empress Theodora from Prokopios' *Secret History* with that we have from other sources.

Frend, W.H.C. *The Rise of the Monophysite Movement.* Cambridge: Cambridge University Press, 1972. A readable and definitive account of the rise of Monophysitism in the eastern Roman Empire.

Greatrex, Geoffrey. "The 'Nika' Riot: A Reappraisal." *Journal of Hellenic Studies* 117 (1997): 60–86. This is the latest study in English of the *Nika* riots of 532.

Greatrex, Geoffrey. *Rome and Persia at War, 502–532.* Leeds: Francis Cairns, 1998. The war was interrupted by an uneasy peace that stretched from 505, in the reign of Anastasius, to the last year of Justin I's reign, and ended in 532 with the "Endless Peace." This book contains good accounts of Belisarios' victory at Dara and his defeat the following year at Callinicum.

Harvey, Susan Ashbrook. *Asceticism and Society in Crisis: John of Ephesus and The Lives of the Eastern Saints.* Berkeley: University of California Press, 1990. The biographical sketches written by John of Ephesus of the Monophysites whom he knew in the eastern provinces give a vivid picture of how they coped with the persecution of the Monophysite clergy that Emperor Justin I unleashed.

Harvey, Susan A. "Theodora the 'Believing Queen': A Study in Syriac Historiographical Tradition." *Hugoye* 4 (July 2001): 1–32. This is an excellent account of how Theodora was seen and still is viewed in the Monophysite tradition. It is available at http://syrcom.cua.edu/Hugoye/Vol4No2/HV4N2Harvey.html.

Herrin, Judith. *The Formation of Christendom*. Oxford: Oxford University Press, 1987. This is a reliable account of the Christian Church in late antiquity and excellent background reading for an understanding of the period.

Hodges, Richard, and William Bowden, eds. *The Sixth Century: Production, Distribution and Demand*. Leiden: Brill, 1998. A collection of essays dealing with the economic aspects of the Justinianic period and after.

Jones, A.H.M. *The Later Roman Empire 284–602: A Social, Economic and Administrative Survey*. 2 vols. Norman: University of Oklahoma Press, 1964. This massive work is a survey of the social and economic structure and of the administration of the later Roman Empire, put into a historical setting. It is a fund of information for subjects as diverse as the slave trade and the wealth of the Christian Church. The work is massively supplied with notes, and good maps are included.

Kaldellis, Anthony. *Procopius of Caesarea: Tyranny, History and Philosophy at the End of Late Antiquity*. Philadelphia: University of Pennsylvania Press, 2004. A sensitive study of the major historian of the period, with a balanced critique of the latest scholarship.

Meyendorff, J. "Justinian, the Empire and the Church." *Dumbarton Oaks Papers* 22 (1968): 43–60. An account of how Justinian attempted to handle the split between Chalcedonians and anti-Chalcedonians.

Moorhead, John. *Justinian*. London and New York: Longman, 1994. A succinct account of Justinian's reign. It contains a chapter on the dangers pressing on the Byzantine Empire from the region of the Danube River, and on Justinian's response to them.

Obolensky, Dimitri. *The Byzantine Commonwealth, 500–1453*. London: Weidenfeld and Nicolson, 1971. Obolensky deals with the spread of Byzantine influence into eastern Europe and Russia from the time of Justinian until the fall of Constantinople to the Turks in 1453.

Pazdernik, Charles. " 'Our Most Pious Consort Given Us by God': Dissident Reactions to the Partnership of Justinian and Theodora, AD 525–548." *Classical Antiquity* 13 (1994): 256–281.

Shahid, I. *Byzantium and the Arabs in the Sixth Century.* Washington, DC: Dumbarton Oaks, 1995. The southern half of the eastern frontier, from Rusafa to the Gulf of Aqaba, was guarded by the Ghassanids, an Arab tribe allied with Byzantium who were Christian, albeit Monophysites. The Persians also had Arab allies, including the Lakhmid tribe, who were pagans. Shahid elucidates Justinian's relations with the Arabs on the imperial frontier.

Ure, Percy Neville. *Justinian and His Age.* Harmondsworth: Penguin, 1951. Ure concentrates on the Greek sources for Justinian's reign, and his chapter on Justinian's laws is still worth reading.

Whitby, Michael, and Bryan Ward-Perkins, eds. *Cambridge Ancient History,* vol. 14, *Late Antiquity: Empire and Successors, A.D. 425–600.* Cambridge: Cambridge University Press, 2000. This is a volume for specialists, but for those with an interest in the period, the essay by Averil Cameron on Justin I and Justinian is a detailed study of the subject.

Internet Resources

Evans, J.A.S. "Justin I" (www.roman-emperors.org/justin.htm), "Justinian" (www.roman-emperors.org/justinia.htm) and "Theodora" (www.roman-emperors.org/dora.htm) on the Web site *De Imperatoribus Romanis.*

De Imperatoribus Romanis, an online encyclopedia of Roman emperors. http://www.roman-emperors.org/indexxxx.htm.

Hugoye: Journal of Syriac Studies. An online journal of Beth Mardutho, The Syriac Computing Institute. http://syrcom.cua.edu/Hugoye.

INDEX

About the Author

JAMES ALLAN EVANS is Professor Emeritus of Classical Near Eastern and Religious Studies at the University of British Columbia, Vancouver. He has published several works on ancient Greece and Rome, including *The Age of Justinian: The Circumstances of Imperial Power*.